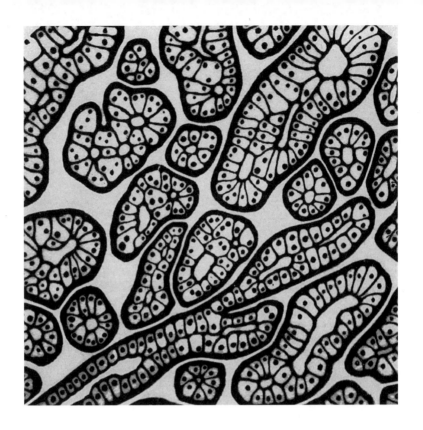

Relational Theories of Urban Form
An Anthology

Daniel Kiss and Simon Kretz (Eds.)

Birkhäuser
Basel

Editors' Preface 13

Daniel Kiss and Simon Kretz
Introduction to Relational Theories 17

Type 67

Christopher Alexander
A Pattern Language 69

Oswald Mathias Ungers
A Thematic Repertoire 113

Process 189

Fumihiko Maki
Collective Form 191

Alison Smithson and Peter Smithson
Spatial Processes 227

Place 263

Gordon Cullen
The Art of Environment 265

Lucius Burckhardt
The Science of Walking 319

Things 351

Bruno Latour
Agency of Things 353

Manuel de Solà-Morales
Urbanity of Things 409

Editors' Preface

Architecture and urban design are disciplines at the intersection of two grand axes: the physical scale ranging from the smallest of architectural details to the vastness of the territory, and the tremendous number of related disciplines and methods. While approaches and modalities are continuously shifting along these axes, the core skill of the discipline remains working with the nexus between the physical environment and society. This compiled volume focuses on the core issue of how this relationship—between physical space and societal action—blossomed in the postwar professional discourse, ultimately emerging to become an integral and constitutive part of the form definitions of some of the most noteworthy theories of architecture and the city. This selection of writings is organized according to specific guiding themes, and the meticulous editing, comparison, and contextualization aims to provide the reader with a theoretical framework and perspective with which to view the world as the totality of relationships between humans, other living creatures, and material elements.

This project stemmed from our shared interest in theories of urban form and a reading seminar we jointly organized and taught at the ETH Zurich in 2016. In our ongoing investigations into questions of form in theory and practice, scientific engagement with methods of design, and teaching of urban design theory, the relationship between the social and the material emerged again and again as one of the momentous central themes of the discipline. Inspired by this observation, and with the motivation of making a case for the relational discourse by distilling it into an easily digestible and discussible form, our research on the topic has culminated in this commented anthology. We hope it proves to be a valuable asset for research, discourse, and teaching, and inspires readers to further investigate the underlying relational perspective. Moreover, this publication also features two delightful world premieres: *Italian Thoughts Followed Further* by Alison and Peter Smithson and *The Dialectical City* by Oswald Mathias Ungers appear here for the first time in English.

Research and writing are not possible without support and collaboration. We wish to express our gratitude to the many individuals, organizations, and institutions who helped make this publication possible. We thank the Department of Architecture at ETH Zurich for their support, which empowered us to bring this project to a fruitful end. Special thanks are due to Professor Kees Christiaanse, who encouraged us to investigate and teach theories of urban form over the past years, provided us with the necessary freedom to conduct our research, and granted us the financial means that made an intensive concluding phase of writing and publishing possible.

We would also like to express our particular gratitude to the numerous individuals, family archives, foundations, publishing houses, and other organizations who assisted us during our research and kindly granted us rights to reproduce materials in their care. We are especially privileged to have received the uncon-ditional support of those still living among the authors of the original written works: Bruno Latour and Fumihiko Maki. We would further like to thank the Manuel de Solà Archive, Rosa Feliu in particular; Martin Schmitz, caretaker of Lucius Burckhardt's legacy; the Smithson Family Collection, especially Soraya Smithson; and the Ungers Archive for Architectural Science.

Finally, we also wish to thank all of our colleagues at ETH Zurich and beyond whose essential input has so greatly enriched this publication, Alice Jauneau and David Vallance for the book's impressive design, and the entire editorial and production team at Birkhäuser for their willingness to back us in our aspirations.

Responsibility for any errors and omissions in this book remains ours alone.

Zurich, January 2021

Daniel Kiss and Simon Kretz
Introduction to Relational Theories

A Relational Lens

The discourse on architecture and urban design is increasingly interwoven with discussions about bringing the physical material qualities of the environment in relation with their human, cognitive, and societal aspects as the very essence and beauty of the discipline. As architecture's main goal is to provide better human habitat and contribute to a symbiosis of the environment's various human and non-human actors and constituents, it seems obvious that mediating between these factors must be inherent to the art of designing and building. This can occur with varying degrees of awareness, but most architectural theories and positions contain traces of the discipline's core skill: working with the nexus between the physical environment and society.

The history of architecture is rich in externally referenced, politically and ethically motivated episodes and self-referential stages driven by form and architecture's own history. An example of the first is the infiltration of other disciplines into the architectural discourse in the 1970s, whereas the second can be exemplified by the gravitation of architectural post-modernism towards historical and visual references and its claim concerning the discipline's autonomy. However relevant such extreme phases have been to architects in their constant search for new ways of dealing with the challenges of each new era, time and again these trajectories have reconnected within the melting pot of the discourse, and the professional debate seems to keep swinging back to the disciplinary backbone—the relationalization of the material and the human.

A common interpretation of "good design" is its ability to contain contextual references and thus to illuminate the way of life it accommodates. On this, Christopher Alexander asserts that any particular well-designed place or building symbolizes the world view that brought it forth. He illustrates this claim by referencing Le Corbusier's new house forms from the 1920s which, according to Alexander, "represented part of the modern attempt to understand the twentieth century's new way of life."[1] This relation between form and culture is fundamental to any politicized interpretation of architecture, as the following example demonstrates: In October of 1943, following the destruction of the chamber of the House of Commons in London by a German air raid, the parliament debated if the chamber was to be rebuilt to its original form. Winston Churchill insisted that the rectangular shape of the old chamber was responsible for the two-party system that is the essence of British parliamentary democracy, and conceived the reciprocal relations between material space and human agency by saying: "We shape our buildings; thereafter they shape us."[2] In more general terms, Churchill's words describe the hypothesis that not only do humans design and transform their spatial environment but the environment also has an impact on the interactions and culture of society. A recent revival of this way of thinking in architectural theory was externally triggered by the sociological discourses that sparked around the philosopher Bruno Latour's actor-network theory[3] and the sociologist Martina Löw's discussion of the interaction between societal actions and material structures in the development of space.[4] What is new in these theories is the treatment of form as the totality of social-material relations. This means, by definition, a refusal of the idea of "container space", which reduces space to a neutral corpus that simply absorbs material objects. In contrast, the concept of relational space describes the reciprocal impacts of material space and social activity in terms of their specification and adaptation. Space is thus established through social activities, and structures these at the same time. That is, according to Latour's and Löw's approach, action has spatial and material attributes, and the material has agency in deeds involving it.

Another development that heightened attention to the topic of social-material relations is the recent democratization of the practice of architecture, not to mention urban design, paralleled by these professions becoming increasingly multidisciplinary. Design proposals are subject to societal exposure, relevant decisions are made through participatory processes, and public discourse socializes concepts of materiality.[5] Consequently, architects are involved in expanding dialogues with actors external to the core discipline, which necessitates that architectural positions and arguments become accessible to laypeople. This has in turn de-heroized the role of the expert, as the notion of expertise has been diversified and distributed among the various actors involved. This trend makes the reading of space and its production as dual social/material structures all the more relevant. In this interpretation, society is comprised of the totality of interactions between humans, other living creatures, and the material world. Consequently, architecture and urban design, disciplines in which mediation between these constituents is inherent, become more relevant.

Urban Form as a Relational Concept

The reciprocity described above is based on the Kantian *duality of meaning* which, in terms of architecture, took shape in Kant's writings on the need for negotiation between aesthetics and ethics[6] or, as Aldo Rossi puts it, between beauty and use.[7] Adhering to this suggestion of the delicate relationship between material form, function, and beauty, let us assume that every *thing* has both a material formulation (medium) related to sensual experience and a social dimension (agency) associated with the way it impacts the actors engaging in a relationship with it. Let us further define *relational form* as the way that the totality of interactions between human and non-human agents takes shape and acts upon the environment. Moreover, let us claim that form, as a cultural concept,

21

not only describes the arrangement of the relations it comprises but also determines what is part of the relational construct, that is, it defines the system boundaries. It describes the reciprocal impacts of physical space and activity in terms of their mutual specification and adaptation, whereby the nexuses may occur within psychological, sociological, and economic spaces, spaces of imagination, or any other space, as well as any combination of spaces. We are now in a position to reiterate that form is established by deeds and structures them at the same time. It is both informed by agency and instructs the constituting agents. In other words, form simultaneously plays a passive and an active role and, accordingly, it is not possible to isolate its material background from the activities it is tied to.

On this, Anthony Giddens writes that the connection between structure and agency is fundamental. In his attempt to explain that the causality goes in both directions, Giddens asserts that "social structures are both constituted by human agency, and yet at the same time are the very medium of this construction."[8] This means that it is impossible to determine which one is changing the other and they must, therefore, be discussed together, without giving primacy to either. These relations are both reciprocal and intertwined. In order the describe the correlation, Giddens coined the term *duality of structure*.

Rooted in the Kantian tradition, the Canadian epistemologist Maurice Lagueux pursues a very similar line of argumentation of reciprocal contingency and mediation when addressing the relationship of aesthetics and ethics in architecture.[9] According to him, ethical problems are decisions that are intrinsic to architectural and aesthetic and thus also ethical judgements. Therefore, Lagueux believes that design is an art of mediation which attempts to solve ethical problems by way of architectural decisions that are at the same time also solutions for aesthetic problems. Lagueux illustrates this dichotomy with questions that have clear ethical implications, where the architectural responses to them also have an aesthetic character. He asks, for example, if architects should "enhance secrecy and individualism inside a dwelling or favor a family's collective life by way of large living and dining rooms"[10] He refers to a "quasi identity" between ethics and aesthetics in architecture, whereby "critical judgement" gradually arises from the oscillating mediation of the two domains.

We can go on to argue that architectural and urban form is not just the result of a creative process, but can also establish, fix, or transform cultural foundations and social environments by producing spaces, times, and media for interaction. In his book *Philosophie der Architektur* [The Philosophy of Architecture] (2009), Ludger Schwarte analyzes exactly these possibilities of architecture. Based on his observation that the French Revolution took place on streets and squares that were originally meant for the representation of the monarchy's power, and that the revolutionist masses were only able to form because these public spaces existed in the first place, Schwarte describes architecture's performative power to enable events through *spaces of possibility* and, thus, contribute to societal change.[11] He associates this capacity with the design and realization of spatial environments being deep-rooted in the discipline of architecture.[12]

Inspired by Giddens' *structuration theory*, Martina Löw approaches urban form over the nexus between space and societal action. She highlights the reciprocity of the relationship by interpreting space and the production thereof as an actuator of societal processes alongside the more common approach of interpreting space as the material outcome of human action. She developed the idea of a *relational spatial model* with the aim of overcoming the separation of spatial theory into absolutist and relativist standpoints.[13] This relational approach focuses on the "arrangements" of living beings and social goods and examines how space is created through processes of perception, memory, and imagination and how it manifests itself as a social structure. In doing so, Löw refers to Giddens and expands his *duality of structure* into what she calls the *duality of space*. Löw's basic idea is that, as social actors, human individuals create spaces but, at the same time, their actions are also dependent on the impacts of economic, legal, social, cultural, and ultimately spatial structures.[14] Thus, spaces are not only the result of actions, they also structure these actions, for example, by enabling them—as seen in Schwarte's argumentation on the nexus between the French Revolution and the public spaces on which it took place.

Hannah Arendt approaches social-material relations from another perspective. Her *space of appearance* concept is based on the conviction that experiencing the other, in this case the mutual physical presence of people in public space, is fundamental to the notion of publicity.[15] For Arendt, *polis* is the space "where I appear to others as others appear to me, where [humans] exist not merely like other living or inanimate things, but to make their appearance explicitly."[16] Such public space of appearance can always be recreated, whenever and wherever individuals gather politically or, in Arendt's terms, "in the manner of speech and action".[17] However, since it is a creation of action, the *space of appearance* is highly fragile and exists only when actualized through the performance of acting or of words. Whereas in a first reading this conception suggests that the material's relation to the social is passive and depends on being actualized by it, analogous to Schwarte's line of reasoning, it is the material that makes the social deed possible in the first place. The way we organize physical space also results in human-material arrangements and, thus, we interpret our encounters—that is, our society—within the framework of this designed, organized space. It is collective experience that turns material space into a political arena and, simultaneously, material space as medium enables the physical encounters to take place at all. Thus, *spaces of appearance*, interpreted through the relational lens, do not simply provide further evidence of the reciprocity of the social and the material, but also suggest that material space empowers human agents, enabling them to act in concert for public political purposes.[18]

The above positions, stemming from philosophy, sociology, and other human sciences, all make claims not only of the existence of a social-material nexus, but also to its reciprocity—some, like Löw, Latour, or Schwarte, do this explicitly, while others, as in the case of Arendt, are more implicit. The attitude towards mutuality is more ambiguous in the discourse rooted in psychology and neuroscience. In her book, *Welcome to Your World: How the Built Environment Shapes Our Lives* (2017), the architecture critic and historian Sarah Williams Goldhagen starts by lamenting on how the built environment affects the way we think, feel, and act.[19] Later, she confidently states that "a design can be deliberately composed to nudge people to choose one action over another."[20] By doing so, Goldhagen refers to the work of Jane Jacobs, William H. Whyte, Oscar Newman, and Jan Gehl to demonstrate the in-depth effects of design on people's social lives.[21] Jacob attacks post-war slum clearance policies for not basing new urban forms on empirical knowledge of how dwellers actually conduct their social and personal lives; Whyte systematizes people's behavior in public space and the role specific design elements play in this; Newman ties the incidence of crime to specific urban forms; and Gehl advocates for walkability, soft edges, and active ground floors as fundamental agents of urban vibrancy. All these ideas are based on considerations of how the design of the built environment shapes the type and character of people's social interactions. In order to better understand how we experience our built environments, i.e. how they shape our actions, Goldhagen suggests turning to developments in neuroscience, neuropsychology, and the emerging field of embodied cognition.[22] To underline her claim, she introduces the orthogonal and hexagonal grids as prime examples of the modular thinking in design that gives disturbingly little attention to how it aligns with the architecture of human experience.[23]

In a response to Goldhagen's theses, architect Richard Buday comes to a different conclusion, claiming that architects have only limited power to shape human behavior.[24] He further asserts that the reason for this is not surprising: most societal problems architects would like their buildings to shape are behavioral, not architectural. "The inconvenient truth facing architectural behavioral shapers is that building users may be uninterested in or possibly antagonistic toward the desired behavior a design is promoting,"[25] Buday argues. He then calls attention to the difference between a building triggering a physiological response—as in the case of novel psychological and neuroscience theories of human response to environments cited by Goldhagen—and architecture actually changing behavior, fueled by the environmental determinism of architects. Buday argues that scientific evidence of the former does not constitute proof of the latter and concludes by quoting anthropologist Margaret Mead: "The notion that we are products of our environment is our greatest sin; we are products of our choices."[26] He does so to make the point that although architecture may influence our decisions, architecture alone cannot lead to long-term behavioral change, at least not without first changing beliefs, intentions, and attitudes.

Robert Lamb Hart, architect and author of *New Look at Humanism in Architecture, Landscapes and Urban Design* (2015), engages in a debate with Buday.[27] He argues that architecture is never experienced by itself but is instead inseparable from its natural or urban setting and the human activity in and around it. He also points to the subjectivity of one's engagement with the built environment, given that it takes place in the context of the person we are at the time of engagement. This includes our beliefs and attitudes, as well as our learning, skills, memories, expectations, and unique personality, all aspects that are accumulated over the course of a lifetime and informed by the surrounding culture. All of these, goes the argument, are latent at a conscious or, more often, unconscious level, until mobilized by the events or emotions of the moment. Hart insists that the built environment itself can shape our beliefs, intentions, skills, and expectations, or activate them through the ways we experience a place. We say we become "a different person" when, for example, we are immersed in the atmosphere of the "divine light" of our place of worship, or at a private retreat such as a "place in the country". And, over a lifetime, we tend to make significant investments of our time and money to be reshaped by the architecture of a place. Hart's argumentation sheds light on the entanglement of the manifold relations between the material, the social, and the psychological dimensions of form. In his view, it is challenging to identify who shapes what in our environment. Instead, the world is best understood as a complex cultural-material network of mutual formation. In response, Hart makes a case for the necessity of transdisciplinary design teams, as only these are in the position to better understand and know how to address the social issues architecture may hope to resolve.

Relational Theories of Urban Form: An Anthology

The anthology in your hands engages the narrative of the social-material and tells the history of architecture as an art of relationalization. The underlying argument is that the *relational*, besides being a topos at the core of many theories, is also a way of interpreting any architectural theory. Therefore, this work suggests employing the "relational lens" to both re-read some of the fundamental theories of urban form and visit newer positions with the aim of offering an organizational raster for the discourse and, at the same time, broadening its horizons.

The eight texts compiled in this volume all describe urban form as a relational bundle of space and action—each in its very specific way and from different individual perspectives. As an assemblage, they both help us understand the evolution of the "relational perspective" on urban form and represent its multiangular approach. Each text is based on positions of dual structures which are all both analytical and normative and thus contribute not only to a better understanding of the discipline and structures of reality, but also provide guiding principles for further action. We distill a key term for the relational discourse from each of the discussed concepts, such as *thematic repertoires* by Oswald Mathias Ungers, *collective form* by Fumihiko Maki, or *matter of things* by Manuel de Solà-Morales. The anthology examines these, discusses them in relation to each other and, finally, portrays a topology of relational concepts by theorizing them under four fundamental topoi of urban design: TYPE, PROCESS, PLACE, AND THINGS. We, the editors, find these four guiding themes to be highly relevant for architecture and urban design, but the selection should not be interpreted as a closed system. It is much rather an open arrangement which allows for reorganization, conversion, and complementation by further perspectives.

The method of text selection and theorization is analogous with the parable of "the blind men and the elephant". As the blind men who have never come across an elephant before learn and conceptualize what the elephant is like by touching its different parts, this book's theoretical backbone also took shape through a process of "blind touching" of a large number of different theories. Our research modus was more inductive than deductive, and did not follow an upfront hypothesis. Studying the many texts has brought us to the conclusion that, one way or another, all these different perspectives can be put in relation to each other using the concept of the social-material nexus—not only those that stem directly and explicitly from it. We selected, edited, and at times combined texts from multiple works of the same author so as to best demonstrate their relatedness both to the theme of their respective chapters and the overarching subject matter of social-material relations as constituents of urban form. At the same time, we took special attention to keep as much of the original texts' formal specificities as seemed necessary in order to maintain their conceptual integrity.

The editors wish to offer a paradigmatic foundation that encourages further research and the continued viewing of our environment through the "relational lens". The relational element is thus treated here not only as an autonomous theme but, above all, as the interpretational perspective of architectural and urban design theory. The following pages walk the reader through the anthology's four chapters with the aim of clarifying the aspects that relate the conception of social-material matters to the guiding themes of TYPE, PROCESS, PLACE, and THINGS, followed by an explanation of their relevance to the contemporary urban design discourse and practice.

1. Typologies of Culture

The book's first chapter revisits theories that interpret urban form as a repository of cultural memory, and thereby see culture as a social-material entity. Along this line, architecture and urban design can be seen as disciplines associated with a cultural repertoire inherent in and exclusive to them. In the late 1960s, this motivated the Italian design collective *Tendenza* to claim that architecture is an autonomous branch of knowledge. According to them, autonomy in architecture meant freedom and independence within a set of rules and repertoires.[28] These derive from architectural history and are completely separate from any personal characteristics of individual architects. Aldo Rossi, in particular, formulated the typological forms and basic elements that define the city in order to identify patterns that have proved enduring and can be turned into elements for a new design. In his book *L'architettura della città* [*The Architecture of the City*] (1966), he presents such patterns as *types*. Rossi defines type as the shared core of various similar individual cases or, expressed metaphorically, the shared DNA that defines their relatedness.[29] Rossi's types are patterns that crystallize from individual experience and, according to Rossi, even more from the collective memory of a society. The term *collective memory* was introduced by the philosopher and sociologist Maurice Halbwachs.[30] His primary thesis was that human memory can only function within a collective context and is an important component of the culture of any society. His work points to the fact that collective memory is territorialized in urban space, making it apparent that remembering, and thus culture, is profoundly shaped by the mutually responsive relationship between social groups and the spaces they inhabit. Particular types, argues Rossi, develop according to both needs (function) and aspirations to beauty (form).[31] Rossi thus emphasizes that in this context type is a cultural fact, and neither an absolute constant nor merely a physical shape or symbol. Rossi coined the term *cultural type* for describing the nexus of the material and societal roles of type and stated that the specific shape of a particular type will vary from society to society, due to the different cultures.

Rossi presents the "Alley of the Washerwomen" as an example of such a *cultural type*.[32] This Alley of the Washerwomen type is a back alley in a densely inhabited city, austere and spatially narrow, that serves as rear access for personnel and infrastructural matters such as trash disposal and deliveries. The façades have French windows and balconies for hanging laundry to dry. The alley smells like soap and wet laundry and echoes with the conversations of washerwomen and cries of errand boys. In order to differentiate the type from the individual case, Rossi presents examples from various Southern European cities, which are similar in their basic principles and together form this cultural type. Rossi defines the uniting basic principle as follows: "The word *type* represents [...] the idea of an element" and also comprises this element's "origins and primary causes".[33] It is therefore not absolutely necessary that exactly the same scent of soap prevails in every alley, but the principal spatial-societal idea of a narrow back alley without a representative function should. Such a cultural type is, accordingly, neither a frozen aesthetic image nor a geometric control diagram to simply copy without questioning, but instead a principle consisting of a material object and its societal role. According to Rossi, "A particular type is associated with a particular form and way of life."[34] The cultural type links various aspects of habitat and therefore psychological, societal, living, and material facts and is thus something like a culturally anchored "social-material scheme".[35] Besides being a device to structure knowledge, this social-material construct can also be accessed for new design actions, not as a blueprint, but instead as a principle, a metaphor, or an idea.

A related cultural typology is Christopher Alexander's highly regarded collection *A Pattern Language* (1977). At its foundation were countless analyses of individual architectural and urban planning situations, which were categorized, examined, and discussed by Alexander with regard to their meaning and usage. The result was a detailed and richly illustrated encyclopedic collection, a so-called *pattern language*, containing evaluated and operatively usable cultural types.[36] Alexander's patterns are not individually delimitable objects, but are instead interrelated complex structures containing several objects, their uses, and their relationships. To further elaborate on this, we turn to sociologist Lucius Burckhardt, who interprets *pattern language* as an attempt to overcome the perception of the world as a realm of objects in which objects are distinguished and labeled according to their external parameters and use, for example as houses, streets, or newsstands.[37] Alexander does not isolate a house, a street, or a newsstand in order to perfect its design and construction, argues Burckhardt. Instead, he distinguishes an integral composite, such as the street corner, from other urban episodes. The street corner, seen here as an integral composite, is thereafter a combination of an intersection, a bus stop, a newsstand, and a crosswalk. These are the visible elements of the street corner, and they are complemented by invisible, organizational factors: the bus timetable, traffic light sequences, and the newsstand's opening hours. The newsstand thrives on the bus that has not yet arrived, causing the rider to buy a newspaper; and the bus happens to stop here, because this is an intersection where passengers can change to other lines. If the newsstand is still closed when the majority of people are waiting for their bus to take them to work, the street corner subsystem fails to function: it lacks an element of livability. This is yet again an important implication of *types* and *patterns* that occupy themselves with social-material habitats rather than with individual objects stripped from their socio-cultural contexts. In this light, Alexander's patterns are cultural types par excellence. As Rossi argued that ways of life were inherent to the definition of type, and as Burckhardt advocates via Alexander for the role of deeds in turning the spatial arrangement of objects into living urban episodes, the urban planner Kevin Lynch defined urban form as the spatial arrangement of people doing different things.[38] After all, the city does not change or take form on its own as a "biological organism". Instead, its form is much rather a product of multiple interacting decisions and actions of agencies, writes Lynch.

Lynch's *A Theory of Good City Form* (1981) is akin to Alexander's approach in that it is the product of a search for patterns that effectively augment the interrelation of human purpose and urban form. Lynch's understanding of form comprises both the social activities and the physical features that encompass and modify them. From this standpoint, Lynch heavily criticizes the majority of patterns and models that existed at the time for referring only to completed forms and, thus, taking no account of the process by which that form was achieved. This emphasis on

32

completed form—he argues—ignores the reality of continuous change, in which no form is a permanent feature. This leads Lynch to the conclusion that "the preoccupation with form is the mark of a mind which focuses on things rather than on their consequences for people"[39] and that process should instead be the key. Accordingly, urban design should rely on a well-developed stock of models that integrate process and form. These models need to be sufficiently independent and abstract to allow for the continuous recasting of aims, analyses, and possibilities. Lynch makes an important distinction between theories and models.[40] For him, a theory should include criteria able to support models which, for their part, are already implementable and thus "worthy of emulation".[41] This differentiation ensures that theories do not run the risk of being promoted to *natural rules*, because the models bind them to reality like an umbilical cord. Lynch further explains the mutual correlation of models and theories by arguing that complex, real problems are not manageable in a limited time without models and prototypes and, at the same time, the creation of these models and prototypes is not possible without the synthesis of merged and ordered experience, knowledge of practice and of principles.[42]

As did Rossi and Alexander, the German architect Oswald Mathias Ungers also expressed his distaste for architecture's treatment as applied art, a trend he accredited to functionalism and the Bauhaus movement more specifically.[43] He argued that architecture that only addresses purpose and practicality is bound to be impoverished and to end up in the dead end of everyday banality. In his architectural manifesto, *Die Thematisierung der Architektur* [The Thematization of Architecture] (1983), Ungers establishes parallels between architecture that does not operate with themes from its own domain and images that are restricted to being photographic copies of reality. Consequently, he aligned with the Tendenza group in advocating autonomous architecture and argued that the "thematization" of architecture contributes to transforming the environment from the pragmatic and trivial reality of the everyday into the metaphysical world of ideas and, thus, to the sensitizing of everyday life.[44] Along these lines, he states that the social potential of architecture can be witnessed in its ability to intensify the meaning of life for the user, in fact not—or not only—through its material utilization, but rather in the sense of a sublimation of the environment molded by and for humanity. He claimed that themes inherent in architectural and urban design thought lead to architectural and, respectively, urban form. This can be exemplified through his themes: "The coincidence of opposites or *coincidentia oppositorum*" and "The Incorporation or *the puppet in the puppet*". In the latter theme, making reference to Russian Matryoshka dolls, Ungers reads the city wall as an example of an envelope that encompasses the city within the larger body of the surrounding landscape. The city encloses other urban elements, such as its neighborhoods, whereas these encapsulate buildings, and so forth. This reflects a basic form of sequential spatial organization that also applies to the Matryoskhas.[45] This leads us to the following conclusions: Firstly, Ungers' themes represent fundamental forms of spatial organization. Secondly, they are based on antetypes, such as the Matryoshka for the "puppet in the puppet" form of spatial organization. Thirdly, by having identified a multitude of different situations where the same spatial organization is applied—as in the case of the Medieval walled city and the Matryoshka doll—Ungers arrives at the idea that these forms are not haphazard occurrences but fundamental themes of the architectural and urban sphere. Finally, he collects these themes and presents them as a thematic typology.

Ungers claims that designers develop their thematic repositories out of ideas, imagination, metaphors, models, analogies, signs, symbols, and allegories.[46] He describes these visual tools as imaginative structures of meaning that pervade all human understanding and thought. The prime matter of these visual tools, according to the philosopher Mark Johnson, is composed of "embodied schemata",[47] physically experienceable patterns that are perceived pre-reflectively, even prior to conceptualization, meaning that they do not have to take the detour of language. They originate from human movements in space and describe situations such as "being inside", "being contained", or "emerging".[48] They not only depict a prescribed reality, but also actively (re-) construct (new) realities from an implicitly available typology rooted in what has been experienced and lived.[49] Thereafter, the development of Ungers' themes is an imaginative discovery and reconstruction of phenomena done in order to conceptualize them. The knowledge used to create them refers not only to a set of facts, but also to a set of constellations derived from perception or, in Ungers' own words, to "something that registers reality through sensual experience and imagination".[50] In a similar manner to the antetypes presented here via Aldo Rossi's concept, Ungers sees his themes as structures that are deeply inscribed in society, join countless different material and human entities, and thus become backbones of our culture. In contrast to types that usually represent finished structures, these themes are to be understood as cultural strategies. Ungers employs them for three purposes: First, to rationalize existing, specific places. Second, to theorize the disciplines of architecture and urban design using their inherent topoi. And third, to lay the foundation of a stimulating repertoire for designers.

The notion of these stimulating repertoires is a key aspect of the philosopher Donald Schön's approach to reflective practice.[51] Practitioners build up a collection of images, ideas, examples, and actions that they can draw upon, something Schön saw as central to reflective thought. In *The Reflective Practitioner* (1983), he suggests that: "When a practitioner makes sense of a situation he perceives to be unique, he *sees* it as something already present in his repertoire. To see *this* site as *that* one is not to subsume the first under a familiar category or rule. It is, rather, to see the unfamiliar, unique situation as both similar to and different from the familiar one, without at first being able to say similar or different with respect to what. The familiar situation functions as a precedent, or a metaphor, or [...] an exemplar for the unfamiliar one."[52] In this way, one engages with a situation. One does not necessarily have a full understanding of all things before acting, but can already establish some sort of orientation within the new situation and is thus more likely to avoid major misconceptions. When looking at a situation one is influenced by, one is able to draw upon certain routines. When reflective practitioners work, it is possible for them to bring fragments of memories into play and to begin to build theories and responses that fit the new situation. This method can be termed *typification*. It is used to bundle similar social-material relations, to understand their cultural dimensions, and to make them useable as urban design tools. In light of this, typification can be understood as the practical genesis of knowledge, encyclopedic wisdom, and plays an important role in the construction of knowledge systems, association networks, and models. Typification is also a model for realization and, thus, pleads for a theory *of* practice instead of a distinct treatment of theory *and* practice. However, it is not an absolute knowledge, a value-neutral episteme, but a practical wisdom aware of its cultural and temporal dependence.

In the "chaos of perception", *types* create a possible order based on familiar patterns. The previously unordered mass of data thus becomes structured, and the countless individual manifestations are incorporated into a structure of meaning. However, these illustrative types, patterns, and themes also stimulate new thoughts, reactions, and actions that reveal potential for innovation.[53] Consequently, they comprise repertoires that are not only ordering reservoirs of similar isolated occurrences but, instead, also stimulate the existing wealth of experience of the designer towards new, experimental designs. In line with this, *type* is both the memory of what has been experienced and the basis for the new, for what is yet to come. At this point, at the very latest, it becomes clear that repertoires are not mere collections of prefabricated solutions but are instead the interfaces between memory and imagination.

In summary, the concepts presented in this section—Alexander's patterns, Rossi's cultural types, Lynch's models, and Ungers' themes—are all indivisible social-material constructs anchored in our collective cultural memory. Not only do they synthesize knowledge about our habitats, they also build up the repertoire of designers and practitioners to create new architectural and urban forms, thus shaping the methodological core of the discipline.

2. Spatial Processes

The book's second chapter introduces theories rooted in the assertion that spatial facts, or *things*, have the ability to trigger processes and that such spatial processes in turn structure urban form. What is important in this conception is the reciprocal relation between space and process, in contrast to the more common human perspective which reads space as the result of processes but does not attribute it with the agency to initiate action. Here, process is understood as a sequence of actions and cognitive patterns, not as a linear timeline. Corresponding to Kevin Lynch's theory on the inseparability of form, process, and management, the positions introduced here also assume that the city's physicality and its organization cannot be discussed individually. In this narrative, space and time are integral: space sparks time and time triggers form. Furthermore—taken that the definition of the urban also implies the aggregation of single individual entities and episodes producing cumulative effects, in other words, forming a collective—the urban form resulting from the spatially triggered processes is a collective form.

In his influential book *Investigations in Collective Form* (1964), the Japanese architect Fumihiko Maki addresses three different approaches to such collective forms.[54] He calls the first *compositional form*, an approach that is two-dimensional and static, for example Oscar Niemeyer's design for Brasilia. Maki identifies the second as *megaform*, a structural approach that provides large frameworks—hierarchical, open-ended, and inter-connected systems—encompassing different functions and elements, as do metabolist megastructures, for example. The third, *group form*, is the result of the incremental accumulation of spatially interconnected elements along an armature, for example a central road or topography lines. In this approach, the notion of linkage between the armature and its proxies is neither implied nor imposed but evolves together with the settlement in its organic development. Maki also points out that the "sequential [or group] form in historical examples developed over a period of time much longer than that in which contemporary cities are being built and rebuilt."[55] He adds that, consequently, the efforts of contempo-rary urban designers are quite different from those of their historical counterparts, and the forms they consciously evolve in a short time span must also differ. He quotes the historical example of traditional Japanese farming villages where a single street is the armature that unifies the community. In this case, the linkage is the controlling idea that orders the buildings and spaces. The two-story street front forms a tight, continuous façade that links individual houses to the larger fabric of houses on the one hand, and connects private family life to village community life on the other. Based on such examples, Maki argues for strong relations between all layers of activity and the physical form of the city, claiming that their linkage is the act by which the two are united in a collective form. Thus, he interprets collective form as a structure

38

determined by social-material relations. Take, for example, his concept of the megastructure form. The megastructure is founded on a basic (infra) structure, or in Maki's words, "a kind of master form which can move into ever new states of equilibrium and yet maintain visual consistency and a sense of continuing order in the long run".[56] On the one hand, these master forms can be infinitely extended and, on the other hand, they can develop over time with subordinate units being plugged into them. What this tells us about spatial processes is that these core structures trigger action which, in turn, result in new spatial phenomena in the form of plug-ins. Accordingly, we can see the megastructure form as a planned version of group form—the latter being a sequential form that develops over a long period of time as a result of the organic processes triggered by spatial phenomena such as geography, topography, and the linking of distinct elements.

Maki's theory can be found in numerous architectural projects and utopias, whereby one must point out that the impact is often mutual or even reversed: Maki theorized what he extracted and systematized from these designs. He explicitly refers to Noriaki Kurokawa's design of a megastructure for an agricultural city in Japan[57] but in an analogous case, one could also mention Frank Lloyd Wright's Broadacre City, a systemic concept of mobility-based autarkic suburban life. Another prime example is, without doubt, Constant Nieuwenhuys' *New Babylon*, a vision of a worldwide network of connected cities of the future, where land is collectively owned and labor fully automated. Emerging from the remarkable Situationist International activist group, Nieuwenhuys' project addressed issues of "unitary urbanism" and the future of art in a techno-cratic society. It suggested replacing the need to work with a nomadic lifestyle of creative play. Inspired by Johan Huizinga's novel of the same title, the proposed urban network was to be inhabited by *homo ludens*,[58] individuals liberated from labor who have no need for art, as they are creative in their daily life.

In Nieuwenhuys' words: "New Babylon offers only minimal conditions for a behavior that should remain as free as possible. Every limitation of movement, of the creation of mood and atmosphere should be inhibited. Everything should remain possible, everything should be able to happen."[59] And, most importantly: "The environment is created by the activities of life not the other way around."[60] Cedric Price's *Fun Palace* for the avant-garde theater producer Joan Littlewood was another unrealized situationist project which, unlike *New Babylon* and other visionary designs of the 1960s and 1970s, was fully intended to be built. It was conceived by Price for the East End of London as a "laboratory of fun" and "a university of the streets",[61] meant to be erected as a temporary project for a time period of ten years. Designed as a flexible framework into which programmable spaces can be plugged, the ultimate goal of the structure was the possibility to change at the behest of its users. The project demonstrated Price's inventive and playful personal vision of the city and expressed his sense of architecture's moral obligations toward its users. He was fascinated by new technology and believed that it should both serve the public and further human freedom. Price was also determined that his *Fun Palace* "shall not impose physical or psychological constraints upon its occupants nor reduce them to a standard form—unlike typical modern architecture."[62] Littlewood's vision of a dynamic and interactive theater provided the programmatic framework on which Price would develop and refine his concept of an interactive performative architecture adaptable to the varying needs and desires of the individual. Thus, the *Fun Palace*'s material spaces would have been both the result of the users' actions and, in turn, would have also triggered further processes.

Another investigation of collective form represented in this anthology is Alison and Peter Smithson's theory of *conglomerate ordering*, with the central issue being territory and architecture's role in constructing territory.[63] It discusses aspects of weaving, connecting, and interlacing, as well as the bodily experience of architecture and of moving through space.[64] The concern with linkage within collective form is central to this work. Peter Smithson once claimed that "buildings should be thought of from the beginning as fragments, containing within themselves a capacity to act with other buildings and be themselves links."[65] Accordingly, the Smithsons also understand urbanization as the product of a linking process that leads from a point to a line, from a line to a surface, and then from a surface to space.

In *Italian Thoughts* (1993), they introduce the gothic way of thinking as a regime of spatial ordering that follows regularities, proportionalities, and spatial rasters, is repetitive, and has the appearance of having been constructed out of flat surfaces. When discussing how medieval city streets differ from those built during the Renaissance, they characterize the streets of the Renaissance as theater, while describing gothic paths as facts.[66] Medieval streets are organically grown and respond to topography, to edges determined by water, land use, and other factors, and function as cohesive armatures. In this, they are similar to the organization of Maki's farming village. The Smithsons claim that receptiveness for the gothic mindset was revived in the 1950s, when the first experiences with highways were made in New York, Boston, and Los Angeles. According to their argumentation, these traffic infrastructures were perceived as geographical facts that gave order to the modern city, just as natural elements did in medieval times.[67] They go on to argue that the gothic mindset shall remain visible in the contemporary city too, for example, through a mechanism they call the *magnetism of the edge*.[68] This describes the ability of topological edges to anchor activities and thus also incremental uncomposed expansion, something they illustrate with the example of the developments along canals in Holland. First, the water's edge triggers trade and the construction of buildings, the critical mass of which in turn leads to the establishment of a market along the canal. The structural analogy to Maki's armature in the form of a village street is conspicuous. However, the Smithsons go on to argue that this conglomerate ordering also has to do with our senses and experiences.[69] Being aliens in a place, we might not exactly know where we are, but we are still able to establish some sort of orientation by following light, temperature, and smells, or by decoding other people's spatial behaviors. Following the idea that the conglomerate order is comprised of all of the above, the structure of a place can be described as the relationship between habitus and material form by way of experience, knowledge, and culture. Process is thus inherent in form. Alison and Peter Smithson also state that a building of the conglomerate ordering is an inextricable part of a larger structure. They present this correlation as the revival of the gothic order, whereby arrangements of spatial facts, both representing themselves and the order of the surrounding territory, determine form.[70] This approach aligns with Oswald Mathias Ungers' *Puppet in a Puppet* theme that likewise explains an urban element's spatial ordering through its relation to the larger whole. As a counterexample to this approach, the Smithsons refer to the Renaissance, interpreting it as a composed and theatrical order of form.

Both the "revival of the gothic way of thinking" in Alison and Peter Smithson's writing and Fumihiko Maki's understanding of group form are based on the idea of a "compelling force" that accompanies processes of organic, non-reflexive, incremental growth, as opposed to the planned, composed nature of compositional forms or of the spaces of the Renaissance. The social-material link lies, thus, in the bundling of space and process and associating them with deeds, through which they can mutually influence and transform each other. In his work *Im Raume lesen wir die Zeit* [*In Space We Read Time*] (2003), the historian Karl Schlögel presents a similar argument, asserting that an appropriate image of the world can only be gained "if we begin to think the long forgotten nexus of space, time, and action together again."[71]

42

3. The Experience of Place

The positions presented in the book's third chapter stem from the conviction that urban design is fundamentally about people and, accordingly, questions about the role of *place* in human life are central to the discipline. Conceptions based on this axiom are collectively referred to as *place theories* and typically investigate physical space based on its cultural and human characteristics or, in other words, on its social-psychological dimension.[72] Place theory embraces the complexity of the urban realm by stating that place is created through the synthesis of different elements rather than through the simple manipulation of spatial form. According to this approach, while space is a purposeful void with the potential to physically link things, place is a space with a distinct character and contextual meaning derived from cultural content. Aldo van Eyck's formulation of the shift from "space and time" to "place and occasion" is significant in this respect. He declared in 1962: "Whatever space and time mean, place and occasion mean more. For space in the image of man is place, and time in the image of man is occasion."[73] While adhering to the concept of the space-time bond, introduced previously with the theories of spatial processes, van Eyck's approach adds a further perceptional layer to this nexus and is grounded on the premise that physical space gains additional richness through unique details that are rooted in its genius loci and use. Accordingly, place is formed by people's manifold relationships with physical settings, individual and group activities, meanings, experiences, and memories.

Christian Norberg-Schulz's concept of the *Genius Loci* (1979) describes the sense people have of a place, understood as the totality of all physical and symbolic values in both the natural and human environments.[74] Turning to Halbwachs' theory, this implies that the power of place is to be found in the collective memory related to it. Norberg-Schulz claims that this is especially important for our sense of identity, which may be bound to a particular place; we refer to this, for example, with the expression "I am a New Yorker."[75] The location itself marks the position of the place, but place further consists of the totality of natural and human-made things assembled in a unique way, and may also include the history and associations attached to the place by those who identify with it. While all places have character, this in itself is not enough to induce genius loci. It is the uniqueness, inherent in the form of a place, which makes it special and with which we can readily associate.

Place attachment, place identity, and sense of place are all concepts that describe the quality of people's relationships with a place and are used to study human-place bonding. Environmental behavior studies became prominent in the urban design discourse in the 1960s and 1970s, making an appearance in such classics as Kevin Lynch's *Image of the City* (1960), Jane Jacob's *Death and Life of Great American Cities* (1961), Gordon Cullen's *The Concise Townscape* (1961), and Oscar Newman's *Defensible Space* (1972). After a shift in the discourse towards technological advancement and ecological sustainability, environmentalists have recently raised their voices again to promote the importance of human desires in spatial design. This is exemplified in Jan Gehl's *Cities for People* (2010), Christine Johnson Coffin and Jenny Young's *Making Places for People* (2017), or the slightly older *Strollology —A New Science* by Lucius Burckhardt (1998).

The two approaches presented in this section of the anthology, by Gordon Cullen and Lucius Burckhardt, are both based on individual human-material relations. However, they treat these individual affiliations within the larger context of collective experience, which they activate in order to expand the physical attributes of *place* to include the social dimension. In this way, they demonstrate a triple reading of space as material, social, and psychological spheres, a concept akin to Henri Lefebvre's trilogy of space. Lefebvre, for his part, suggested three perspectives in order to understand the fundamental relationships involved in urban relational space: the perceived space, *l'espace perçu*; the lived space, *l'espace vécu*; and the conceived space, *l'espace conçu*.[76] The perceived space, which signifies people's direct perception of the space, and the lived space, which refers to the use of the space as a part of the everyday world, describe relationships between the space and the human being, implying the concrete physical presence of people within the physical space. The conceived space, in contrast, is an indirect relationship that is also possible without a concrete physical presence and encompasses the idea of the space but also such things as its planning, regulation, supervision, and funding.

Gordon Cullen claimed that one's identification with place is triggered by visual impacts that activate memories and experiences and coined the term *art of relationship*[77] to describe this relation on a rather small local scale. In contrast, the sociologist Lucius Burckhardt discusses the cognitive appropriation of space in a regional context, from the perspective of strollers and voyagers that move in the space being investigated. His approach can be associated with the neo-Kantian cultural philosopher Ernst Cassirer's thesis, according to which experiencing—as an extension to the concept of knowledge—provides the actual foundation for our reference to the world, both within and beyond science proper: "It is not just observation but action that forms the epicenter from which the mental organization of reality starts for human beings."[78] This *experiencing* expresses itself in language, as well as in myths, religion, art, and architecture.[79] For the latter, experiencing can also be understood as an analytical and normative concept that contributes both to a better understanding of the world and experimental changes to it. The concept of experience is thus not only anchored as a richness of experience in the past, but is also based in the present as an inquisitive experiment in the sense of something to be newly discovered. Resting on these foundations, Burckhardt's *strollology* is a cultural-scientific and aesthetic method of research that aims to make people aware of the conditions for experiencing the environment and further expanding their perception. It is based both on a cultural-historical analysis of forms of environmental perception and on experimental practices such as "reflexive walks".[80] These explorations attempt to clarify planning issues using the example of typical and everyday situations. In addition, "reflexive walks" are connected to the questions of what one sees and why one sees it, and how and why one behaves certain ways in specific situations. Burckhardt's aim was for planners to have personal experiences relevant to planning. To this end, he initiated per-formative art projects, such as hosting a seminar in a parking lot or strolling on busy streets at an incredibly slow pace—aiming in both cases to provoke and examine the reactions of drivers and passers-by.[81] His aesthetic interventions in everyday situations are therefore not only to be understood in an artistic sense, but are also aimed at making the participants aware of certain perceptual and behavioral habits and making familiar situations perceptible in new ways. This is because many planning issues are ultimately aesthetic problems that result from established perception patterns.[82]

Although his cultural-historical research was clearly scientific, Burckhardt did not conceive the science of walking in the sense of a strictly academic science with a paradigmatic core and established methodology. In his opinion, a purely scientific methodology would not be appropriate for a discipline that also includes design aspects.[83] Hence, his down-to-earth method disassembles the demarcation line between professionals and laypeople and makes way for the participative co-construction of a shared reality, with the joint narration of experiences acting as a first step towards mutual understanding.

In *The Concise Townscape* (1961), Gordon Cullen discusses the visual impact the city has on its users and their activities, and how this becomes a force of spatial organization. He claims that, in an urban conglomeration, buildings can collectively provide visual pleasure which none could give separately. This is made possible through what Cullen calls the *art of relationship* that takes all elements of the environment—buildings, plants, water, traffic, billboards and so on—and weaves them together in such a way that drama is released.[84] This is illustrated in his book by the experience of climbing up a hill on a winding road to find yourself in a tiny village street at the summit. If you then enter a restaurant and are served on the veranda, you might find—with exhilaration or horror—that this veranda is cantilevered out over a several-hundred-meter drop. Cullen argues: "By this device of the containment (street) and the revelation (cantilever) the fact of height is dramatized and made real."[85]

As opposed to Alison and Peter Smithson who maintain in *Italian Thoughts* that it is the combination of our different senses that allow us to orient in unknown territories, Cullen says that the environment is almost entirely comprehended through vision. He coined the term *serial vision* to describe the notion of the pedestrian strolling through town at a uniform speed, perceiving the scenery as a series of impulses and revelations.[86] In addition to the perception of place and the image of space, Cullen implicitly addresses the relationship between object and movement or, in other words, the city's psychic content. This can be exemplified by Cullen's drawings that explore the event of arriving at or leaving different "city rooms" by illuminating contrasts and transitions.[87] *The Concise Townscape* strives to define place and context through the individual's relationship to material space. By having a sense of identity with the environment, one feels a street or a square when in it or when entering or leaving it. Cullen argues that the introduction of *here* automatically means that there has to be a *there* and that some of the greatest townscape effects are provided by the charged relationship of these two.[88] These are represented in Cullen's casebook with a set of spatial patterns, each comprised by a variety of different architectural aspects—similar to Christopher Alexander's collection of patterns. The aim here is to assist in charting the structure of the subjective world, which can also be understood as the form of the city. Furthermore, both Alexander's and Cullen's ordering patterns contribute to the differentiation of a place from its surroundings, the advancement of its legibility, and the creation of coherence. In her discussion of how the built environment changes our lives, Sarah Williams Goldhagen asserts that humans are ever on the lookout for iterative patterns because they want to quickly assign meaning to the things they encounter, and recognizing and identifying patterns of place produces a sensation of pleasure.[89] In a similar vein, Robert Hart suggests that recognizing familiar places that we can associate with patterns culminating from our experience has a warm emotional power that biases our actions. "The feeling is easy to rationalize," he postulates.[90] Something that worked in the past is considered safe and reassuring. This is one of the main reasons why Cullen also incorporates the subjective values of inhabitants and space-users into his "art of the environment" and makes the case for patterns of comforting perceptions, such as enclosure or the notion of here and there.

Despite their conspicuous differences in approach and time of origin, both Cullen's and Burckhardt's work can be contextualized in the domain of phenomenology, which introduces the idea of how the environment affects the fundamental character of our lived experience. In this approach, *place* does not refer to the locality, but consists of factors that together consolidate to form the environment's character, also described as its perceptible atmosphere. The German philosopher Gernot Böhme expands on the topic of architectural atmosphere in his essay on *Atmosphere as the Subject Matter of Architecture* (2005). He addresses the "nature of space" as the combination of the physicality of an actual space and the atmospheric qualities that are embedded within the space. Böhme states that one must thus be physically present in space to experience it in its entirety.[91] A handful of contemporary architects share this attitude, amongst them Peter Zumthor, who emphasizes the sensory aspects of architecture. He argues that every design should expand its considerations to the perception of atmospheres and should therefore mediate between "composure and seduction".[92] He proceeds to explain that architecture is not merely an automated, apathetic process but one that involves emotive feelings and human understanding. It is an art that engages people and highly influences their state of mind, activating all senses based on processes of perception and appreciation—precisely like Burckhardt's participatory observations or Cullen's recognition of one's identity with the environment.

Whether related to the nexus between objects and movements, material space and behavior patterns, or experience and the psychological dimension of space, at the core of all these considerations lie the social-material relations that constitute the urban form of each place.

4. The Agency of Things

The conception of social-material relations being core constituents of form is further expanded by theories that endow non-human actors with agency, which are introduced in the fourth chapter. In *Things Theory* (2001), the linguist Bill Brown writes about human-object interactions, challenging the apolitical approach that is often taken in the discourse of things by contesting the commonplace notion that things should exist outside of social theory.[93] French sociologist Bruno Latour goes even further by arguing that agency, or involvement in social relationships, should not be limited to humans. He claims that objects have agency too and, accordingly, should be appreciated as actors in any course of action that involves them. His argument is based on the fact that "Any thing that does modify a state of affairs by making a difference is an actor—or, if it has no figuration yet, an actant."[94] Thus, according to Latour, the question that must be asked about any agent is if it makes a difference in the course of another agent's action or not. Things create social relations through their inherent power to produce both disagreement and attachment to the extent that it is actually things that make us public. Consequently, any material form should be understood as social assembly—an arena in which human and non-human actors both perform. In Latour's words: "As Heidegger recognized, a thing is first and foremost a gathering of relations that has an existential bearing upon us."[95] In this way, humans and things always form a social network seamlessly woven together by what Latour famously termed "Ariadne's thread".[96] Stemming from the same roots as Alison and Peter Smithson's theory on the ability of things to spark spatial processes, Churchill's famed statement on the agency of buildings in shaping the way their human users act, or Maurice Lagueux's argument on architecture's performance in influencing social deeds through design, Latour's interpretation goes a step further by explicitly placing things in bundles of relationships with humans, and these relationships—in turn—constitute any urban form.

Ludwig Wittgenstein heralded the birth of philosophical modernism when asserting in his *Tractatus* (1921) that the world is the totality of facts, not things.[97] In contrast, Latour argues for a philosophical post-modernism where the world is the totality of things, not facts, and where facts give way to intricate entanglements and are, thus, to be understood as products of the activities of things. According to Latour, we live in an age of endless innovation where things are increasingly taking on a life of their own—the recent pinnacle of this trend being the emergence of artificial intelligence. Therefore, goes the argument, we cannot rely on traditional notions and definitions of things as mere inert objects that exist in isolation from ourselves as controlling subjects. Matters of fact should give way to matters of concern. This leads Latour to ask what exactly is a *thing* in today's context and to suggest examining the *thing* itself, instead of prioritizing its representation or biased understanding. In his essay on *Dingpolitik* (2005), he claims that: "Objects—taken as so many issues—bind all of us in ways that map out a public space profoundly different from what is usually recognized under the label of the political."[98] According to this politicized understanding of public space, the city's spaces are established through social activities, while structuring them at the same time, making it impossible to isolate material background (things) from relevant activities (social network). Latour goes on to claim that, despite this conspicuous relevance of things (or issues) to our socio-political structures, the political discourse remains on the rather abstract level of opinions, positions, and problem solving that he calls *Realpolitik*. His idea is to bring politics back to *things* and to see what happens when the various assemblies in which things are shaped and decided are compared to the traditional vocabulary of politics. Accordingly, he pleads for a shift from *Realpolitik* to *Dingpolitik*.

Motivated by the desire of paying attention to the many urban things and their correlations, the Catalan urban planner Manuel de Solà-Morales converted Latour's relational theory into a things-based design approach he calls *material urbanity*.[99] He uses the term *skin of the city* to describe the accumulation of all things we can perceive with our senses and through which we experience the city.[100] In addition to human users of space, this also includes actants of all forms and dimensions, such as "a pavement, a glass façade, a wall, a ramp or a distant perspective […], a closed patio […] [or] unfinished roads half-occupied by provisional pieces of furniture". De Solà-Morales argues that the materiality of the city's skin and its physical sensations determine the form of any urbanity. According to him, skin—and thus form—shall be defined as the materialization of the density of specific elements and episodes that relate people to things.

De Solà starts his argument with the observation that the contemporary city is undergoing such rapid transformation that the establishment of a lasting catalogue or typology of its spaces is hardly possible. However, in *A Matter of Things* (2008), he refutes the resulting "worn out mantra" that the city is in retreat and has become a virtual territory without actual place. He claims the contrary, namely that there are more places and more contacts every day. He goes on to suggest the establishment of new perspectives in order to accommodate ourselves to this new multiplicity, stating his belief that contemporary urban territory cannot be understood by applying century-old patterns of clear-cut spaces and cemented relations. Instead, de Solà argues, one needs to pay attention to the many urban things and decode their kaleidoscopic correlations. All of these, together, determine the form of the ever-changing metropolis.

More precisely, de Solà-Morales proposes urban projects on different scales and settings that shape the skin of the city. His approach is based on the social-material nexus and goes beyond mapping existing relationships, as many humans, other living beings, and things are not yet involved in episodes. Some may seem impossible to integrate, yet often have a high potential for engaging in new relationships, which can be activated through targeted design. De Solà's conception aims at a state in which different and conflicting perceptions and activities by different actors are embedded in a diverse and manifold context of meaning, hence tying things into multiple relationships through urban design. This also makes it possible for urban situations to have several interpretations. The aforementioned has three essential effects that provide a description of the urban qualities of a place.[101] The first effect is an increase in resource efficiency due to the multiple use of things by different users for different purposes. The second effect is that various diverse people and groups are assembled—even if these encounters do not actually take place in physical space, but instead through a shared awareness of the space. The juxtaposition of these manifold uses and meanings leads to a third effect, in which the diversity of relationships may cause rivalry and therefore conflict, for example if different uses disturb or contradict one another in terms of their ideas about the meaning and importance of the space. Thus, the richness and diversity of relationships causes things to become matters of concern, that is, more disputed which in turn valorizes public life. The precise configuration of the skin of the city can generate and enable new relationships, but it can also destroy or prevent them. According to de Solà-Morales, there are three different connection techniques that can be used to harness existing potential, depending on the prevailing situation:

1. If there is a lack of elements to connect, it is appropriate to "create a place". This can be done by generating relationship potential or "inventing things", for example in the form of temporary uses or events that link different actors in a shared urban episode.
2. If there is sufficient relationship potential, it is often appropriate to connect or "overlap things" in order to achieve a "condensed form", which brings together different movement streams, uses, and programs.
3. If there is a high level of diversity, perhaps even to the degree of chaos or confusion, it is necessary to isolate certain elements or to place things in productive conflict in order to produce urban complexity, or a "heterogeneous accumulation" of various agencies.

From an urban design point of view, de Solà's urban project is concerned with the social angle and thus with the power, effect, and suggestiveness of things in their precise geometry and material nature. The skin of the city is therefore an intrinsic, active part of the urban. Its characteristics determine whether urbanity is possible.[102] One example is the design concept of the city's porosity, as described by the sociologist Richard Sennett.[103] Sennett demonstrates that spatial proximity alone is not enough to enable sensual relationships. Porosity, or the permeable configuration of boundaries between different urban spaces, is a decisive factor. He illustrates this idea using the transition from the street to the ground floor, via transition zones. Sennett notes that various aspects of buildings make them unapproachable—they may feature smooth, opaque, or mirrored façades, as well as deterrent enclosures and green strips. Conversely, a porous design includes openings that allow visual and physical contact (readability, accessibility) or transition zones that are used (viability, usability), maintained (controllability), and—over time—transformed (adaptability), and thus invite various and dynamic relationships. Sufficient porosity within the city is a vital physical characteristic of the urbanity of things, one that enables the skin of the city to have a multitude of different relationships.

In contrast to Alexander, Rossi, and similar thinkers, de Solà's skin approach denounces lasting catalogues of spatial types and patterns, offering instead a new perspective for dealing with contemporary urban spaces that transform at a rapid pace. While modernism approached the city's skin as being independent of the supporting structure, and post-modernists criticized this suggestion for degrading skin to a mere decoration with no real meaning, Bruno Latour claims that there is no underlying structure at all, only the visible skin exists, with political structures attached to the objects themselves.[104] De Solà joins Latour in this debate, claiming that skin itself is the principle structure of the organism, that is, of the city. For de Solà, skin is also the "Lebensraum", a form that comprises the city's many social-material relations. In this approach, the human users of space are inseparable from the things they engage in relationships with, and physical changes to the membrane—its acupuncture, in de Solà's vocabulary—also have a transformative effect on societal activities, for instance, by altering streams of people. Consequently, mindsets can also be changed and material transformation can ultimately lead to systemic change, such as new forms of political organization.

While Latour's concept of extending agency to non-human actors and interpreting them as integral constituents of any social network is probably the most radical approach to social-material relations presented in this anthology, its application by de Solà-Morales sheds light on its practicability for the urban design praxis. It is only through this understanding that the designer becomes able to identify, manipulate, multiply, and enrich the many relationships humans, other living entities, and material things engage in.

Epilogue: Relevance for the Contemporary Discourse

As the above introduction attempts to demonstrate, the relational perspective guides us back to the core of the discipline, offering a particular way of looking at the world and providing a method with which to undertake the challenges and problems of our times. Hereinafter, we hope to clarify the relevance the "relational approach" has for the contemporary discourse and to identify its main lessons for the practices of architecture and urban design.

The first chapter, TYPE, introduces us to the significance of practice-related wisdom in avoiding "misunderstood scientifications" of the art of building. As Lucius Burckhardt pointed out: a purely scientific methodology is not appropriate for a design discipline.[105] Given that the problems tackled by architecture, not to mention urban design, are complex and vexing, often containing unclarity and contradiction, they cannot be uniformly processed or even objectified in methodological terms. In his book *Thinking Design* (1996), the design theoretician Horst Rittel explains that such "wicked problems" mostly manifest themselves as a bundle of ambiguous, individual issues from different disciplines, existing in obvious contradiction with one another.[106] They recognize no clearly right or wrong solution but can instead only be solved for better or for worse. Therefore, the design practice calls for an independent form of knowledge, a form that must be differentiated from the principles of epistemic science independent of context. Alexander's *pattern language*, Rossi's *cultural types*, and Ungers' *themes* are all just such forms of knowledge, culturally informed theories of practice. They demonstrate that establishing a repertoire does not follow standardized, epistemic techniques and is based on organizing factors inherent in the production of space. In this respect, the Danish economist and planning theorist Bent Flyvbjerg points out that the foundations of such forms of knowledge are "not rules, but instead thousands of examples, comparative, direct, and intuitively based on experience".[107] He goes on to term these repertoires *holistic patterns* which, according to him, comprise countless examples that are compared with each new situation in the search of analogies and differences.[108]

In his magnum opus *How We Think* (1910), the philosopher John Dewey describes the difference between the application of rules in the sense of scientific principles and a reflective practice that cannot be understood in deductive rules due to its inconsistency and complexity and finds an example for the latter in Aristotle's *phronesis*.[109] Aristotle describes *phronesis* as a specific type of wisdom relevant to practical action, implying both good judgement and excellence of character and habits, sometimes referred to as "practical virtue"—as opposed to the factual knowledge encompassed by *epistemes*.[110] In keeping with this tradition of thought, the holistic patterns presented in the anthology provide a hermeneutical description of architecture and urban design anchored both culturally and in the practice of building. They equip the discipline with comprehensive models which, being transdisciplinary figures of thought, allow for a shared cultural understanding of space and habitat.

The second chapter, PROCESS, sheds light on the spatialization of time or, in other words, space's capacity for temporal action. Such conceptions can be contextualized in the spatial turn of the humanities and social sciences. Recent study in these fields has rejuvenated inquiries by engaging spatial praxis across time and, in doing so, contributed to the interdisciplinary perspective that has transformed the methodology of related disciplines. Critical geographers, such as David Harvey, Doreen Massey, and Edward Soja, amongst many others, offer a perspective in which space is every bit as important as time in the unfolding of human affairs, a view in which space is not relegated to an afterthought of social relations, but is intimately involved in their very construction.[111] Martina Löw demonstrates in *Raumsoziologie* [Sociology of Space] (2001) that one can only gain an appropriate understanding of space when its existence is seen as the relation between things and human action. In line with this, space should be understood as an actor capable of triggering processes.

Approaches such as Alison and Peter Smithson's *gothic way of thinking* or Fumihiko Maki's *collective form* are associated with theories of spatial emergence. These denounce the arbitrary composition of physical space and claim that the form of the environment should rather be understood as being the result of time-based, multifaceted, highly interconnected, and evolutionary processes that are triggered by "facts". The relevance of these approaches to the discourse lies in their conceptualization of the emergent nature and nonlinear dynamics of spatial processes, and in their understanding of the world as an incremental reality, where the totality of the many analogous deeds is always more valuable than their simple sum. Although coming from a very different perspective, Gordon Cullen sees the relationship between the city and its constituting episodes similarly when proclaiming that the visual pleasure provided collectively by the conglomerate of buildings is not to be understood as an aggregate of the satisfactions each building could provide individually.[112]

It is much more than that and this surplus lies in the manifold complex relations between the distinctive elements and in the users' perception of the resulting spatial patterns and atmospheres.

Finally, the Smithsons' interpretation of contemporary highway infrastructure and pipelines as geographical facts[113] and Maki's idea of linkage in road and other infrastructures in his group and megastructure forms[114] both discuss infrastructure's ability of giving order to spatial development. This makes another important contribution to the discourse by valorizing infrastructures as important spatial actors with agency in the development of urban form.

The pertinence of the anthology's third chapter, PLACE, is manifest in that it provides the discourse with an apparatus for a democratized understanding of the role of experts within the fields of design and planning. The down-to-earth methods presented in this section, including Burckhardt's *strollology* and Cullen's *art of environment*, de-heroize professionals and reframe reality through participative co-construction based on shared everyday experience. The emerging polyphony of various pragmatic methods and approaches is more suited to dealing with the complex and multi-faceted problems that involve a large diversity of actors and their often conflicting motivations—goes the argument here.

In addition, this chapter also highlights the relevance of the psychological and psycho-geographical dimensions of urban design. This encompasses the individual experience of urban space, as well as the collective imagination of the shared living environment. In this context, one should reiterate the relevance of Henri Lefebvre's trilogy of space, which distinguishes perceived, lived, and conceived spaces, and thus diversifies the urban design discourse by integrating into it the various spatial concepts of the many different actors involved.

The most important contribution of the book's fourth chapter, THINGS, is to be found in its establishment of a hybrid human-technology unity, or the attribution of agency to things in any societal action they are involved in. Bruno Latour's "Parliament of

Things" interprets anything "real" that an actor claims as a source of motivation for action.[115] This also implies a new understanding of the relation between human and non-human entities as opposed to the common interpretation of the first being controlling subjects, while the latter controlled objects within a shared environment. In the course of this paradigm shift, the hard boundary between "human-made" and "natural" is dissolved, giving way to an ecological approach that treats nature and culture as realms mutually inherent within each other.

"Things theory" also lends itself as a valuable paradigmatic foundation of design methods that have the goal of providing urban life with enhanced diversity, vitality, and sustainability by shaping the city's skin and laying the foundations for productive relationships between humans, other living beings, and material artifacts. De Solà's "Urban Projects", for example, are concerned with the social angle, the atmosphere, and the suggestiveness of things, through manipulating their geometrical and material qualities. The skin of the city, claims de Solà, is an active part of the urban and, like an epidermis for living beings, it has a central role in the social-material reality of cities and landscapes.[116] It can internalize traces of use, can be appropriated and changed over time—or can have an aseptic and evasive effect. De Solà thus reminds us that the shape and materiality of the city's surfaces should by no means be underestimated in the production of space, and that this aspect of space is still highly topical.

In conclusion, we wish to argue that many fundamental issues of contemporary urban design can be understood along and historically derived from the narrative of space as an amalgam of the social and the material. Thus, the compass this anthology presents should not only be helpful in organizing different themes into a coherent body of knowledge and anchoring them to the disciplinary core, but also in providing a theoretical framework for evaluating new phenomena and positions in the practice and discourse of urban design.

1. Christopher Alexander, *Notes on the Synthesis of Form*, (Cambridge: Harvard University Press, 1964), 91.

2. Winston Churchill, in his speech to the meeting in the House of Lords, 28 October 1943.

3. Bruno Latour, *Reassembling the Social. An Introduction to Actor-Network-Theory* (Oxford: Oxford University Press, 2005).

4. Martina Löw, *Raumsoziologie* (Frankfurt am Main: Suhrkamp, 2001).

5. See for example: Diana MacCallum, *Discourse Dynamics in Participatory Planning: Opening the Bureaucracy to Strangers* (Farnham: Ashgate Publishing, 2009).

6. Immanuel Kant, *Kritik der Urteilskraft [Critique of the Power of Judgment]* (Berlin: Verlag Lagarde und Friedrich, 1790).

7. Aldo Rossi, *The Architecture of the City* (Cambridge, MIT Press, 1982), 40. First published as *L'architettura della città* (1966).

8. Anthony Giddens, *New Rules of Sociological Method: A Positive Critique of Interpretative Sociologies* (London: Hutchinson, 1976), 128–129.

9. Maurice Lagueux, "Ethics Versus Aesthetics in Architecture", in: *The Philosophical Forum*, Vol. 35, No. 2 (2004), 117–133.

10. Ibid., 131.

11. Ludger Schwarte, *Philosophie der Architektur* (Munich: Fink Wilhelm GmbH + Co. KG, 2009), 9.

12. Ibid., 10.

13. Löw, *Raumsoziologie*, 24–35.

14. Ibid., 167–168.

15. Hannah Arendt, *The Human Condition* (Chicago: University of Chicago Press, 1958).

16. Ibid., 198–199.

17. Ibid.

18. Hannah Arendt, *Crises of the Republic* (New York: Harcourt Brace Jovanovich, 1972), 143–155.

19. Sarah Williams Goldhagen, *Welcome to Your World – How the Built Environment Shapes our Lives* (New York: HarperCollins Publishers, 2017), xiii–xiv.

20. Ibid., 62.

21. Ibid., xxvii.

22. Ibid., 45–52.

23. Ibid., 62–66.

24. Richard Buday, "We Shape Buildings, But Do Buildings Really Shape Us?" in: CommonEdge.org, accessed 13 October 2020, https://commonedge.org/we-shape-buildings-but-do-buildings-really-shape-us/.

25. Ibid.

26. Ibid.

27. Robert Lamb Hart, *How Buildings Shape Us*, in: CommonEdge.org, accessed 13 October 2020, https://commonedge.org/how-buildings-shape-us/.

28. The key figures of *Tendenza* were Aldo Rossi, Giorgio Grassi, Massimo Scolari, and Ezio Bonfanti. See: Geoffrey Broadbent, *Emerging Concepts in Urban Space Design* (London: Van Nostrand Reinhold, 1990), 178–183.

29. Aldo Rossi, *The Architecture of the City* (Cambridge, MIT Press, 1982), 35–40. First published as *L'architettura della città* (1966).

30. Maurice Halbwachs, "On Collective Memory" (Chicago: The University of Chicago Press, 1992). First published as "*Les cadres sociaux de la mémoire*", in: Félix Alcan (ed.), *Les Travaux de L'Année Sociologique* (Paris, 1925).

31. Rossi, *The Architecture of the City*, 40.

32. Ibid., 39.

33. Ibid., 40.

34. Ibid.

35. Mark Johnson, *The Body in the Mind. The Bodily Basis of Meaning, Imagination, and Reason* (Chicago: University of Chicago Press, 1987).

36. Christopher Alexander, Sara Ishikawa, Murray Silverstein, *A Pattern Language* (Oxford: Oxford University Press, 1977).

37. Lucius Burckhardt, "Design Is Invisible", in Jesko Fezer and Martin Schmitz (eds.), *Lucius Burckhardt Writings. Rethinking Man-made Environments. Politics, Landscape & Design* (Vienna/New York: Springer, 2012), 153–165 (153–154).

38. Kevin Lynch, *A Theory of Good City Form* (Cambridge: MIT Press, 1981), 48.

39. Ibid., 280.

40. Ibid., 285.

41. Ibid., 277.

42. Ibid., 288.

43. Oswald Mathias Ungers, *Die Thematisierung der Architektur* (Zurich: Niggli Verlag, 2011), 15. First published by the Technical University of Dortmund in 1983.

44. Ibid., 16.

45. Ibid., 63.

46. Oswald Mathias Ungers, *Morphologie. City Metaphors* (Cologne: Verlag der Buchhandlung WalterKönig, 1982), 9.

47. Johnson, *The Body in the Mind*, 29.

48. Ibid., 37.

49. Elisabeth List, "Die Kreativität des Lebendigen und die Entstehung des Neuen", in: Daniel Gethmann, Susanne Hauser (eds.), *Kulturtechnik Entwerfen. Praktiken, Konzepte und Medien in Architektur und Design Science* (Bielefeld: Transcript Verlag), 319–332.

50. Ungers, *Morphologie*, 8.

51. Donald Schön, *The Reflective Practitioner: How Professionals Think in Action* (New York: Basic Books, 1983).

52. Ibid., 138.

53. Oswald Mathias Ungers, "Über das Denken und Entwerfen in Bildern und Vorstellungen", in: Manfred Sundermann, Claudia Lang, Maria Schwarz (eds.), *Rudolph Schwarz, Architektur und Denkmalpflege* 17 (Düsseldorf/Bonn: Akademie der Architektenkammer Nordrhein-Westfalen, 1981), 23. See also: Wolfgang Pehnt, *Die Plangestalt des Ganzen. Der Architekt und Stadtplaner Rudolph Schwarz (1897–1961) und seine Zeitgenossen* (Cologne: Verlag der Buchhandlung Walther König, 2011), 178.

54. Fumihiko Maki, *Investigations in Collective Form*, Special Publication of the School of Architecture (St. Louis: Washington University, 1964).

55. Ibid., 16.

56. Ibid., 11.

57. Ibid., 13–14.

58. Johan Huizinga, *Homo ludens. Proeve eener bepaling van het spel-element der cultuur* [*Homo Ludens. A Study of the Play-Element in Culture*] (Leiden: Leiden University Press, 1938).

59. Constant, *The Decomposition of the Artist: Five Texts by Constant* (New York: The Drawing Center, 1999), a12.

60. Ibid.

61. Bevin Cline and Tina di Carlo, "The Megastructure", in Terence Riley (ed.), *The Changing of the Avant-Garde: Visionary Architectural Drawings from the Howard Gilman Collection* (New York: The Museum of Modern Art, 2002), 44.

62. Gallery label from *9+1 Ways of Being Political: 50 Years of Political Stances in Architecture and Urban Design*, 12 September 2012–25 March 2013, MoMa, New York.

63. Alison Smithson and Peter Smithson, *Italian Thoughts* (London: Alison and Peter Smithson Architects, 1993), 58–69.

64. Max Risselada, "Conglomerate Ordering, Growing Houses", in: Dirk van den Heuvel, Max Risselada (Eds.), *Alison and Peter Smithson—from the House of the Future to a House of Today* (Rotterdam: 010 Publishers, 2004), 180.

65. Peter Smithson, manuscript in: Baker, John (Ed.), "A Smithson File", *Arena. The Architectural Association Journal*, February 1966,21.

66. Alison Smithson and Peter Smithson, *Italian Thoughts Followed Further*, manuscript (London: Alison and Peter Smithson Architects, 1997), 8.

67. Ibid., 9.

68. Ibid., 33.

69. Smithson and Smithson, *Italian Thoughts*, 58, 60.

70. Smithson and Smithson, *Italian Thoughts Followed Further*, 27.

71. Karl Schlögel, *Im Raume lesen wir die Zeit: Über Zivilisationsgeschichte und Geopolitik* [In Space We Read Time: On the History of Civilization and Geopolitics] (Munich: Carl Hanser Verlag GmbH & Co. KG, 2003), 24.

72. Roger Trancik, *Finding Lost Space* (New York: Van Nostrand Reinhold Company, 1986), 112.

73. Herman Hertzberger, *Lessons for Students in Architecture* (Rotterdam: Nai Publishers, 2009), 193.

74. Christian Norberg-Schulz, *Genius Loci—Towards a Phenomenology of Architecture* (New York: Rizzoli International Publications, 1979), 6–23.

75. Ibid., 21.

76. Henri Lefebvre, *The Production of Space* (Hoboken: Blackwell Publishing, 1991), 38–40. First published as *La production de l'espace* (Paris: Anthropos, 1974).

77. Gordon Cullen, *The Concise Townscape* (Oxford: The Architectural Press, 1961), 7–8.

78. Ernst Cassirer, *Philosophie der symbolischen Formen. Band II: Das mythische Denken* [The Philosophy of Symbolic Forms. Vol. 2: Mythical Thinking] (Darmstadt: Wissenschaftliche Buchgesellschaft, [1925] 1994), 187.

79. Ibid.

80. Lucius Burckhardt, "Die Spaziergangswissenschaft", in Markus Ritter and Martin Schmitz (eds.), *Warum ist Landschaft schön? Die Spaziergangs-wissenschaft* (Berlin: Martin Schmitz Verlag, 2006), 257–300.

81. See, for example: Lucius Burckhardt, *Autofahrer-spaziergang* [Car Drivers' Walk], Kassel 1993, seminar "Wahrnehmung und Verkehr" [Perception and Traffic].

82. Lucius Burckhardt, "Promenadologische Betrachtungen über die Wahrnehmung der Umwelt und die Aufgaben unserer Generation" [Strollological Observations on the Perception of the Environment and the Tasks Facing Our Generation], in Markus Ritter and Martin Schmitz (eds.), *Warum ist Landschaft schön? Die Spaziergangswissenschaft* [Why Is Landscape Beautiful? The Science of Strollology] (Berlin: Schmitz, 2006), 251.

83. Lucius Burckhardt, "Promenadologie—Eine neue Wissenschaft" [Strollology—A New Science], in: *Passagen/Passages* No. 24, 1998, 3–5.

84. Cullen, *The Concise Townscape*, 8.

85. Ibid., 10.

86. Ibid., 9.

87. Trancik, *Finding Lost Space*, 122.

88. Cullen, *The Concise Townscape*, 11.

89. Goldhagen, *Welcome to Your World*, 220–221.

90. Robert Lamb Hart, *A New Look at Humanism in Architecture, Landscapes and Urban Design* (Middletown: Meadowlark Publishing, 2015), 95.

91. Gernot Böhme, "Atmosphere as the Fundamental Concept of a New Aesthetics", in: *Thesis Eleven*, 1993; 36 (1): 113–126 (122).

92. Peter Zumthor, *Atmospheres: Architectural Environments. Surrounding Objects* (Basel: Birkhäuser Verlag, 2006), 41–45.

93. Bill Brown, "Things Theory", in: *Critical Inquiry*, Vol. 28, No. 1, Things (Autumn, 2001), 1–22.

94. Latour, *Reassembling the Social*, 71.

95. Neil Turnbull, "The Thing and its Politics", in: *Writing Technologies*, Vol. 3 (2010), 100–104 (102).

96. Bruno Latour, *Science in Action: How to Follow Scientists and Engineers Through Society* (Cambridge: Harvard University Press, 1987).

97. Ludwig Wittgenstein, "Tractatus, Logisch-philosophische Abhandlung", in: Wilhelm Ostwald (ed.), *Annalen der Naturphilosophie*, Band 14, 1921, 185–262.

98. Bruno Latour, "From Realpolitik to Dingpolitik or How to Make Things Public", in: Bruno Latour, Peter Weibel, *Making Things Public—Atmospheres of Democracy*, exhibition catalogue (Cambridge: MIT Press, 2005), 4–31 (5).

99. Manuel de Solà-Morales, *A Matter of Things* (Rotterdam: Nai Publishers, 2008), 146–153.

100. Ibid., 23–26.

101. Simon Kretz, Christian Salewski, "Urbanity of Things", in: Tim Rieniets, et.al. (eds.), *The City as Resource* (Berlin: Jovis Verlag, 2014), 167–180 (170–171).

102. Ibid., 178.

103. Richard Sennett, "The Open City", in: Ricky Burdett (ed.), *Towards an Urban Age*, catalogue of the Urban Age Summit (Berlin, 2006), unnumbered pages.

104. Latour, "From Realpolitik to Dingpolitik", 6.

105. Burckhardt, "Promenadologie".

106. Horst W. J. Rittel, *Planen, Entwerfen, Design. Ausgewählte Schriften zu Theorie und Methodik* (Stuttgart: Kohlhammer Verlag, 1996), 75.

107. Bent Flyvbjerg, *Making Social Science Matter. Why Social Inquiry Fails and How It Can Succeed Again* (Cambridge: Cambridge University Press, 2001), 21.

108. Ibid., 20.

109. John Dewey, *How We Think: A Restatement of the Relation of Reflective Thinking to the Educative Process* (Boston: DC Health, 1910), 30, 66, 78.

110. See Patsy Healey, "The pragmatic tradition in planning thought", in: *Journal of Planning Education and Research*, Vol. 28, No. 3 (2009), 277–292.

111. See, for example: David Harvey, "Between Space and Time: Reflections on the Geographical Imagination", in: *Annals of the Association of American Geographers*, Vol. 80, No. 3 (Sep. 1990), 418–434; Doreen B. Massey, *Space, Place, and Gender* (Minneapolis: University of Minnesota Press, 1994); Edward W. Soja, "The Socio-Spatial Dialectic", in: *Annals of the Association of American Geographers*, Vol. 70, No. 2 (Jun. 1980), 207–225.

112. Cullen, *The Concise Townscape*, 7.

113. Smithson and Smithson, *Italian Thoughts Followed Further*, 9, 24–26.

114. Maki, *Investigations*, 8–18.

115. Latour, "From Realpolitik to Dingpolitik", 21–27.

116. De Solà-Morales, *A Matter of Things*, 23.

Type

The first chapter presents two positions that both describe the nexus of the material and societal roles of type. Accordingly, these positions interpret types neither as absolute constants nor as mere physical shapes, but instead as cultural facts. Christopher Alexander compiles an encyclopedic *Pattern Language* of good examples of architectural and urban forms, while Oswald Mathias Ungers explores visual thinking and suggests a pertinent *Thematic Repertoire* for urban design.

Christopher Alexander
A Pattern Language

i. Christopher Alexander, *The Timeless Way of Building* (New York: Oxford University Press, 1979), 81–100.

ii. Christopher Alexander, Sara Ishikawa, and Murray Silverstein, *A Pattern Language: Towns, Buildings, Construction* (New York: Oxford University Press, 1977), x–xviii, xxxvii, xli, 163–167–270–275, 310–314, 451–453.

Suppose I want to understand the "structure" of something. Just what exactly does this mean?

It means, of course, that I want to make a simple picture of it, which lets me grasp it as a whole.

And it means, too, that as far as possible, I want to paint this simple picture out of as few elements as possible. The fewer elements there are, the richer the relationships between them, and the more of the picture lies in the "structure" of these relationships.

And finally, of course, I want to paint a picture which allows me to understand the patterns of events which keep on happening in the thing whose structure I seek. In other words, I hope to find a picture, or a structure, which will, in some rather obvious and simple sense, account for the outward properties, for the pattern of events of the thing which I am studying.

What then, is the fundamental "structure" of a building or a town?

In the crudest sense, we know roughly what the structure of a town or building is.

It is made up of certain concrete elements, with every element associated with a certain pattern of events.

On the geometric level, we see certain physical elements repeating endlessly, combined in an almost endless variety of combinations.

A town is made of houses, gardens, streets, sidewalks, shopping centers, shops, workplaces, factories, perhaps a river, sports fields, parking ...

A building is made up of walls, windows, doors, rooms, ceilings, nooks, stairs, staircase treads, door handles, terraces, counter tops, flowerpots ... repeated over and again.

A gothic cathedral is made of a nave, aisles, west door, transept, choir, apse, ambulatory, columns, windows, buttresses, vaults, ribs, window tracery.

A modern metropolitan region in the United States is made of industrial areas, freeways, central business districts, super-markets, parks, single-family houses, gardens, high-rise housing, streets, arteries, traffic lights, sidewalks ...

And each of these elements has a specific pattern of events associated with it.

Families living in the houses, cars and buses driving in the streets, flowers growing in the flower pots, people walking through the doors, opening and closing them, traffic lights changing, people gathering for mass on Sundays in the nave of the cathedral, forces acting on the vaults, when the wind sways the building, light coming through the windows, people sitting at the windows in their living rooms and looking at the view ...

But this picture of space does not explain how—or why—these elements associate themselves with definite and quite specific patterns of events.

What is the relation between a church, say, taken as an element— and the pattern of events which happens in the church? It is all very well to say that they are connected. But unless we can see some kind of common sense in the connection, it explains nothing.

It is certainly not enough merely to say glibly that every pattern of events resides in space. That is obvious, and not very interesting. What we want to know is just how the structure of the space supports the patterns of events it does, in such, a way that if we change the structure of the space, we shall be able to predict what kinds of changes in the patterns of events this change will generate.

In short, we want a theory which presents the interaction of the space and the events, in a clear and unambiguous way.

Further, it is very puzzling to realize that the "elements", which seem like elementary building blocks, keep varying, and are different every time that they occur.

For among the endless repetition of elements we also see an almost endless variation. Each church has a slightly different nave, the aisles are different, the west door is different ... and in the nave, the various bays are usually different, the individual columns are different; each vault has slightly different ribs; each window has a slightly different tracery and different glass.

And just so in an urban region. Each industrial area is different; each freeway is different; each park is different; each supermarket is different—even the smaller individual elements like traffic lights and stop signs, although very similar, are never quite the same—and there is always a variety of types.

If the elements are different every time that they occur, evidently then, it cannot be the elements themselves which are repeating in a building or a town: these so-called elements cannot be the ultimate "atomic" constituents of space.

Since every church is different, the so-called element we call "church" is not constant at all. Giving it a name only deepens the puzzle. If every church is different, what is it that remains the same, from church to church, that we call "church"?

When we say that matter is made of electrons, protons, and so forth, this is a satisfying way of understanding things, because these electrons seem, indeed, to be the same each time that they occur, and it therefore makes sense to show how matter can be built up from combinations of these "elements", because the elements are truly elementary.

But if the so-called elements of which a building or a town is made—the houses, streets, windows, doors—are merely names, and the underlying things which they refer to keep on changing, then we have no solidity at all in our picture, and we need to find some other elements which truly are invariant throughout the variation, in a way that we can understand a building or a town as a structure made up by combination of these elements.

Let us therefore look more carefully at the structure of the space from which a building or a town is made, to find out what it really is that is repeating there.

We may notice first that over and above the elements there are relationships between the elements which keep repeating too, just as the elements themselves repeat ...

Beyond its elements each building is defined by certain patterns of relationships among the elements.

In a gothic cathedral, the nave is flanked by aisles which run parallel to it. The transept is at right angles to the nave and aisles; the ambulatory is wrapped around the outside of the apse; the columns are vertical, on the line separating nave from aisle, spaced at equal intervals. Each vault connects four columns, and has a characteristic shape, cross-like in plan, concave in space. The buttresses are run down the outside of the aisles, on the same lines as the columns, supporting the load from the vaults. The nave is always a long thin rectangle—its ratio may vary between 1:3 and 1:6, but is never 1:2 or 1:20. The aisles are always narrower than the nave.

74

And each urban region, too, is defined by certain patterns of relationships among its elements.

Consider a typical mid-twentieth-century American metropolitan region. Somewhere towards the center of the region, there is a central business district, which contains a very high-density office block; near these there are high density apartments. The overall density of the region slopes off with distance from the center, according to an exponential law; periodically there are again peaks of higher density, but smaller than the central ones; and subsidiary to these smaller peaks, there are still smaller peaks. Each of these peaks of density contains stores and offices surrounded by higher density housing. Towards the outer fringe of the metropolis there are large areas of freestanding one-family houses; the farther out from the center they are, the larger their gardens. The region is served by a network of freeways. These freeways are closer together at the center. Independent of the freeways, there is a roughly regular two-dimensional network of streets. Every five or ten streets, there is a larger one, which functions as an artery. A few of the arteries are even bigger than the others: these tend to be arranged radially, branching out from the center in a star-shaped fashion. Where an artery meets a freeway, there is a characteristic cloverleaf arrangement of connecting lanes. Where two arteries intersect, there is a traffic light; where a local street meets an artery, there is a stop sign. The major commercial areas, which coincide with the high density peaks in the density distribution, all fall on the major arteries. Industrial areas all fall within half a mile of a freeway; and the older ones are also close to at least one major artery.

Evidently, then, a large part of the "structure" of a building or a town consists of patterns of relationships.

For both the city of Los Angeles and the medieval church get their respective characters as much from these repeating patterns of relationships, as they do from the elements themselves.

At first sight, it seems as though these patterns of relationships are separate from the elements.

Think of the aisle of the cathedral. It is parallel to the nave, and next to it, it shares columns with the nave, it runs east–west, like the church itself, it contains columns, on its inner wall, and windows on its outer wall. At first sight, it seems that these relationships are "extra", over and above the fact of its being an aisle.

When we look closer, we realize that these relationships are not extra, but necessary to the elements, indeed a part of them.

We realize, for instance, that if an aisle were not parallel to the nave, were not next to it, were not narrower than the nave, did not share columns with the nave, did not run east to west ... that it would not be an "aisle" at all. It would be merely a rectangle of space, in a gothic construction, floating free ... and what makes it an aisle, specifically, is just the pattern of relationships which it has to the nave, and other elements around it.

When we look closer still, we realize that even this view is still not very accurate. For it is not merely true that the relationships are attached to the elements: the fact is that the elements themselves are patterns of relationships.

For once we recognize that much of what we think of as an "element" in fact lies in the pattern of relationships between this thing and the things in the world around it, we then come to the second even greater realization, that the so-called element is itself nothing but a myth, and that indeed, the element itself is not just

76

embedded in a pattern of relationships, but is itself entirely a pattern of relationships, and nothing else.

In short, the aisle, which needs the pattern of relationships to the nave and the east window to define it, is itself also a pattern of relationships between its length, its width, the columns which lie on the boundary with the nave, the windows which lie on the outer boundary ...

And finally, the things which seem like elements dissolve, and leave a fabric of relationships behind, which is the stuff that actually repeats itself, and gives the structure to a building or a town.

In short, we may forget about the idea that the building is made up of elements entirely, and recognize instead, the deeper fact that all these so-called elements are only labels for the patterns of relationships which really do repeat.

The freeway, as a whole, does not repeat. But the fact that there are cloverleafs which connect the freeway to roads at certain intervals—that does repeat. There is a certain relationship between the freeway and its crossing arteries and cloverleafs, which does repeat.

But once again, the cloverleaf itself does not repeat. Each cloverleaf is different. What does repeat is that each lane forms a continuously curving off ramp to the right—there is a relationship between its radius, its tangency, the fact that it is banked, which does repeat.

Yet once again the "lane" which figures in this pattern of relationships does not repeat. What we call a lane is itself a relationship among still smaller so-called elements—the edges of the road, the surface, the lines which form the edge ... and these again, although they function temporarily as elements, in order to make these relations clear, themselves evaporate when we look closely at them.

Each one of these patterns is a morphological law, which establishes a set of relationships in space.

This morphological law can always be expressed in the same general form:

$X \rightarrow r$ (A, B, ...), which means:
Within a context of type X, the parts A, B, ... are related by the relationship r.

Thus, for example:
Within a gothic cathedral → the nave is flanked on both sides by parallel aisles.

or:
Where a freeway meets an artery → the access ramps of the interchange take the rough form of a cloverleaf.

And each law or pattern is itself a pattern of relationships among still other laws, which are themselves just patterns of relationships again.

For though each pattern is itself apparently composed of smaller things which look like parts, of course, when we look closely at them, we see that these apparent "parts" are patterns too.

Consider, for example, the pattern we call a door. This pattern is a relationship among the frame, the hinges, and the door itself: and these parts in turn are made of smaller parts: the frame is made of uprights, a crosspiece, and cover moldings over joints; the door is made of uprights, crosspieces and panels; the hinge is made of leaves and a pin. Yet any one of these things we call its "parts" are themselves in fact also patterns, each one of which may take an almost infinite variety of shapes, and color and exact size—without once losing the essential field of relationships which make it what it is.

78

The patterns are not just patterns of relationships, but patterns of relationships among other smaller patterns, which themselves have still other patterns hooking them together—and we see finally, that the world is entirely made of all these inter-hooking, interlocking nonmaterial patterns.

Further, each pattern in the space has a pattern of events associated with it.

For instance, the pattern of the freeway contains a certain fabric of events, defined by rules: drivers drive at certain speeds; there are rules governing the way that people may change lanes; the cars all face the same way; there are certain kinds of overtaking; people drive a little slower on the entrances and exits …

And the pattern of a kitchen, in any given culture, also contains a very definite pattern of events: the way that people use the kitchen, the way that food is prepared, the fact that people eat there, or don't eat there, the fact that they wash the dishes standing at the sink … and on and on …

Of course, the pattern of space, does not "cause" the pattern of events.

Neither does the pattern of events "cause" the pattern in the space. The total pattern, space and events together, is an element of people's culture. It is invented by culture, transmitted by culture, and merely anchored in space.

But there is a fundamental inner connection between each pattern of events, and the pattern of space in which it happens.

For the pattern in the space is, precisely, the precondition, the requirement, which allows the pattern of events to happen. In this sense, it plays a fundamental role in making sure that just this pattern of events keeps on repeating over and over again, throughout the space, and that it is, therefore, one of the things which gives a certain building, or a certain town, its character.

Take, for example, the porch, and the pattern of events we may call "sitting on the porch, watching the world go by."

What aspect of the space is it which is connected to this pattern of events? Certainly it is not the whole porch, in its entirety: it is instead, just certain specific relationships.

For instance, in order for the pattern of events "watching the world go by" to happen, it is essential that the porch should be a little raised above the level of the street; it is essential that the porch be deep enough, to let a group of people sit there comfortably; and it is essential, of course, that the front of the porch be open, pierced with openings, and that the roof is therefore supported on columns.

It is this bundle of relationships which is essential, because these are the ones which are directly congruent with the pattern of events.

By contrast, the length of the porch, its height, its color, the materials of which it is made, the height of the side walls, the way the porch connects up with the inside of the house, are less essential—so they can vary, without altering the fundamental and essential nature of the porch.

And in this same sense, each pattern of relationships in space is congruent with some specific pattern of events.

The pattern of relationships we call a "freeway" is just that pattern of relationships required by the process of driving fast with limited access to and from side roads: in short, it is the pattern of events.

The pattern of relationships we call a Chinese "kitchen" is just that pattern of relationships required for cooking Chinese food: again, the underlying pattern of events.

And insofar as there are different "kinds" of kitchens, there are different patterns of relationships, responsible for slightly different patterns of events, in different cultures, which have different patterns of cooking.

In every case the pattern of relationships in space is that invariant which must repeat itself with some pattern of events, because it is exactly these relationships which are required to sustain that pattern of events.

We realize then that it is just the patterns of events in space which are repeating in the building or the town: and nothing else.

Nothing of any importance happens in a building or a town except what is defined within the patterns which repeat themselves.

For what the patterns do is at the same time seize the outward physical geometry, and also seize what happens there.

They account entirely for its geometrical structure: they are the visible, coherent stuff that is repeating, and coherent there: they are the background of the variation, which makes each concrete element a little different.

And, at the same time, they are also responsible for those events which keep repeating there, and therefore do the most to give the building or a town its character …

Each building gets its character from just the patterns which keep on repeating there.

This is not only true of general patterns; it is true of the entire building: all its details; the shape of rooms, the character of ornament, the kind of windowpanes it has, the boards of which the floor is made, the handles on the doors, the light, the height, the way the ceilings vary, the relationship of windows to the ceiling, the connection of the building to the garden and the street, and to the spaces and the paths and to the detailed seats, and walls which are around it …

Each neighborhood is defined, too, in everything that matters, by the patterns which keep on repeating there.

Again, it is just those details which give the neighborhood a "character" which are defined by patterns: the kind of streets which it has, the kind of lots the houses are; the typical size of houses, the way that the houses are connected or distinct …

Isn't it true that the features which you remember in a place are not so much peculiarities, but rather the typical, the recurrent, the characteristic features: the canals of Venice, the flat roofs of a Moroccan town, the even spacing of the fruit trees in an orchard, the slope of a beach towards the sea, the umbrellas of an Italian beach, the wide sidewalks, sidewalk cafes, cylindrical poster boards and pissoirs of Paris, the porch which goes all the way around a plantation house in Louisiana …

The qualities which make Paris a special place, which make Broadway and Times Square exciting, the qualities which make Venice special, the qualities which make an eighteenth-century London square so peaceful and refreshing—indeed, the qualities in any environment which give it the character you like it for—are its patterns.

A barn gets its structure from its patterns.

It has a certain overall shape, roughly a long rectangle; there is a central portion where the hay is stored, with aisles along the sides where the cows stand; there is a row of columns between the center and the aisle; along these columns are the feeding troughs where the cows feed; there are great doors or double doors at one end; perhaps smaller doors at the other end, in the aisle, for cattle to pass in and out ...

And an expensive restaurant gets its structure and character from its peculiar patterns too.

Small tables, each one with a few chairs; small individual lights at the tables; the head waiter's desk at the entrance, with a light and a place for his reception book. Dark perhaps inside, reds, deep colors, often no windows. A swinging door leading to the kitchen ...

Venice gets its life and structure from its patterns.

A large number of islands, typically about 1,000 feet across, packed together houses, three to five stories high, built right up to the canals; each island with a small square in the middle of it, the square usually with a church; narrow, irregular paths cutting across the islands; hump-backed bridges where these paths cross canals; houses opening onto the canals and onto the streets; steps at the canal entrance (to take care of variations in water level) ...

Venice is the special place it is, only because it has those patterns of events in it, which happen to be congruent with all these patterns in the space.

London gets its life and structure from its patterns too.

First, at the regional scale: the characteristic conglomeration of boroughs, the characteristic location of major railway stations on an inner ring, with the railways radiating outwards, the characteristic location of industry at the periphery. Then, at the next smaller scale there are the characteristic rows of semi-detached "villas", the characteristic interior details of the railway stations, the characteristic squares, with oval or rectangular green parks in the center, the use of roundabouts, traffic moving on the left. Then to more detail:

the interior layout of a typical row house, the particular English character of "filling" stations, the London club, Lyons and Marks, and Spencer's, the shape and height and placing of advertisement boards on bridges and outside railway stations, and their particular characteristic shape and height. Then to more detail: the special kind of staircase baluster, the use of two-inch bricks in Georgian houses, the ratio of bathroom area to house area, compared with that typical of an American house, the use of flagstones on the sidewalks. Then, down to the tiniest details of all—the special shape of English faucets, the kinds of handles on an English metal window, the shape of the insulators on a telegraph pole.

Again, in each case, the patterns define all the typical events which happen there. So "London", as a way of life, lies there completely in these patterns which the Londoners create, and fill with the events that are exactly congruent with them.

And, what is most remarkable of all, the number of the patterns out of which a building or a town is made is rather small.

One might imagine that a building has a thousand different patterns in it; or that a town has tens of thousands …

But the fact is, that a building is defined, in its essentials, by a few dozen patterns. And, a vast town like London, or Paris, is defined, in its essence, by a few hundred patterns at the most.

In short, the patterns have enormous power and depth; they have the power to create an almost endless variety, they are so deep, so general, that they can combine in millions upon millions of different ways, to such an extent, that when we walk through Paris we are mainly overwhelmed by the variety; and the fact that there are these deep invariants, lying behind the vast variety, and it, is really an amazing shock …

In this sense, the patterns are perhaps still deeper and more powerful than the discussion has made clear so far. From a handful of patterns, a vast, almost incalculable variety can be made: and a

84

building, with all of it; complexity and variety, is generated, actually, by a small number of them.

They are the atoms of our man-made universe.

In chemistry, we learn that the world, in all of its complexity, is made up from combinations of some 92 elements, or atoms. This is an extraordinary fact, amazing to a person who learns chemistry for the first time. It is true that our conception of these atoms has changed repeatedly—far from being the little billiard balls we once thought, we know that they are shifting patterns of particles and waves—and that even the most "elementary" particle—the electron—is itself merely a ripple in the universe, not a "thing". However, all these changing views do not alter the fact that at the level of scale where atoms occur, they do occur, as identifiable recurrent entities. And even if vast changes occur in physics, and we one day recognize that these so-called atoms are also merely ripples in a deeper field, the fact that there are entities of some kind which correspond to the things we once called atoms will remain.

Just so, we realize now, that at the larger scale of towns and buildings, the world is also made of certain fundamental "atoms"—that each place is made from a few hundred patterns—and that all of its incredible complexity comes, in the end, simply from the combinations of these new patterns.

Of course the patterns vary from place to place, from culture to culture, from age to age; they are all man-made, they all depend on culture. But still, in every age and every place the structure of our world is given to it, essentially, by some collection of patterns which keeps on repeating over and over and over again.

These patterns are not concrete elements, like bricks and doors—they are much deeper and more fluid—and yet they are the solid substance, underneath the surface, out of which a building or a town is always made.

The elements of what we will call "pattern language" are the II. 163 previously described entities, identified here as patterns of space. Each such pattern describes a problem which occurs over and over again in our environment, and then describes the core of the solution to that problem, in such a way that you can use this solution a million times over, without ever doing it the same way twice.

For convenience and clarity, each pattern has the same format. First, there is a picture, which shows an archetypal example of that pattern. Second, after the picture, each pattern has an introductory paragraph, which sets the context for the pattern, by explaining how it helps to complete certain larger patterns. Then there are three diamonds to mark the beginning of the problem. After the diamonds there is a headline, in bold type. This headline gives the essence of the problem in one or two sentences. After the headline comes the body of the problem. This is the longest section. It describes the empirical background of the pattern, the evidence for its validity, the range of different ways the pattern can be manifested in a building, and so on. Then, again in bold type, like the headline, is the solution—the heart of the pattern—which describes the field of physical and social relationships which are required to solve the stated problem, in the stated context. This solution is always stated in the form of an instruction—so that you know exactly what you need to do, to build the pattern. Then, after the solution, there is a diagram, which shows the solution in the form of a diagram, with labels to indicate its main components.

After the diagram, another three diamonds, to show that the main body of the pattern is finished. And finally, after the diamonds there is a paragraph which ties the pattern to all those smaller patterns in the language, which are needed to complete this pattern, to embellish it, to fill it out.

There are two essential purposes behind this format. First, to present each pattern connected to other patterns, so that you grasp the collection of all 253 patterns as a whole, as a language, within which you can create an infinite variety of combinations. Second, to present the problem and solution of each pattern in such a way that you can judge it for yourself, and modify it, without losing the essence that is central to it.

Let us next understand the nature of the connection between patterns.

The patterns are ordered, beginning with the very largest, for regions and towns, then working down through neighborhoods, clusters of buildings, buildings, rooms and alcoves, ending finally with details of construction.

This order, which is presented as a straight linear sequence, is essential to the way the language works. What is most important about this sequence, is that it is based on the connections between the patterns. Each pattern is connected to certain "larger" patterns which come above it in the language; and to certain "smaller" patterns which come below it in the language. The pattern helps to complete those larger patterns which are "above" it, and is itself completed by those smaller patterns which are "below" it.

Thus, for example, you will find that the pattern ACCESSIBLE GREEN (60), is connected first to certain larger patterns: SUBCULTURE BOUNDARY (13), IDENTIFIABLE NEIGHBORHOOD (14), WORK COMMUNITY (41), and QUIET BACKS (59). These appear on its first page. And it is also connected to certain smaller patterns: POSITIVE OUTDOOR SPACE (107), TREE PLACES (171), and GARDEN WALL (173). These appear on its last page.

What this means, is that IDENTIFIABLE NEIGHBORHOOD, SUBCULTURE BOUNDARY, WORK COMMUNITY, and QUIET BACKS are incomplete, unless they contain an ACCESSIBLE GREEN; and that an ACCESSIBLE GREEN is itself incomplete, unless it contains POSITIVE OUTDOOR SPACE, TREE PLACES, and a GARDEN WALL.

And what it means in practical terms is that, if you want to lay out a green according to this pattern, you must not only follow the instructions which describe the pattern itself, but must also try to embed the green within an IDENTIFIABLE NEIGHBORHOOD or in some SUBCULTURE BOUNDARY, and in a way that helps to form QUIET BACKS; and then you must work to complete the green by building in some POSITIVE OUTDOOR SPACE, TREE PLACES, and a GARDEN WALL.

In short, no pattern is an isolated entity. Each pattern can exist in the world, only to the extent that is supported by other patterns: the larger patterns in which it is embedded, the patterns of the same size that surround it, and the smaller patterns which are embedded in it.

This is a fundamental view of the world. It says that when you build a thing, you cannot merely build that thing in isolation, but must also repair the world around it, and within it, so that the larger world at that one place becomes more coherent, and more whole; and the thing which you make takes its place in the web of nature, as you make it.

Now we explain the nature of the relation between problems and solutions, within the individual patterns.

Each solution is stated in such a way that it gives the essential field of relationships needed to solve the problem, but in a very general and abstract way—so that you can solve the problem for yourself, in your own way, by adapting it to your preferences, and the local conditions at the place where you are making it.

For this reason, we have tried to write each solution in a way which imposes nothing on you. It contains only those essentials which cannot be avoided if you really want to solve the problem. In this sense, we have tried, in each solution, to capture the invariant property common to all places which succeed in solving the problem.

But of course, we have not always succeeded. The solutions we have given to these problems vary in significance. Some are more true, more profound, more certain, than others. To show this clearly, we have marked every pattern, in the text itself, with two asterisks, or one asterisk, or no asterisks.

In the patterns marked with two asterisks, we believe that we have succeeded in stating a true invariant: in short, that the solution we have stated summarizes a property common to all possible ways of solving the stated problem. In these two-asterisk cases we believe, in short, that it is not possible to solve the stated problem properly, without shaping the environment in one way or another according to the pattern that we have given—and that, in these cases, the pattern describes a deep and inescapable property of a well-formed environment.

In the patterns marked with one asterisk, we believe that we have made some progress towards identifying such an invariant: but that with careful work it will certainly be possible to improve on the solution. In these cases, we believe it would be wise for you to treat the pattern with a certain amount of disrespect—and that you seek out variants of the solution which we have given, since there are almost certainly possible ranges of solutions which are not covered by what we have written.

Finally, in the patterns without an asterisk, we are certain that we have *not* succeeded in defining a true invariant—that, on the contrary, there are certainly ways of solving the problem different from the one which we have given. In these cases we have still stated a solution, in order to be concrete—to provide the reader with at least one way of solving the problem—but the task of finding the true invariant, the true property which lies at the heart of all possible solutions to this problem, remains undone.

We hope, of course, that many of the people who read, and use this language, will try to improve these patterns—will put their energy to work, in this task of finding more true, more profound invariants—and we hope that gradually these more true patterns, which are slowly discovered, as time goes on, will enter a common language, which all of us can share.

You see then that the patterns are very much alive and evolving. In fact, if you like, each pattern may be looked upon as a hypothesis like one of the hypotheses of science. In this sense, each pattern represents our current best guess as to what arrangement of the physical environment will work to solve the problem presented. The empirical questions center on the problem—does it occur and is it felt in the way we have described it? —and the solution—does the arrangement we propose in fact resolve the problem? And the asterisks represent our degree of faith in these hypotheses. But of course, no matter what the asterisks say, the patterns are still hypotheses, all 253 of them—and are therefore all tentative, all free to evolve under the impact of new experience and observation.

Let us finally explain the status of this language, why we have called it "A Pattern Language" with the emphasis on the word "A", and how we imagine this pattern language might be related to the countless thousands of other languages we hope that people will make for themselves, in the future.

The Timeless Way of Building says that every society which is alive and whole, will have its own unique and distinct pattern language; and further, that every individual in such a society will have a unique language, shared in part, but which as a totality is unique to the mind of the person who has it. In this sense, in a healthy society there will be as many pattern languages as there are people—even though these languages are shared and similar.

The question then arises: What exactly is the status of this published language? In what frame of mind, and with what intention, are we publishing this language here? The fact that it is published as a book means that many thousands of people can use it. Is it not true that there is a danger that people might come to rely on this one printed language, instead of developing their own languages, in their own minds?

The fact is, that we have written this book as a first step in the society-wide process by which people will gradually become conscious of their own pattern languages, and work to improve them. We believe, and have explained in *The Timeless Way of Building*, that the languages which people have today are so brutal, and so fragmented, that most people no longer have any language to speak of at all—and what they do have is not based on human, or natural considerations.

We have spent years trying to formulate this language, in the hope that when someone uses it, they will be so impressed by its power, and so joyful in its use, that they will understand again what it means to have a living language of this kind. If we only succeed in that, it is possible that each person may once again embark on the construction and development of their own language—perhaps taking the language printed in our book as a point of departure.

And yet, we do believe, of course, that this language which is printed in *A Pattern Language* is something more than a manual, or a teacher, or a version of a possible pattern language. Many of the patterns here are archetypal—so deep, so deeply rooted in the nature of things, that it seems likely that they will be a part of human nature, and human action, as much in five hundred years, as they are today. We doubt very much whether anyone could construct a valid pattern language, in their own mind, which did not include the pattern ARCADES (119) for example, or the pattern ALCOVES (179).

In this sense, we have also tried to penetrate, as deep as we are able, into the nature of things in the environment: and hope that a great part of this language will be a core of any sensible human pattern language, which any person constructs for themselves, in their own mind. In this sense, at least a part of the language we present here, is the archetypal core of all possible pattern languages, which can make people feel alive and human.

ACTIVITY NODES (PATTERN 30)

… this pattern forms those essential nodes of life which help to II. 270 generate IDENTIFIABLE NEIGHBORHOOD (14), PROMENADE (31), NETWORK OF PATHS AND CARS (52), and PEDESTRIAN STREET (100). To understand its action, imagine that a community and its boundary are growing under the influence of COMMUNITY OF 7000 (12), SUBCULTURE BOUNDARY (13), IDENTIFIABLE NEIGHBORHOOD (14), NEIGHBORHOOD BOUNDARY (15), ECCENTRIC NUCLEUS (28), and DENSITY RINGS (29). As they grow, certain "stars" begin to form, where the most important paths meet. These stars are potentially the vital spots of a community. The growth of these stars and of the paths which form them need to be guided to form genuine community crossroads (Fig. 1).

Community facilities scattered individually through the city do nothing for the life of the city.

One of the greatest problems in existing communities is the fact that the available public life in them is spread so thin that it has no impact on the community. It is not in any real sense available to the members of the community. Studies of pedestrian behavior make it clear that people seek out concentrations of other people, whenever they are available.[1]

To create these concentrations of people in a community, facilities must be grouped densely round very small public squares which can function as nodes—with all pedestrian movement in the community organized to pass through these nodes. Such nodes require four properties.

First, each node must draw together the main paths in the surrounding community. The major pedestrian paths should converge on the square, with minor paths funneling into the major

Fig. 1 An activity node.

ones, to create the basic star-shape of the pattern. This is much harder to do than one might imagine. To give an example of the difficulty which arises when we try to build this relationship into a town, we show the following plan—a scheme of ours for housing in Peru—in which the paths are all convergent on a very small number of squares (Fig. 2).

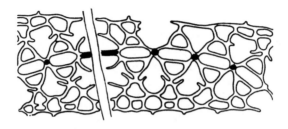

This is not a very good plan—it is too stiff and formal. But it is possible to achieve the same relationship in a far more relaxed manner. In any case the relationship between paths, community facilities, and squares is vital and hard to achieve. It must be taken seriously, from the very outset, as a major feature of the city.

Second, to keep the activity concentrated, it is essential to make the squares rather small, smaller than one might imagine. A square of about 45 × 60 feet can keep the normal pace of public life well concentrated. This figure is discussed in detail under SMALL PUBLIC SQUARE (61).

Third, the facilities grouped around any one node must be chosen for their symbiotic relationships. It is not enough merely to group communal functions in so-called community centers. For example, church, cinema, kindergarten, and police station are all community facilities, but they do not support one another mutually. Different people go to them, at different times, with different things in mind. There is no point in grouping them together. To create intensity of action, the facilities which are placed together round any one node must function in a cooperative

94

Fig. 2 Public paths converge on centers of action.

manner, and must attract the same kinds of people, at the same times of day. For example, when evening entertainments are grouped together, the people who are having a night out can use any one of them, and the total concentration of action increases— see NIGHT LIFE (33). When kindergartens and small parks and gardens are grouped together, young families with children may use either, so their total attraction is increased.

Fourth, these activity nodes should be distributed rather evenly across the community, so that no house or workplace is more than a few hundred yards from one. In this way, a contrast of "busy and quiet" can be achieved at a small scale—and large dead areas can be avoided (Fig. 3).

Therefore:
Create nodes of activity throughout the community, spread about 300 yards apart. First identify those existing spots in the community where action seems to concentrate itself. Then modify the layout of the paths in the community to bring as many of them through these spots as possible. This makes each spot function as a "node" in the path network. Then, at the center of each node, make a small public square, and surround it with a combination of community facilities and shops which are mutually supportive (Fig. 4).

95

Fig. 3 Nodes of different size.

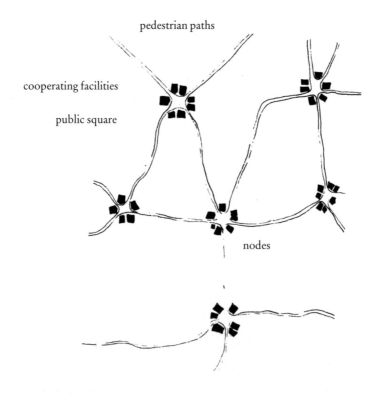

pedestrian paths

cooperating facilities

public square

nodes

Fig. 4 Mutually supportive nodes within a path network.

Connect those centers which are most dense with a wider, more important path for strolling—PROMENADE (31); make special centers for night activities—NIGHT LIFE (33); whenever new paths are built, make certain that they pass through the centers, so that they intensify the life still further—PATHS AND GOALS (120); and differentiate the paths so they are wide near the centers and smaller away from them—DEGREES OF PUBLICNESS (36). At the heart of every center, build a small public square—SMALL PUBLIC SQUARES (61), and surround each square with an appropriate mix of mutually self-reinforcing facilities—WORK COMMUNITY (41), UNIVERSITY AS A MARKETPLACE (43), LOCAL TOWN HALL (44), HEALTH CENTER (47), BIRTH PLACES (65), TEENAGE SOCIETY (84), SHOPFRONT SCHOOL (85), INDIVIDUALLY OWNED SHOPS (87), STREET CAFE (88), BEER HALL (90), FOOD STANDS (93) ...

96

... roads may be governed by PARALLEL ROADS (23), LOOPED LOCAL ROADS (49), GREEN STREETS (51); major paths by ACTIVITY NODES (30), PROMENADE (31), and PATHS AND GOALS (120). This pattern governs the interaction between the two (Fig. 5).

Cars are dangerous to pedestrians; yet activities occur just where cars and pedestrians meet.

It is common planning practice to separate pedestrians and cars. This makes pedestrian areas more human and safer. However, this practice fails to take account of the fact that cars and pedestrians also need each other: and that, in fact, a great deal of urban life occurs at just the point where these two systems meet. Many of the greatest places in cities, Piccadilly Circus, Times Square, the Champs-Élysées, are alive because they are at places where pedestrians and vehicles meet. New towns like Cumbernauld, in Scotland, where there is total separation between the two, seldom have the same sort of liveliness.

The same thing is true at the local residential scale. A great deal of everyday social life occurs where cars and pedestrians meet. In Lima, for example, the car is used as an extension of the house: men, especially, often sit in parked cars, near their houses, drinking beer and talking. And in one way or another, something like this happens everywhere. Conversation and discussion grow naturally around the lots where people wash their cars. Vendors set themselves up where cars and pedestrians meet; they need all the traffic they can get. Children play in parking lots—perhaps because they sense that this is the main point of arrival and departure; and of course because they like the cars (Fig. 6). Yet, at the same time, it is essential to keep pedestrians separate from vehicles: to protect children and old people; to preserve the tranquility of pedestrian life.

Fig. 5   Where cars and pedestrians meet.

To resolve the conflict, it is necessary to find an arrangement of pedestrian paths and roads, so that the two are separate, but meet frequently, with the points where they meet recognized as focal points. In general, this requires two orthogonal networks, one for roads, one for paths, each connected and continuous, crossing at frequent intervals (our observations suggest that most points on the path network should be within 150 feet of the nearest road), meeting, when they meet, at right angles (Fig. 7).

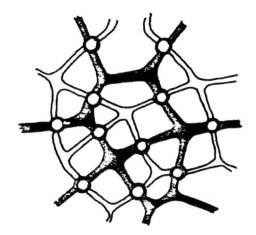

Fig. 6 Children like cars.
Fig. 7 Two orthogonal networks.

In practice, there are several possible ways of forming this relationship between the roads and paths. It can be done within the system of fast one-way roads about 300 feet apart described in PARALLEL ROADS (23). Between the roads there are pedestrian paths running at right angles to the roads, wiwth buildings opening off the pedestrian paths (Fig. 8). Where the paths intersect the roads there are small parking lots with space for kiosks and shops.

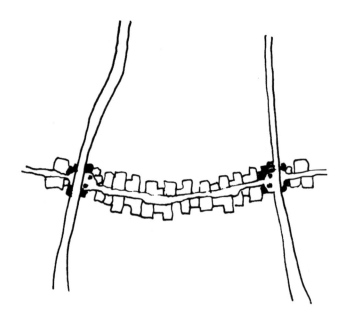

It can be applied to an existing neighborhood—as it is in the following sequence of plans drawn by the People's Architects, Berkeley, California. This shows a beautiful and simple way of creating a path network in an existing grid of streets, by closing off alternate streets, in each direction. As the drawings show, it can be done gradually (Fig. 9).

100

Fig. 8 Path between parallel roads.

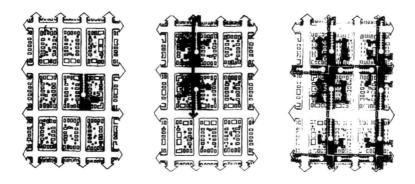

Different again, is our project for housing in Lima. Here the two orthogonal systems are laid out as follows (Fig. 10).

In all these cases, we see a global pattern, in which roads and paths are created more or less at the same time—and therefore brought into the proper relationship. However, it is essential to recognize that in most practical applications of this pattern, it is not necessary to locate the roads and paths together. Most typically of all, there is an existing road system: and the paths can be put in one by one, piecemeal, at right angles to the existing roads. Slowly, very slowly, a coherent path network will be created by the accumulation of these piecemeal acts.

Finally, note that this kind of separation of cars from pedestrians is only appropriate where traffic densities are medium or medium high. At low densities (for instance, a cul-de-sac gravel road serving half-a-dozen houses), the paths and roads can obviously be combined. There is no reason even to have sidewalks—GREEN STREETS (51). At very high densities, like the Champs Elysées, or Piccadilly Circus, a great deal of the excitement is actually created by the fact that pedestrian paths are running along the roads. In these cases the problem is best solved by extra wide sidewalks—RAISED WALKS (55)—which actually contain the resolution of the conflict in their width. The edge away from the road is safe—the edge near the road is the place where the activities happen.

101

Fig. 9 The growth of a path network in a street grid.

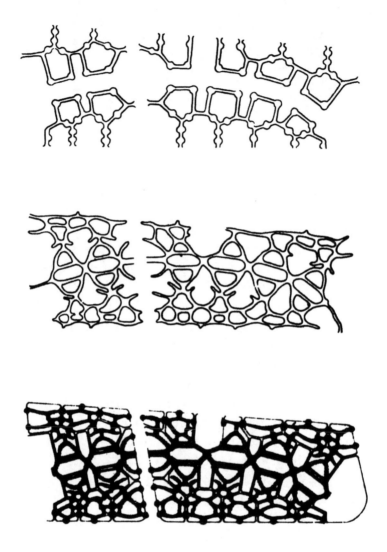

Fig. 10　Roads, pedestrian paths, and the two together.

Therefore:
Except where traffic densities are very high or very low, lay out pedestrian paths at right angles to roads, not along them, so that the paths gradually begin to form a second network, distinct from the road system, and orthogonal to it. This can be done quite gradually even if you put in one path at a time, but always put them in the middle of the "block", so that they run across the roads (Fig. 11).

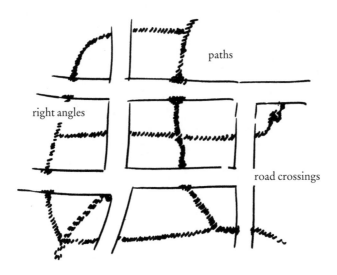

Where paths have to run along major roads—as they do occasionally—build them 18 inches higher than the road, on one side of the road only, and twice the usual width—RAISED WALK (55); on GREEN STREETS (51) the paths can be in the road since there is nothing but grass and paving stones there; but even then, occasional narrow paths at right angles to the green streets are very beautiful. Place the paths in detail according to PATHS AND GOALS (120); shape them according to PATH SHAPE (121). Finally, treat the important street crossings as crosswalks, raised to the level of the pedestrian path—so cars have to slow down as they go over them ROAD CROSSING (54) …

103

Fig. 11 Network of paths and cars.

SMALL PUBLIC SQUARES (PATTERN 61)

... this pattern forms the core which makes an ACTIVITY NODE (30): it can also help to generate a node, by its mere existence, provided that it is correctly placed along the intersection of the paths which people use most often. And it can also help to generate a PROMENADE (31), a WORK COMMUNITY (41), an IDENTIFIABLE NEIGHBORHOOD (14), through the action of the people who gather there. But it is essential, in every case, that it is not too large (Fig. 12).

A town needs public squares; they are the largest, most public rooms, that the town has. But when they are too large, they look and feel deserted.

It is natural that every public street will swell out at those important nodes where there is the most activity. And it is only these widened,

Fig. 12 A small public square.

swollen, public squares which can accommodate the public gatherings, small crowds, festivities, bonfires, carnivals, speeches, dancing, shouting, mourning, which must have their place in the life of the town.

But for some reason there is a temptation to make these public squares too large. Time and again in modern cities, architects and planners build plazas that are too large. They look good on drawings; but in real life they end up desolate and dead.

Our observations suggest strongly that open places intended as public squares should be very small. As a general rule, we have found that they work best when they have a diameter of about 60 feet—at this diameter people often go to them, they become favorite places, and people feel comfortable there. When the diameter gets above 70 feet, the squares begin to seem deserted and unpleasant. The only exceptions we know are places like the

105

Fig. 13 The squares in Lima: one huge and deserted (top), the other small and alive (bottom).

Piazza San Marco and Trafalgar Square, which are great town centers, teeming with people (Fig. 13).

What possible functional basis is there for these observations? First, we know from the pattern, PEDESTRIAN DENSITY (123), that a place begins to seem deserted when it has more than about 300 square feet per person.

On this basis, a square with a diameter of 100 feet will begin to seem deserted if there are less than 33 people in it. There are few places in a city where you can be sure there will always be 33 people. On the other hand, it only takes 4 people to give life to a square with a diameter of 35 feet, and only 12 to give life to a square with a diameter of 60 feet. Since there are far far better chances of 4 or 12 people being in a certain place than 33, the smaller squares will feel comfortable for a far greater percentage of the time.

The second possible basis for our observations depends on the diameter. A person's face is just recognizable at about 70 feet; and under typical urban noise conditions, a loud voice can just barely be heard across 70 feet. This may mean that people feel half-consciously tied together in plazas that have diameters of 70 feet or less—where they can make out the faces and half-hear the talk of the people around them; and this feeling of being at one with a loosely knit square is lost in the larger spaces. Roughly similar things have been said by Philip Thiel[2] and by Hans Blumenfeld.[3] For example, Blumenfeld gives the following figures: a person's face can be recognized at up to 70 or 80 feet; a person's face can be recognized as "a portrait", in rich detail, at up to about 48 feet.

Our own informal experiments show the following results. Two people with normal vision can communicate comfortably up to 75 feet. They can talk with raised voice, and they can see the general outlines of the expression on one another's faces. This 75-foot maximum is extremely reliable. Repeated experiments gave the same distance again and again, +/- 10 percent. At 100 feet it is uncomfortable to talk, and facial expression is no longer clear. Anything above 100 feet is hopeless.

Therefore:

Make a public square much smaller than you would at first imagine; usually no more than 45 to 60 feet across, never more than 70 feet across. This applies only to its width in the short direction. In the long direction it can certainly be longer (Fig. 14).

An even better estimate for the size of the square: make a guess about the number of people who will typically be there (say, P), and make the area of the square no greater than 150 to 300P square feet—PEDESTRIAN DENSITY (123); ring the square around with pockets of activity where people congregate—ACTIVITY POCKETS (124); build buildings round the square in such a way that they give it a definite shape, with views out into other larger places—POSITIVE OUTDOORS PACE (106), HIERARCHY OF OPEN SPACE (114), BUILDING FRONTS (122), STAIR SEATS (125); and to make the center of the square as useful as the edges, build SOMETHING ROUGHLY IN THE MIDDLE (126) ...

107

Fig. 14 Square 45–70 feet across.

BUS STOP (PATTERN 92)

II. 451

... within a town whose public transportation is based on MINI-BUSES (20), genuinely able to serve people, almost door to door, for a low price, and very fast, there need to be bus stops within a few hundred feet of every house and workplace. This pattern gives the form of the bus stops (Fig. 15).

Bus stops must be easy to recognize, and pleasant, with enough activity around them to make people comfortable and safe.

Bus stops are often dreary because they are set down independently, with very little thought given to the experience of waiting there, to the relationship between the bus stop and its surroundings. They are places to stand idly, perhaps anxiously, waiting for the bus, always watching for the bus. It is a shabby experience; nothing that would encourage people to use public transportation.

The secret lies in the web of relationships that are present in the tiny system around the bus stop. If they knit together, and reinforce each other, adding choice and shape to the experience, the system is a good one: but the relationships that make up such a system are extremely subtle. For example, a system as simple as a traffic light, a curb, and street corner can be enhanced by viewing it as a distinct node of public life: people wait for the light to change, their eyes wander, perhaps they are not in such a hurry. Place a newsstand and a flower wagon at the corner and the experience becomes more coherent.

The curb and the light, the newspaper stand and the flowers, the awning over the shop on the corner, the change in people's pockets—all this forms a web of mutually sustaining relationships.

The possibilities for each bus stop to become part of such a web are different—in some cases it will be right to make a system that will draw people into a private reverie—an old tree; another time one that will do the opposite—give shape to the social possibilities—a coffee stand, a canvas roof, a decent place to sit for people who are not waiting for the bus (Fig. 16).

Fig. 15   Advertising pillar in a bus stop.

Fig. 16   Two bus stops.

Therefore:
Build bus stops so that they form tiny centers of public life. Build them as part of the gateways into neighborhoods, work communities, parts of town. Locate them so that they work together with several other activities, at least a newsstand, maps, outdoor shelter, seats, and in various combinations, corner groceries, smoke shops, coffee bar, tree places, special road crossings, public bathrooms, squares ... (Fig. 17)

Make a full gateway to the neighborhood next to the bus stop, or place the bus stop where the best gateway is already—MAIN GATEWAY (53); treat the physical arrangement according to the patterns for PUBLIC OUTDOOR ROOM (69), PATH SHAPE (121), and A PLACE TO WAIT (150); provide a FOOD STAND (93): place the seats according to sun, wind protection, and view—SEAT SPOTS (241) ...

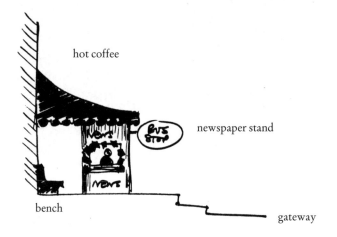

Summary of the Language

A pattern language has the structure of a network. However, when II., xviii we use the network of a language, we always use it as a sequence, going through the patterns, moving always from the larger

Fig. 17 Section of a bus stop.

patterns [e.g. ACTIVITY NODES] to the smaller [e.g. BUS STOP], always from the ones which create structures, to the ones which then embellish those structures, and then to those which embellish the embellishments ... You can see, from this short example, how powerful and simple a pattern language is. If you read through the sentences which connect the groups of patterns to one another, you will get an overview of the whole language. And once you get this overview, you will then be also able to find the patterns which are relevant to your own project.

II., xxxvii
II., xviii
II., xli

Finally, a note of caution. This language, like English, can be a medium for prose, or a medium for poetry. In an ordinary English sentence, each word, and the sentence too, has one simple meaning. In a poem, the meaning is far more dense. Each word carries several meanings; and the sentence as a whole carries an enormous density of interlocking meanings, which together illuminate the whole. The same is true for pattern languages. It is possible to make buildings by stringing together patterns, in a rather loose way. A building made like this, is an assembly of patterns. It is not dense. It is not profound. But it is also possible to put patterns together in such a way that many many patterns overlap in the same physical space. This makes the building very dense. It has many meanings captured within a small space and, through this density, it becomes profound.

1. For instance, Jan Gehl, "Mennesker til Fods (Pedestrians)", *Arkitekten*, no. 20, 1968.

2. Philip Thiel, "An Architectural and Urban Space Sequence Notation", unpublished manuscript, University of California, Department of Architecture, August 1960, 5.

3. Hans Blumenfeld, "Scale in Civic Design", *Town Planning Review*, April 1953, 35–46.

Oswald Mathias Ungers
A Thematic Repertoire

I. Oswald Mathias Ungers, *Morphologie: City Metaphors* (Cologne: Verlag der Buchhandlung Walther König, 1982), 7–14. First published in "MAN transFORMS: An International Exhibition on Aspects of Design", curated by Hans Hollein for the opening of the Smithsonian Institution's National Museum of Design Cooper-Hewitt Museum (New York: Cooper-Hewitt Museum, 1976).

II. Oswald Mathias Ungers et al., *Architettura come tema/Architecture as theme* (Milan: Electa, 1982), 8–10, 29–39, 50–53, 125.

III. Oswald Mathias Ungers, "Die dialektische Stadt", in Oswald Mathias Ungers and Stefan Vieths, *Die dialektische Stadt* (Braunschweig/Wiesbaden: Vieweg, 1999), 7–18, 81–91, 105–115, translated to English by Ada St. Laurent.

Designing and Thinking in Images,
Metaphors, and Analogies

I. 7 Apparently, all thinking processes happen in two different ways. Each is claimed to be the only way in which thought processes occur in science, arts, and philosophy.

The first is commonly known as the empirical way of thinking. It is limited to the study of physical phenomena. The actual concern is with facts that can be measured and justified. This intellectual concern concentrates on separate elements and isolated facts, deriving from direct practical experience. Thinking is strictly limited to technical and practical processes as they are most strongly formulated in the theories and methodologies of pragmatism and behaviorism.

The other way of thinking seeks out phenomena and experiences which describe more than just a sum of parts, paying almost no attention to separate elements which would be affected and changed through subjective vision and comprehensive images anyway. The major concern is not the reality as it is but the search for an all-around idea, for a general content, a coherent thought, a leading theme, or an overall concept that ties everything together. It is known as holism or Gestalt theory and has been most forcefully developed during the age of humanism in the philosophical treatises of morphological idealism.

Kant postulates that knowledge has its origin in two basic components: intuition and thought. According to Kant, all our thinking is related to imagination, which means it is related to our senses, because the only way to describe an object is through imagination. The intellect is incapable of perceiving anything, and the senses cannot think. Only through a combination of both can knowledge arise. Imagination has to precede all thinking processes since it is nothing less than a synopsis, an overall ordering principle bringing order into diversity. If we accept that thinking is an imaginative process of a higher order, then, argues Kant, it means all sciences are based on imagination.

In more recent philosophical debates, Herman Friedman replaces Kant's concept of imagination and thought as the basic components of knowledge with the argument that the sense of sight—the vision—and the sense of touch—the haptic—are the two competing polarities, and that all intellectual activity happens either in an optical or haptic way. Friedman argues that the sense of touch is nonproductive; it measures, is geometrical, and acts in congruity. The sense of sight, however, is productive; it interpolates, is integral, and acts in similarities. The sense of sight stimulates spontaneous reactions of mind; it is more vivid and more far-reaching than the sense of touch. The sense of touch proceeds from the specific condition to the general, the sense of vision from the general to the specific. The visionary process, whose data are based on imagination, starts out with an idea, looking at an object in the most general way, to find an image from which to descend to more specific properties.

In every human being there is a strong metaphysical desire to create a reality structured through images in which objects become meaningful through vision and which does not, as Max Planck believed, exist because it is measurable. Most of all, the question of imagination and ideas as an instrument of thinking and analyzing has occupied artists and philosophers. Only in more recent history has this process of thinking been undervalued because of the predominance of quantitative and materialistic criteria. It is obvious, however, that what we generally call thinking is nothing other than the application of imagination and ideas to a given set of facts and not just an abstract process but a visual and sensuous event. The way we experience the world around us depends on how we perceive it. Without a comprehensive vision the reality will appear as a mass of unrelated phenomena and meaningless facts—in other words, totally chaotic. In such a world it would be like living in a vacuum: Everything would be of equal importance, nothing could attract our attention, and there would be no possibility to utilize the mind.

As the meaning of a whole sentence is different from the meaning of the sum of single words, so is the creative vision and ability to grasp the characteristic unity of a set of facts, and not just to analyze them as something which is put together by single parts. The consciousness that catches the reality through sensuous perception and imagination is the real creative process because it achieves a higher degree of order than the simplistic method of testing, recording, proving, and controlling. This is why all traditional philosophy is a permanent attempt to create a well-structured system of ideas in order to interpret, to perceive, to understand the world, as other sciences have done. There are three basic levels of comprehending physical phenomena: first, the exploration of pure physical facts; second, the psychological impact on our inner self; and third, the imaginative discovery and reconstruction of phenomena in order to conceptualize them. If, for instance, designing is understood purely technically, then it results in pragmatic functionalism or in mathematical formulas. If designing is exclusively an expression of psychological experiences, then only emotional values matter, and it turns into a religious substitute. If, however, the physical reality is understood and con-ceptualized as an analogy to our imagination of that reality, then we pursue a morphological design concept, turning it into phenomena which, like all real concepts, can be expanded or condensed; they can be seen as polarities contradicting or comple-menting each other, existing as pure concepts in themselves like a piece of art. Therefore we might say, if we look at physical phenomena in a morphological sense, like Gestalten in their meta-morphosis, we can manage to develop our knowledge without machine or apparatus. This imaginative process of thinking applies to all intellectual and spiritual areas of human activities, though the approaches might be different in various fields. But it is always a fundamental process of conceptualizing an unrelated, diverse reality through the use of images, metaphors, analogies, models, signs, symbols, and allegories.

Image and Perception

Probably all of us remember the story of the man in the moon which occupied our childhood fantasies, producing all sorts of images of an old man, carrying a bundle on his back, and whose face used to change depending on the clarity of the night. He helped to fulfil secret wishes, and he became the friendly companion of romantic couples. Before human intelligence managed to uncover his secret, he was the subject of so many desires and wishes that he became part of our life while existing only in our imagination.

The human mind created a vivid fantasy not only about the moon, but also about the whole firmament. It probably took a long time to structure the wide starry sky, and to develop a coherent system within a chaotic reality long before science was capable of calculating and measuring the orbits, the gravity, the intensity and speed of light of the stars and to register all relevant data. Before that, understanding was based entirely on imaginative concepts. Instead of a set of facts, knowledge referred to a set of constellations derived from perception. The firmament was filled with figures and images, such as Orion, Castor and Pollux, the Great Bear, and others. Those star images represented a sensuous reality in the human consciousness. Therefore we might conclude: Reality is what our imagination perceives it to be. In a general sense, an image describes a set of facts in such a way that the same visual perception is connected with the conditions as with the image itself.

Metaphors

In everyday language, we are constantly using metaphorical expressions without paying any attention to them. For instance, we talk about the foot of the mountain, the leg of a chair, the heart of the city, the mouth of the river, the long arm of the law, the head of the family, and a body of knowledge. We use many words that are vivid metaphors although they exist as common expressions.

In addition to the words, everyday language abounds in phrases and expressions of metaphorical character, such as: straight from the horse's mouth, the tooth of time, or the tide of events, a forest of masts, the jungle of the city.

Metaphors are transformations of an actual event into a figurative expression, evoking images by substituting an abstract notion for something more descriptive and illustrative. It usually is an implicit comparison between two entities which are not alike but can be compared in an imaginative way. The comparison is mostly done through a creative leap that ties different objects together, producing a new entity in which the characteristics of both take part. The meaning of metaphors is based on comparison and similarities most often of anthropomorphical character, like the human body as a metaphor for the shape of a Romanesque cathedral or the conformation of the universe (Figs. 1–4). Designers use the metaphor as an instrument of thought that serves the function of clarity and vividness predating or bypassing logical processes. "A metaphor is an intuitive perception of similarities in dissimilars," as Aristotle defined it.

Models

A model is commonly understood as somebody who poses as a prototype representing an ideal form. In a more general sense a model is a structure, a pattern, along the lines of which something is shaped. As an artist paints their painting after the lines of a model, a scientist builds their theory of natural events on the basis of a concept or a plan which acts as a model. This is all the more true when the complexity of something increases or the scientific sphere becomes so minute that any kind of observation would fail. In chemistry or physics, for instance, models are built to demonstrate the position of atoms in molecules, or biological models are used to represent the organic formation in which every organ has its function in relation to the whole system. Such models serve as instructions for technical intrusion with the reality.

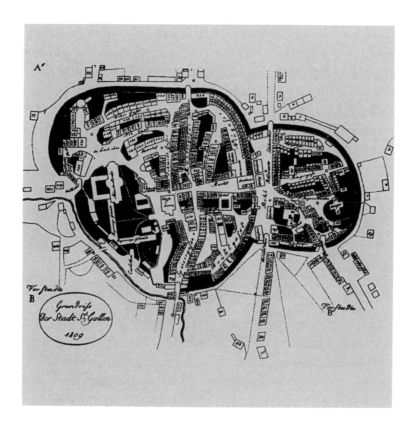

Fig. 1 Enclosure.

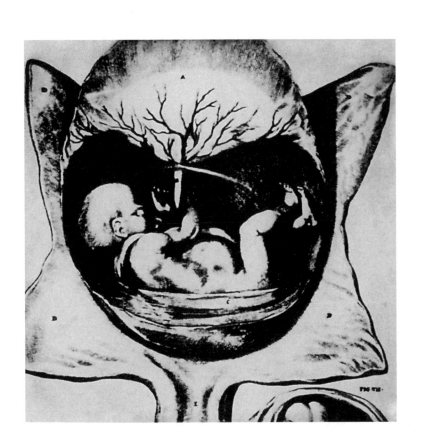

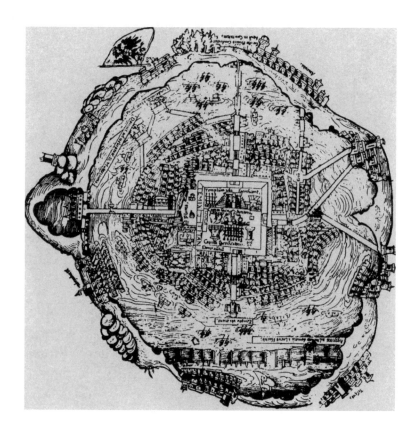

Fig. 2 Growth.

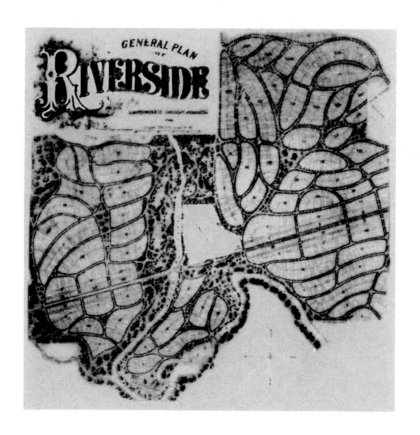

Fig. 3 Cell Structure.

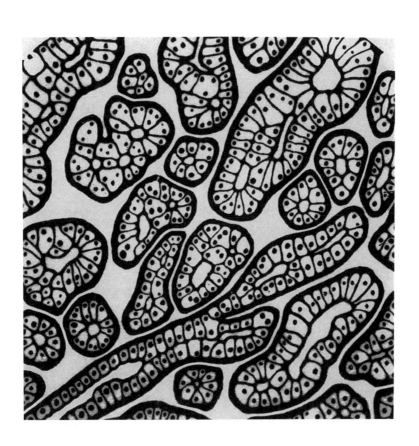

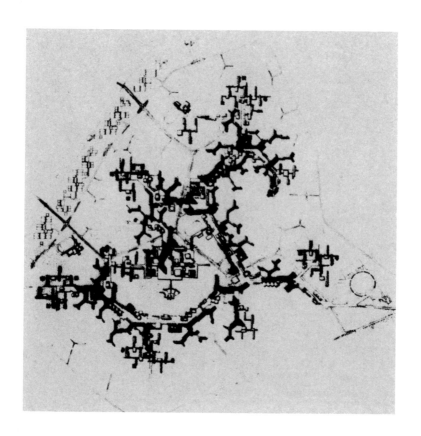

Fig. 4 Branching.

Generally, a model is a theoretical complexity in itself which either brings a visual form or a conceptual order into the components of complex situations. In such a model the external form is the expression of an internal structure. It shows the way something is put together. To make a model means to find coherence in a given relationship of certain combinations and fixed dispositions, usually done with two types of models, visual models and thinking models. They serve as conceptual devices to structure our experience and turn them into functions or make them intentional.

By means of these two models we formulate an objective structure that turns facts into something more certain and therefore more real. It is nothing other than a formal principle which makes it possible to visualize the complexity of appearances in a more ordered way, and which in reverse is a creative approach to structured reality along the knowledge of a model. Not least, the model is an intellectual structure setting targets for our creative activities, just like the design of model buildings, model cities, model communities, and other model conditions supposedly are setting directions for subsequent actions.

Analogies

When Le Corbusier compared the edifice with a machine, he saw an analogy where nobody had seen one before. When Aalto compared the design of his organically shaped vases with the Finnish landscape, or his design for a theater in Germany with a tree stump, he did the same; and when Haring designed with anthropomorphic images in mind he again did just that—seeing an analogy where nobody had seen one before. In the course of the twentieth century it has become recognized that analogy taken in the most general sense plays a far more important role in architectural design than that of simply following functional requirements or solving pure technical problems. All the constructivist designs, for instance, have to be seen as a reference to the dynamic world of machines, factories, and industrial components to which they are analogous. Melnikov once produced a series of designs for workers' clubs in Moscow, which are analogies to pistons, tubes, gears, and bearings.

It has been said that scientific discovery consists in seeing analogies where everybody else sees just bare facts. Take, for instance, the human body: A surgeon perceives it mainly as a system of bones, muscles, organs, and a circulatory system. A football coach appreciates the performance capacity of the body, the lover has a romantic notion about it, a businessman calculates the working power, a general the fighting strength, and so on. Architects, like Cattaneo, Haring, Soleri, and others perceive the human body as a Gestalt which is analogous to their plans either for buildings or cities. They draw an inference by analogy from one to the other. The analogy establishes a similarity, or the existence of some similar principles, between two events which are otherwise completely different. Kant considered the analogy as something indispensable to extend knowledge. By employing the method of analogy, it should be possible to develop new concepts and to discover new relationships.

Signs, Symbols, and Allegories

Almost all our communication is based on signs, signals, symbols, and allegories which structure not only most aspects of our daily routine but also are most often carriers of religious and metaphysical systems. Riding in a motorcar, for example, is only possible because of the regulating effect of traffic signals, signs, and symbols, and it would be a most daring and deadly adventure without them. The modern scientific world is full of complicated symbolic codes and systems of synthetic signs and symbols which are more advantageous because they are unambiguous, distinct, and shorter than regular language. But beyond the objective world, symbols also represent a metaphysical world as magical illuminations and cult symbols in various religions, such as the wheel of life in Buddhism, the fish as a symbol of Christianity, and the phoenix as a sign of regeneration in ancient mythology.

While signs point to something that they represent, as words are artificial signs for ideas and thoughts, symbols are a penetration of mind and image characterized by mystery, depth, and inexhaustible interpretation. To express and visualize something abstract, transcendental, or spiritual, either symbols or allegories are used. The transition between symbols and allegories is flexible and cannot be strictly separated. Allegory is regarded as a dimension of controlled indirectness and double meaning. The original meaning of the term suggests the direction of its development; it comes from the Greek words "allos" and "agorein", which mean an "other speaking" and suggests a more deceptive and oblique language. The method of allegory is represented in art whenever it emphasizes thematic content and ideas rather than events and facts. The abiding impression left by the allegorical mode is one of indirect, ambiguous, and sometimes even emblematic symbolism which inevitably calls for interpretation. The allegory arouses in the contemplator a response to levels of meaning, and provides the designer with a tool that goes beyond pragmatic representation. Particularly art and mythology make wide use of allegories, both in subject matter and in its imagery. Quite often, personifications are employed to visualize abstract ideas and events, such as death as reaper, justice as the blindfolded woman, the goddess of luck sitting on a flying wheel; even in allegories like "John Bull" as the representative of the British nation, "Michael" for the Germans, "Marianne" for the French, and good old "Uncle Sam" who stands for America.

The allegorical mode, however, has not only been of major importance in the past as representing the Cosmos in the ancient world or speculating on the nature of the Universe in the Middle Ages, it also plays a significant role in modern literature, exhibiting incomprehensible and unconceivable dimensions rooted in the depth of the unconscious as in Beckett's *Waiting for Godot* or in Kafka's novels.

130

What all that means—thinking and designing in images, metaphors, models, analogies, symbols, and allegories—is nothing more than a transition from purely pragmatic approaches to a more creative mode of thinking. It means a process of thinking in qualitative values rather than quantitative data, a process that is based on synthesis rather than analysis. Not that analytical methods are opposed but more in the direction that analysis and synthesis alternate as naturally as breathing in and breathing out, as Goethe put it. It is meant to be a transition in the process of thinking from a metrical space to the visionary space of coherent systems, from the concepts of homology to the concepts of morphology. All of the different modes described are part of a morphological concept which is understood as a study of formations and transformations whether of thoughts, facts, objects, or conditions as they present themselves to sentient experiences.

This approach is not meant to act as a substitute for the quantitative sciences which break down forms, as we know them, into functions to make them controllable, but it is meant to counteract the increasing influence of those sciences that claim a monopoly of understanding.

Therefore, the city images as they are shown in this anthology are not analyzed according to function and other measurable criteria—a method which is usually applied—but they are interpreted on a conceptual level demonstrating ideas, images, metaphors, and analogies. The interpretations are conceived in a morphological sense, wide open to subjective speculation and transformation. The book shows the more transcendental aspect, the underlying perception that goes beyond the actual design. In other terms, it shows the common design principle which is similar in dissimilar conditions. There are three levels of reality exposed: the factual reality—the object; the perceptual reality—the analogy; and the conceptual reality—the idea, shown as the plan—the image—the word

Architecture as Theme

Ever since the term functionalism was introduced in the 1920s, the II. 8 opinion that architecture is not to be considered as part of the arts possessing their own autonomy has become widespread. This conception of architecture as an applied art dates back to the distinction that Kant made between pure art—*pulchritudo vaga*—and applied art—*pulchritudo adhaerens*. Semper, in his book *Style in the Technical and Tectonic Arts*, adopted this double meaning of the concept of art and placed architecture not among the genuinely creative arts, but among the applied ones. A definitive confirmation of this attitude was provided by the Bauhaus with its teaching based on the assumption that architecture is exclusively defined by its functions, by adherence to purpose, and by technology and that, as a consequence, it can in no way rise to the level of pure art, but is only an applied art. He maintained that there was no difference at all between the design of an object and the plan of a city or, in the words of Gropius: "The approach to any kind of project, be it a chair, a building, a city or a regional plan should in principle be identical." In this way architecture became only a part of the general process of production.

If in antiquity architects had held a position in the foreground with respect to all the others arts, now they were even denied the right to their own language, to any possibility of artistic expression. The role was reduced to one of pure functionalism, to the satisfaction of needs based on utility, on the fulfillment of purpose and on the containment of cost.

This attitude has endured up to the present day. The discussion of functional objects is still at the heart of the architectural debate. It becomes generally accepted as obligatory and, once adopted in isolation as such, the exclusive criterion for the evaluation of architecture. All architectural expression reduces to adherence to purpose: One might think that architecture's sole right to existence falls under this aspect.

Nevertheless, an architecture that devotes itself exclusively to the fulfillment of functional requirements is inevitably bound to grow poorer and to end up in the blind alley of everyday routine. Nor is the situation changed by the overlaying of a stylistic superstructure. On the contrary, if architecture renounces its artistic expression, the only outlet left to it is the narrow field of action of the stylistic exercise; if this is taken on too lightly, then the two extremes condition each other reciprocally.

An architecture that does not derive its themes from itself is like a painting that tries to be nothing more than a photographic reproduction. The theme and the content of architecture can only be architecture itself; just as painting makes use of its own language and poetics to give expression to images, or music is represented in tonal compositions, there is a possibility, or even a necessity, for architecture to make ideas visible and testable in the form of spatial compositions by the use of the language of architecture.

While painting and sculpture can—though do not necessarily have to—reproduce an external reality and even literature can describe perceptions, architecture—in a manner not unlike music—should propose, deriving them from itself, the themes that it wishes to express. The identification and definition of a theme are indispensable premises for architecture. Once a theme has been identified, it may undergo variations and be transformed at will, yet it is fundamental that there should always be a theme as a basis for the project.

The need for a thematization of architecture means nothing if not moving away from the blind alley of pure functionalism or—at the other end of the spectrum—from stylistic aberrations and a return to the essential content of architectural language. A building without a theme, without a supporting idea, is an architectural work without theoretical foundation. Buildings put up in this way lack all sense; they have no meaning and serve solely for the banal satisfaction of needs. Yet any need, even one relating to the simplest hut, can be given a theme and is represented in the process of thematic elaboration, as a house that has itself for a theme and that at its highest level culminates in the ancient temple (Fig. 5).

When speaking of architecture, it is not necessarily a matter of expressing its purpose "to the letter", but rather one of understanding in what form it is possible to thematize its functional requirements. Therefore it is necessary to go beyond pure satisfaction of functions by transforming them conceptually; that is by grasping them from a thematic point of view. Consequently, the content and premise of the architectural project is also formed by the search for a theme for a building. This is the really creative, conceptual act that must be carried out in designing. In the same way as the working hypothesis determines the direction of thought in scientific research, the theme defines ideation, content, and artistic expression in architecture. Just as scientific research would soon begin to dry up without identification of hypotheses, a purely empirical architecture—that is to say an architecture without fantasy and ideas—descends into the extreme banality of purely functional adaptation.

In this connection the need for themes in architecture should also be seen as an exquisitely human question, since it helps to transform the environment from pragmatic reality to the metaphysical world of ideas, i.e., to sensitize the world of everyday affairs, causing it to emerge from triviality. So the social potential of architecture can also be seen in its ability to intensify the meaning of life for the user; not—or not just—through its material utilization, but in the sense of a sublimation of the environment molded by and for humanity as well.

The possibilities for singling out a theme in architecture are numerous, although perhaps—because of its tie with functions and materials not so unlimited as in other arts. Naturally the theme can be more or less evident in each individual project but at times several themes are interwoven in the same project.

It is essential however that the intention of setting a main theme as the basis for a work of architecture, with a view to bestowing artistic expression on it, should be clear and recognizable.

134

ICH KAN MICH NIT SVBTILER MACHE DARVM GLEICHT MAN MICH ZV GROBE Saf

Fig. 5 The metamorphosis of the column by Gabriel Krammer, from "Architectura von den fünf Säulen samt ihren Ornamenten und Zierden", Prague, 1600.

The Dialectical City

Cities have always been conceived and built as unified systems. III. 7
Amongst these, the urban block structure has proven to be particularly durable and robust. Freestanding buildings and row patterns are seen less often, as they have been only rarely implemented. From ancient Miletus to nineteenth-century Manhattan, nothing of true significance has changed but the proportions within the grid system. The structure of Celtic settlements is hardly different from highly civilized St. Petersburg, and the basic principles of any given atavistic row village are no different from those of Bern or the rational strivings of Modernism. The only question was if the row was to run north–south or east–west, and does it follow the topography or the traffic flows (Fig. 6).

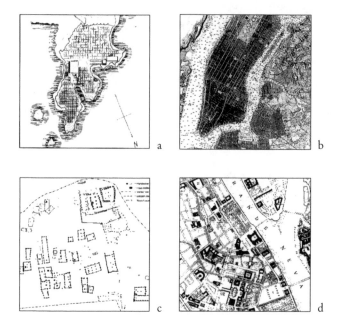

a

b

c

d

Fig. 6 Basic urban planning patterns (a: Miletus, b: Manhattan,
c: Neolithic settlement in Hallstadt, Germany, d: St. Petersburg).

For thousands of years, urban planning and development has been limited to a few fundamental patterns that are then varied in an infinite number of ways. Sometimes the blocks are regular, like in antiquity and the colonial era, sometimes they are more or less arbitrary, as in the Middle Ages, or massive, like in 1930s Vienna. The basic types remain the same: blocks, streets and avenues, atria, courtyards, and squares.

Another topos is that of the freestanding single building, the solitaire. Every archaic homestead, every farmyard is made up of isolated, mutually interrelated buildings, arranged according to function and need: the residence, storage, stables, and annexes. The concept is loose, a more or less differentiated conglomerate of different architectures. Pathways connect these structures and their individual uses, as processional paths to churches did in the medieval city. Village structures follow the same principles, supplemented by public buildings such as churches, community centers, or schools. Modern business parks are similar clusters, pragmatic smorgasbords of industrial and commercial buildings, sometimes mixed with residential and other facilities. The urban order or—better—the basic pattern of the disorder resembles the empirical distribution structures of rural and historical settlements. The same type of arbitrary scattering of freestanding buildings is visibly demonstrated by the random dispersion of high-rise buildings in modern urban areas. They stand in vicinity to one another, entirely lacking any reference to a differentiated overall system. This lack of association is determined only by the independent and generous distribution and material autonomy of the structures.

Each epoch has selected a few suitable basic building blocks from this set of models and adapted them to the purposes and needs of the era.

This would be reasonable if a claim to exclusivity were not made at the same time as each particular system declared its exclusive supremacy. Orderly block development or anarchic freestanding structures, egalitarian housing slabs or hierarchically organized geometric figures, centralized or decentralized arrangements. All are systems of urban development that have proven their practicality throughout the course of history, and their various realms of application will be reconfirmed over and over again as we move into the future. The problem arises when these systems are alienated from their context and used exclusively, without taking topographical, social, economic, political, and technical requirements into consideration, turning them into ideological weapons.

Modern cities are complex structures and, due to the convoluted demands they must fulfill, can no longer be captured under the umbrella of a single, uniform, and pure system. In the heroic period of early Modernism propagated by Le Corbusier, Mies van der Rohe, and Gropius, belief in the discovery of a viable binding system for a uniformly structured city was still held. The urban planning proposals by protagonists of a new era—be it the ribbon developments of the 1920s, Le Corbusier's colossal Ville Radieuse, the Constructivists' linear urban networks, or the patterns of Mies and Hilberseimer—all failed miserably and entered into the history of urbanism as mere fragments. Such well-intentioned, highly ideological attempts can, at best, be seen as laboratory experiments along the difficult path to gaining some sort of control over the complex problems faced by cities (Fig. 7).

We have reached a point where any attempt to create a complete, self-contained system for the city is doomed to failure. This is where Modernism miscarried, its logic determined by outdated thought structures. It became impossible to seriously discuss fulfilling the hope of Modernism to find a system suitable for all. The failure, however, does not lie in any lack of effort or dearth of opportunities, but in the intellectually erroneous approach of all these efforts. The designers were thinking in opposites, in antagonisms—old against new, traditional against modern, progressive against reactionary—instead of in supplementing, layering, and complementing.

138

Instead of intertwining thesis with antithesis, they are confronted as excluding alternatives to one another. Modernist urban planning failed due to the exclusivity of its thesis and has led, in a de-ideological reality, to the heterogeneous sprawl and familiar phenomena that shape the anti-image of contemporary cities. The modernist ideology of clean and egalitarian cities has resulted in the exact opposite: a chaotic and bewildering urban mix that one no longer dares to appreciate, hopelessly deteriorated and falling apart. It is no coincidence that architects repeatedly fall back on reactionary activism, plunging all their energy into façades and materials in a vain attempt to disregard the urban disaster that has been created and to restore their lost alibis as creators of the urban environment.

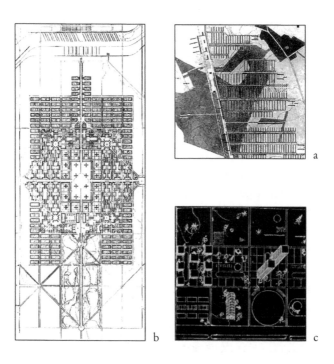

139

Fig. 7 Modernist ideal cities (a: Walter Gropius, large housing project, 1929,
b: Le Corbusier, Ville Contemporaine, 1922, c: Ivan Leonidov, Magnitogorsk, 1930).

The most recent discourse on the "media city"—intended to suggest a new, future-focused vision of the city—is, however, nothing more than a continuation of the attempt to grasp the urban phenomenon by technical means, and to once again see the city as a unified *Gesamtkunstwerk*. Here, traditional methods appear as old wine in new skins, fascinating the experts. The declared design goal is still a uniform city, whether medial or conceptual. In their helplessness and despair, architects and so-called "urban designers" start working out their own private theories of the city. Bricolage is the order of the day. Some discuss the city of the future as a field of communication in which a multimedia network of traffic is incessantly humming. Railway stations, airports, conference halls, hotels, and motorway service stations—laden with crisscrossing and coalescing traffic—are programmed to become transitory social connection hubs. Urban life is to take place only during brief encounters between two stations or within the network. Real relationships between people are replaced by an urban menu, subject to permanent change and exchangeable at any time. Urbanity exists, at best, on a screen or on the subway platform. Cities are like airports, they say. In other words, there are no more cities, they have instead disintegrated into stations of more or less random encounters. There are no more places of permanence. Continuance is replaced by communication. Locations once characterized by constancy, tradition, and duration are dissolved into non-binding information systems. Places, sites, are replaced by network hubs, points at which arbitrary bits of information converge for a short time. The media city has no actual places. With neither history nor name, it is subject to constant change. It is impossible for anything lasting to develop. It is the irrepressible trust in a constantly changing future without a face, without a personality, without recognizable characteristics, that has an impact.

Piazza Navona does not yield to such a network. It is a place with a unique history, where continuity is manifest and change embraces visible forms. A place that persists. Not a media mirage.

140

A very real and unique place meant to spend time in, instead of just rushing past (Fig. 8). Cities are not like airports, even if they seem that way on the internet. They are places with lasting designs and forms.

While some seek salvation in a nomadic architecture intended to heal the world from its hectic improvisations, others enter into a kind of historical trance, digging up old, forgotten cityscapes. They rely solely on their aesthetic and emotional instincts. Their artistic and metaphorical powers of imagination replace any reasonable, rational consideration. Urban space becomes subject to abstract speculation and accidental ideas for images that clearly do not need explanation, that are based exclusively on the personal experience of each respective genius. Amazing accomplishments come to light, achievements that fully satisfy all touristic and voyeuristic desires. One is taken to the threshold of a fantasy land and kitschy mimicry.

These two extreme poles of urban concentration exercises—the virtual city on the one hand and Fantasia on the other—are complementary strategies, both of which claim to have discovered a way out of the prevailing dilemmas of urban planning. In reality, they are nothing more than extremely helpless efforts to tame the chaos of our modern cities. Both strategies have exhausted themselves with academic bluffing and keep on mutually stimulating one another. The more one side loses itself in visionary speculations

141

Fig. 8 Beyond the network (a: Promenade on the flooded Piazza Navona, Rome, painting by Giovani Paolo Pannini, 1756, b: Piazza Navona, Rome).

on the future, the deeper the other buries itself in a historical morass of misunderstood models and metaphors—unrealistic ideas that are miles away from answering even one single factual issue related to complex urban systems. Both strategies are useless, neither utopia nor regression provide a glimmer of hope for being useful. Dispensing with both strategies is therefore an easy step. Their speculations can be left to the media and to art historians.

The time of ideal cities ended with the Renaissance, at the latest. Later efforts, during the nineteenth century in particular, attempted to force the city into a corset of idealism and failed not least due to the rampant spread of industrial and social development. Even Modernists, especially in fascist Italy, failed in their attempt to create a generally binding concept of what constitutes the ideal and, in the end, were unable to make headway in building new cities. The results that emerged from encounters with the ideals of car-friendly or socially balanced cities following the Second World War are no different. These fiascos demonstrated that cities of the late twentieth century are far too heterogeneous and contradictory to be grasped with a single concept, however dominant (Fig. 9). The cities of our time are not just one place; rather, they consist of many places. They are complex, multi-layered diverse structures in which it is possible for a wide range of different ideas, concepts, and systems to complement and supplement each other.

a   b

142

Fig. 9   Failed ideal cities (a: Cancellotti, Montuori, Piccinato, Scalpelli: Sabaudia New Town, 1933–1934, b: Hans Bernhard Reichow, diagram of a neighborhood, 1948).

a   b

 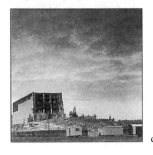

c   d

The problem of cities today, regardless of size, is not to be found exclusively in the center. It also concerns the peripheries, or, to put it better: the interaction of the center and the periphery. Paris is perhaps the most extreme example of a European city surrounded, and almost suffocated, by a peripheral ring of *banlieues*. Even small and medium-sized cities wrestle with the phenomenon of sprawl, with uncontrolled growth developing into an urban plague that seems entirely unsurmountable. Like cancerous growths on the outskirts, industrial zones, commercial facilities, and shopping malls are increasingly defining the cities of today, gradually threatening to shift the face of classic urbanity. This mixture of traffic routes, outsourced services, production facilities, and distribution centers creates an accumulation of entirely disorganized building masses, impossible to aesthetically or rationally assess (Fig. 10). At the same time, an indisputable drive to preserve the historical building stock of city centers is becoming an economic and a barely solvable formal problem.

143

Fig. 10   The contemporary city (a: Rostock-Reutershagen, b: Humboldthafen, Berlin, c: Neuss outskirts, d: Spreeinsel, Berlin).

The dilemma of cities is not only social, economic, and technical, it is above all a dilemma of planning. The main focus of urban planning is to bring order to a whole that is created by chance, factual constraints, and social givens, to propose methods for bringing often mutually exclusive facts and processes under the umbrella of a rational system and logical strategies. The planning methods used so far are no longer sufficient to create strategies applicable to today's city.

In contrast to previous attempts to standardize, we will discuss the following two urban strategies, both of which address dichotomies and unresolved contradictions—strategies based on the concepts of Nikolaus von Kues formulated in his *Docta de ignorantia* and which focus on the coincidence of opposites or "*coincidentia oppositorum*":

1. the strategy of a city of complementary places;
2. the strategy of the city as a foil.

Unlike villages, small towns, and ideal cities in particular, today's metropolises no longer have a uniform shape. Instead, they are a heterogeneous collection of different elements, systems, and functions. Big cities extend out into the surrounding regions, are made up of fragments. They have a fragmented open structure that, due to the great diversity of contradicting needs, can no longer be bound into a coherent whole. Today's cities are dialectical, thesis and antithesis at once. Contemporary cities reveal the contradictions not only of society, but of technical systems as well. It is no longer possible to find coherent forms or solutions without discrepancy, solutions that could, as in historic cities and even until the nineteenth century, be entirely encompassed by a single system. The city as a unifying concept has increasingly dissolved over the course of history. What remains is an unmanageable, barely controllable apparatus steering towards ever larger excesses and increased dissolution. Individual,

144

identifiable places play an important role in this trend towards the dissolution of centralized cities.

The city as a unified concept is replaced by the city as a system of complementary places. Many mutually contradictory places, sites for relaxation, culture, business, living, and working all form a loose network of urban density. It is not the widespread mixing, but the supplementary, mutually complementary system of significant places that characterizes the modern city, a city defined by technology and the high requirements of civilization. It is therefore important to develop a method suited to exploring the character of highly diverse places, defining them and developing their uniqueness—either by adding missing functions or by improving the existing ones.

The city of complementary places has a large number of different parts, each of which develops a special urban aspect in context with the whole, a "city within a city" system, so to speak. Each sub-area is unique in and of itself, yet is neither complete nor encapsulated. Single aspects—housing, culture, and commerce for example—are highly developed and, when brought together with other highly developed places, create a complex system, a type of alliance or federation. Complementary places are, for example, historical city centers with their newly founded peripheries or industrial complexes alongside extensive recreation areas. These places are organized hierarchically. Some places are more important and some less so. The valuation is derived only from the place itself, not from an ideal. For this reason, all types of construction—high-rise or low-rise, large block or solitary—are fundamentally possible. The building structure is not exclusive, but diverse and heterogeneous instead. The search is for diversity and plurality, not for uniformity. Opposition becomes part of the system, con-tradictions are left unresolved. The aim is not to resolve them, but to make differences as clear and unambiguous as possible. Each section, each place, initially exists in and of itself, only evolving within a complementary relationship to another self-contained

145

a b c

place. The places are like monads, small microcosms, independent worlds with a diversity of peculiarities, advantages, and disadvantages integrated into a larger urban macrocosm made up of all these many small worlds to form a metropolis (Fig. 11).

The art of urbanity lies in finding these places within the urban chaos, naming them and honing their uniqueness: an urban architecture of discovery, not invention. New systems—technical and otherwise—are unnecessary. The existing state, whether arisen by accident, through constraints, or from shortcomings, is fully accepted and seen as a foil, a layer. A new and different city structure is built from these preexisting elements and segments, from the pieces and fragments. New spaces and places are built and developed. A city of complementary places is both open and accessible to interpretation, diverse and adaptable at the same time, useful, unideological, and unpretentious, accessible to innovation, and preserves the existing substance.

The second approach to structuring and organizing today's cities is that of the city as a foil. Cities are made up of different layers and overlays, which are either mutually complementary or diametrically opposed. The various systems—traffic, supply and disposal, parks, rivers and lakes, building development—are each taken into consideration individually and seen as contributing to the complexity of the urban structure. They can be isolated, thus becoming available and operational. They can be supplemented, reduced, perfected, and changed. Each individual

146

Fig. 11 The city as the sum of complementary places
(a: Berlin, b: Edinburgh, c: Wiesbaden).

system influences, interferes, or transforms the others. The ideal case is superimposed by conditions, constraints, and demands, disturbances that cause fragmentary structures to arise. Even highly autocratic technical systems like the last century's railway networks, which burst upon cities like wild hurricanes, were realized ideally. They were just changed by topographical and historical circumstances. This caused contradictions and difficulties in assimilation that led to unique and unpredictable results. The railways turned their cities into a continuum of unresolved mutual conflict. Conflicts, fragments, and unresolved contradictions are the characteristic criteria of the city as a foil. The structures overlap like the building layers of a historic city (Fig. 12).

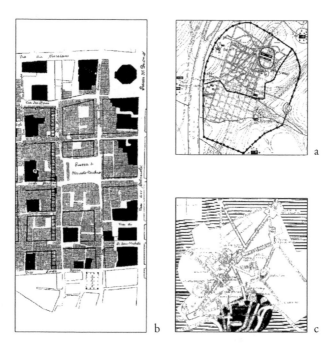

Fig. 12 The city as the result of layering (a: Treves: topography, Roman city, medieval city, b: Florence: medieval city, renaissance city, c: Rome according to Giedion: Roman city, medieval city, baroque city).

The method is to repeatedly layer new and more complete systems like foils over the existing ones, monitoring the impacts and effects and exploiting the formal outcomes. Urban design is thus transformed from a purely emotional process into a rational procedure in which every decision, each additional degree of complexity can be monitored and understood. The various foils, the layers, can be weighted and emphasized according to priority. Urban design is therefore absolved of the usual need to beautify, something which depends solely on emotions and "brilliant" ideas. The trick lies in finding sensible arrangements and recognizing and evaluating the mutual effects of the various layered systems. Rational decision-making processes take the place of subjective feelings and inventions. This strategy of layering can be seen as supplementing the morphological approach of the city of complementary places with a structural approach, and presupposes that the city is understood as a complex whole and that the existing city is being addressed in a specific and concrete manner. Only when a city is seen as a whole can the tensions and contradictions of diversity and complexity become clear. The unfinished or, if you prefer, provisional character of the city acts both as the basis and the goal of planning. This creates a diversity of forms and spaces that are desired, the result of a clear and strictly defined process. This process encompasses topographical situations, historical influences, technical processes, social facts, and formal visions. Nothing is predetermined; instead, everything is decided case-by-case.

This planning approach of the city as a foil aims to create an instrument and at the same time a vocabulary with which the chaotic conglomerate of today's cities can be transformed into orderly, manageable structures—while still maintaining and, if possible, even intensifying the high degree of their complexity. The method aims to emphasize the discursive nature of the city by creating hypotheses and testing them experimentally, working to guide and carry forth the orderly planning and development of the city—as exemplified by the following two previously introduced strategies.

Strategy 1: The Theme of Assemblage or the City of Complementary Places

II. 29 The theme of assemblage primarily concerns the aspect of time, but also that of discontinuity and of contradiction. In general, one strives to see things and objects as a whole. The achievement of a unitary image for the city is considered of particular value for example. In an urban plan, uniformity—whether one meets it in the organization of space or of form—is considered an indispensable element for all architecture on a high level of quality. Yet one often forgets that this demand for unity, in its exclusivity, too easily becomes an imposition on project studies. There is no doubt that a totalitarian plan is unitary, and so to speak "all of a piece". The demand for a non-unitary plan, for architecture that contradicts itself, seems almost absurd.

The criteria by which one makes an evaluation of architecture usually aim at a homogeneous, definitive, and complete situation, while contradictions are seen as something that have to be eliminated. The complete form stands in the middle and provides simultaneously both measure and limit. All value judgements would be overturned if what is incomplete, or in other words the unresolved contradiction, was placed at the center of the conception and of the plan and hence of architectural studies. Is it possible—or even necessary—to produce artificially, and therefore consciously, the contradiction that is usually determined by chance? In this connection, a more profound examination of history can help to clear away a prejudice: In fact, the opinion that historically formed cities are unitary is a myth. These cities—with the exception of a few museum cities—are created through a discontinuous process of growth and are therefore contradictory in themselves. Different epochs have left their traces on the city at different times. Theses are followed by antitheses, so that the city turns out to be a dialectical structure as far as its essence and its image are concerned.

This can be seen to be as true for individual works of architecture as it is for the historic city as a whole. The finest example of the great number of architectural works of this type that are in existence is the cathedral of Trier (Figs. 13 and 14). Over the course of their history, these buildings have always been subjected to a continuous process of modification, completion, enlargement, reduction, or improvement. They have the appearance of a collage of different pieces and parts and reflect the individual epochs and their respective styles of architecture. Even ruins—created by a violent act or by the passing of time—reveal the different aspects and stages of architectural works that differ substantially from complete and homogeneous buildings (Fig. 15).

The building as a fragment, as discontinuous object, composed of different unrelated parts, is not, if looked at historically, unusual. Nevertheless the fragment as a theme and deliberate plan seems to

150

Fig. 13 Remains from several historical periods in the wall of a church in Trier.
Fig. 14 Vestiges and ancient fragments combined to form an "ensemble" in a wall of Glienicke Schlosspark.

be a genuine contradiction. One is only prepared to accept the idea of an architectural work that looks like a fragment by referring it to a romantic kind of architecture—one thinks of ruins, or towns and houses in ruins (Fig. 16). Yet fragmentary architecture only partly fits with this romantic vision. In fact there are modern cities that are contradictory and fragmentary, like present-day Frankfurt for example. Could it be called romantic as a result? The definition of romantic is certainly not appropriate for Frankfurt, but rather for a city like Rothenburg, which presents a substantially homogeneous image. The concept of fragmentary in this context does not at all mean the same thing as the concept of romantic. Rather it unfailingly contains a stratification, a degree of complexity not met with in an architectural work or urban structure that is conceived as a unity. The element of surprise, of intellectual and visual challenge is much stronger in a contradictory setting as in one created by a homogeneous order.

Hence the theme of fragmentation, of dialectical contradiction, by no means needs to be romantic. Instead it adds to the awareness of a process that makes the individual object, or even the urban structure, stand out, freeing it from dependence on time or from formal rigidity. Here we have a principle that brings together, in a higher conception based on the unresolved contradiction, both creative contradiction and continuity, spontaneity and plan, chance as much as the established order (Fig. 17).

151

Fig. 15 Fragments of ancient columns and architraves in Glienicke Schlosspark.

Fig. 16 Castle on the Pfaueninsel in Berlin by J. G. D. Brendel, 1794.
The castle is a document of Romantic classicism, and with it the concept
of "memory" was added to architecture.

Fig. 17 General plan of Rome from the 18th century with the principal fragments of the ancient city.

Fig. 18 View of the cathedral of Trier which grew into a whole from the fragments of different historical epochs.

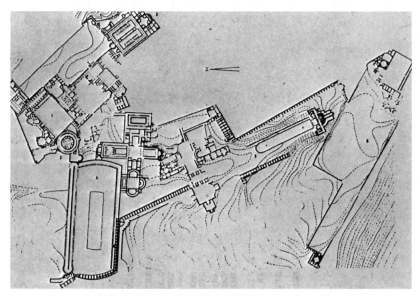

Fig. 19 Plan of the Villa Adriana in Tivoli, in which fragments from historic memory are gathered into an ensemble.

Fig. 20 The Teufelsbrücke by Persius, in Glienicke Schlosspark 1838. The bridge was made up of fragments with different meanings.

Fig. 21 The Teufelsbrücke in the "restoration" of the 1930s. The parts deliberately left in a fragmentary state were "completed" in the restoration. This error can be blamed on the conservationists.

The "*coincidentia oppositorum*", as Nikolaus von Kues called it, the coincidence of opposites and not their overcoming, lies at the bottom of the theoretical conception that defines the theme of fragmentation. These contradictions do not shut themselves up in their antithetical nature, but are integrated into an all-inclusive image (Fig. 18). This does not only apply to the contradictions between individual works of architecture, and hence between architectural forms and styles, or to the contradictions present in the urban environment relating to spaces, places, and settings, but also to those between designed and natural environment, and therefore between culture and nature (Fig. 19).

A new dimension of thought and perception is opened up if the world is experienced in all its contradictions, that is in all its multiplicity and variety, if it is not forced into the concept of homogeneity that shapes everything to itself. Only collectivized thought can aspire to unity; the free, individual spirit seeks contradictions, antitheses, heterogeneity. Von Kues's conception was, at that time of mediaeval dogmatic scholasticism, a first move in the direction of enlightenment at the beginning of a new, conscious age, that places man at the center of the world.

On the same level of philosophical thinking Persius overcame the constriction of the unitary style when he designed the Teufelsbrücke [Devil's Bridge] in the Glienicke Palace park by combining different fragments (Fig. 20). He made use of the archaic, natural element as well as the technical, refined one, original elements along with the most sophisticated ones; the complete work is an abridgement of the whole spectrum between the natural and the artistic. Similarly, in life, workdays and holidays, triviality and important events make up part of a whole, being nothing but different aspects of the same totality. So the Teufelsbrücke in Berlin is an illustration of an enlightened age that aimed at synthesis. A creative, universal spirit is manifested in this work that refuses to be restricted to a dogmatic principle. A century later we have moved so far away from this encyclopedic conception of Humanism that not only are we not capable of following it, but even the meaning of Persius's bridge has been misunderstood. It is seen as an incomplete rudiment because it is not homogeneous. Consequently it has been "restored" so as to turn it into a homogeneous and "complete" work of architecture in which the original meaning is no longer recognizable (Fig. 21). The demand for an urban restoration, which is so much talked about today, derives from the same theoretical position. Instead of "restoring", the contradictions of the place should be recognized and accepted, turning them into the poetry of the design.

The theme of assemblage is not to be confused either with arbitrary decomposition or with the casual products of a pluralistic conception based on laissez faire. It is also in opposition to the present-day tendency towards a faithful and literal restoration of the past. Instead it is a question of making an attempt, in the sense of a humanistic concept to comprehend thought and action as a morphological whole made up of many different relations, and to give all intellectual potentialities a place to unfold.

Project for the Tiergarten Museum in Berlin:
A "Forum" of Contradiction (1965)

This project for the museums of Berlin is not based on any homogeneous plan. The image to which it refers is provided by the model of a forum for spirit and culture (Fig. 22). Like in a Roman forum, where the individual buildings each express what they represent, the buildings take on forms here that correspond to the use for which they are intended (Fig. 23). Each building has its own identity and exists in a contradictory relationship with the others. Just as the contents of the museums range from the antique collection to the modern picture gallery and, with the exhibitions of applied art, sculpture and a library, encompass many different aspects of culture, the buildings are conceived here in different ways, each according to its specific context (Fig 24). This is both true for form and material—an almost archaic building stands by the side of one of

156

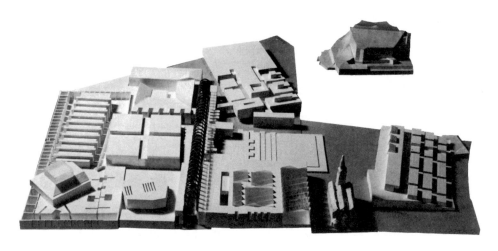

Fig. 22 The Tiergarten Museum in Berlin: An analogy to the design for the Acropolis. Model, 1965.

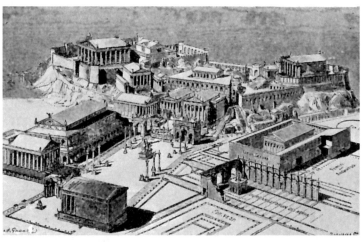

Fig. 23 View of a Roman forum. A complex made up of different building types, forms, and fragments.

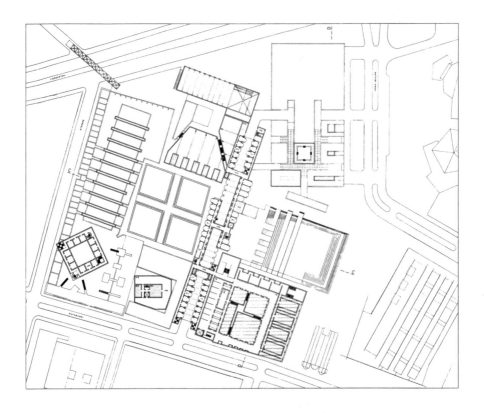

Fig. 24 General plan of the Tiergarten Museum project.
Each individual museum has a plan suitable to its content.

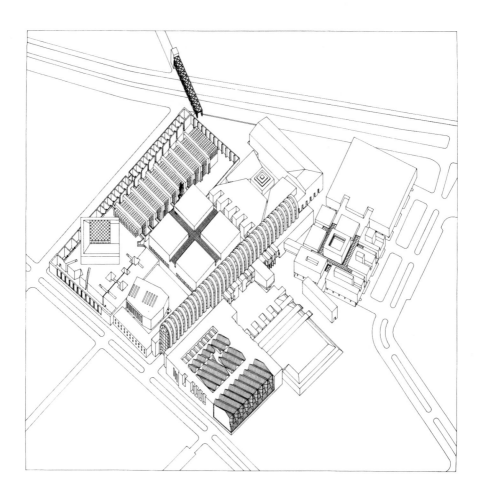

Fig. 25   Axonometric view of the Tiergarten Museum project
that is made up of different buildings treated as fragments.

the highest technological perfection, a classical building by the side of a monumental one, a building of very small structure next to a monumental one, a glass building next to one of steel, an anonymous architecture alongside a stylized one (Fig. 25). Each construction has its own language and the repertory of forms is manifold and contradictory, as is the exhibition material brought together in a single museum. The whole might be described as a garden of culture in which grow plants of different kind. The individual buildings are fragments, in part pieces of memory as well, set in a contextual place, a place of spirit and of culture, an island of museums.

The theme of the project, fragmentation, fits with the surrounding landscape of Tiergarten Park, which includes buildings of different architectural character: Mies van der Rohe's Nationalgalerie [National Gallery] and Scharoun's Philharmonie [Philharmonic] stand against one another in a dialectical relationship, as thesis and antithesis; yet another thesis is made by Stüler's church, which was built around 1850 (Fig. 26). Along with these architectural documents there are various minor buildings—urban houses that have survived the war or remained in a state of ruin, each of which has its own characteristics (Fig. 27). This contradiction between ceremonial and simple architecture, between different conceptions and historical epochs, between the complete and the fragmentary, gives rise to an architectural variety that at the same time is an expression

160

Fig. 26 View of the Kulturforum on Kemperplatz in Berlin showing the Nationalgalerie by Mies van der Rohe, Stühler's church, and the Philharmonie by Scharoun. A newly cast cultural forum.

of the quality of urbanity. While the situation of a village is a homogeneous one, the life of the urban place derives from its wealth of discontinuity, of contradictions. The ideal model of an urban center is the forum, just as Schinkel used it in his plan for the Acropolis, and it also forms the basis of the idea of the Museumsinsel [Museum Island] in Berlin (Fig. 28). The project for the museums in Tiergarten is an attempt to give formal expression to a spiritual and cultural forum.

Project for the Court of Justice in Berlin:
The Discontinuity of Spatial Relationships (1979)

II. 50 The concept of the forum as an expression of the highest urban expression also forms the basis for the project for the Berlin Court of Justice. Three different complexes of buildings are arranged on a triangular plot of land on the Landwehrkanal: a residential building along the canal, the law court at the center, and the Turkish consulate at the vertex of the site (Fig. 29). The conception of the plan and the architectural design correspond to the different contents of the buildings (Figs. 30 and 31). In the design for the Court of Justice the volume of the building and the space that it encloses are identical and form a clearly identifiable structure, determined by the functional needs. In the project for the Turkish consulate the open space has been treated as if it was an object and

161

Fig. 27 View of the site intended for the Berlin museums. The individual buildings are fragments of the old perimetrical structure.

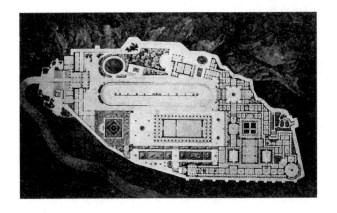

has been practically cut out of the surrounding volume; in this way a differentiation of space has been achieved (Fig. 32). These two design concepts can be seen as analogous to the visible contrast between Scharoun's Library and Philharmonie and Mies van der Rohe's Nationalgalerie, which derive from totally antithetical conceptions of architecture (Fig. 26). In the projects for the Court of Justice and for the consulate, the inherent historical dichotomies have been put in relation in a creative sense, integrating them into a concept of a higher order. The residential building has been divided into four blocks of the same size, which are oriented towards the watercourse. To give the residence an individual character, each block retains its own identity thanks to a definite theme—forming a square, or an internal road, or on a crossroads, or even a garden with single-family houses set in it. The four complexes are arranged on a slope that runs down to the water. The different design of the three architectural works that face onto the Landwehrkanal not only corresponds to the diversity of functional programs on which they are based, but it is also an attempt, above and beyond pure fulfillment of function, to individualize or thematize each of their different tasks. Only this made it possible to reconcile their contrasting functional aims and contrasting forms of expression in a theoretical conception of higher order, whose own content is the theme of contradiction.

162

Fig. 28 Schinkel's design for the Acropolis in which different fragments of plans, existing and planned, were brought together to form a unified whole.

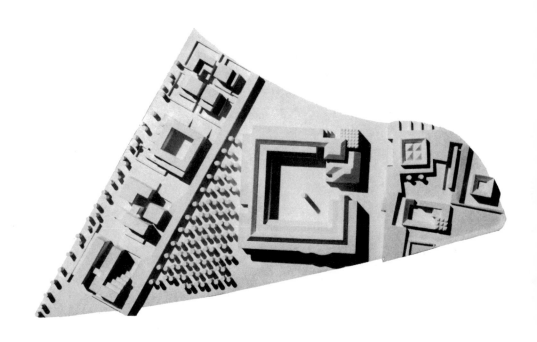

Fig. 29 Photograph of the model. Court of Justice, Berlin, 1979.

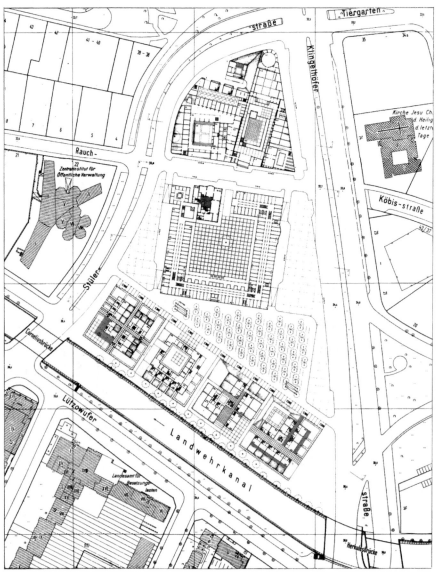

Fig. 30 General plan of the project's ground floor in the zone of the Court of Justice, of the residential building on the Landwehrkanal, and of the Turkish cultural center to the north.

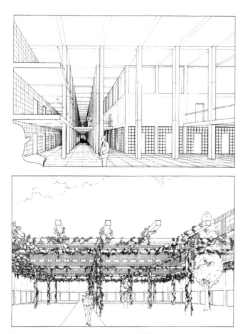

Fig. 32 Perspective views of the internal space.

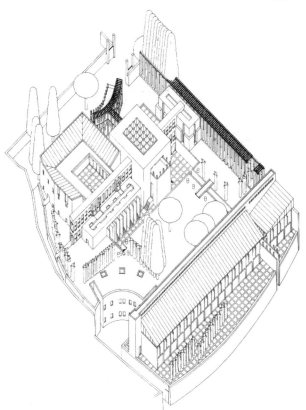

Fig. 31 Axonometric of the project for the Court of Justice. It consists
of three distinct architectural zones: the Turkish consulate to the north,
the Court of Justice at the center, and the residential block to the south.

Fig. 33   Photographic view of the Spreeinsel at the time of the project.

Strategy 2: The Theme of the City as a Foil

Project for the Spreeinsel in Berlin (1994)

III. 81 The Spreeinsel [Spree Island] is an essential part of Berlin's historic center that, as such, has a lively and eventful history (Figs. 33 and 34). This was the site of one of the early settlements that germinated into the city we know today. The Berliner Stadtschloss [Castle of Prussian Kings] was built here, followed by elements of a humanistic "Spree Athens". Some of Karl Friedrich Schinkel's most important buildings can be found here: the Friedrichswerder Church, the Bauakademie [Building Academy], and the Altes Museum [Old Museum] (Fig. 35).

After the Second World War, the Spreeinsel became a place of state representation for the GDR. The castle, partially destroyed during the war, was demolished and replaced by the out-of-scale expanse of the Marx-Engels-Platz and the Palace of the Republic.

Seen in light of this background, the complexity of the competition assignment becomes clear. Besides the many issues the urban reorganization of the desolate area entails, the question of how to approach the site's history and monuments also emerges. The latter already crystallized prior to the competition in the form of a fierce public debate on the pros and cons of demolishing the Palace of the Republic and reconstructing the historic Berliner Stadtschloss.

The competition proposal assumes that—out of respect for history—neither can the Palace of the Republic be demolished nor the Berliner Stadtschloss rebuilt. Instead, the Palace of the Republic should be placed under heritage protection. However, this decision means that an attempt should be made to relativize the monumental positioning of the building. It should be freed from its representative position and integrated into a unified urban whole. This is achieved by treating it not as a freestanding building, but as an urban block, which results in its integration into the overall structure of the city (Figs. 36 and 37).

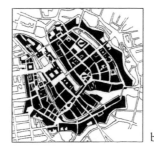

Fig. 34 The historic urban development process of the
Spreeinsel area (a: 1650, b: 1850, c: 1990).

Fig. 35 Solitary buildings and urban structure, buildings by Schinkel in the Spreeinsel
area (a: Friedrichswerder Kirche, b: Bauakademie, c: Altes Museum, d: Neue Wache
[New Guardhouse]).

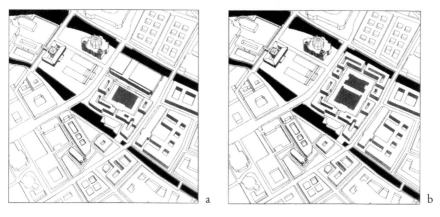

Fig. 36 Projected axonometric view of the Spreeinsel
(a: Building phase 1, b: Building phase 2).

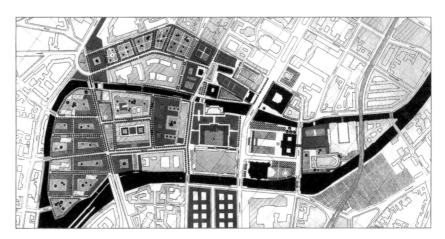

Fig. 37 Site plan of the Spreeinsel project.

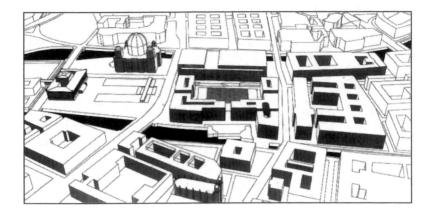

Carrying this idea forward, the block development is extended all the way to the Unter den Linden boulevard, forming a closed backdrop to the Lustgarten park together with the front of the Palace of the Republic (Figs. 38). The achievements of this move are dual: It creates an edge to which the dense network of buildings on the Spreeinsel extends, while the Lustgarten is provided with a spatial framework into which the freestanding buildings of the cathedral, the Altes Museum, and the Zeughaus [Armory] are set (Fig. 39 and 40).

However, as history prevents building on the site and grounds of the former Berliner Stadtschloss, its footprint is left as an open void within the block structure. This creates a negative space where the castle once stood. Thus, the site stands out in the plans— an open space enclosed by buildings on all sides that can be used as a historical park, even if initially a fragmented one (Fig. 41).

The amalgamation of two ideologies that historically mutually extinguished one another into a single urban planning unit would not only stage the historical process, but would also continue to be functional if the proponents of demolition prevailed. If one assumes, on the one hand, that the palace were to be demolished for whatever reason, while on the other hand, the castle was not

170

Fig. 38 Axonometric view, seen from Kupfergraben.

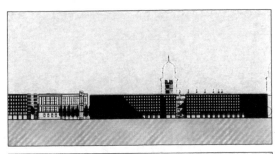

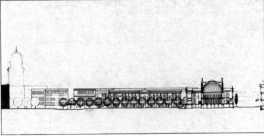

Fig. 39 Design proposal: view of the Spreekanal.

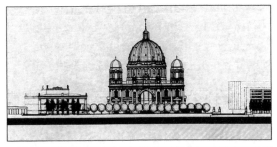

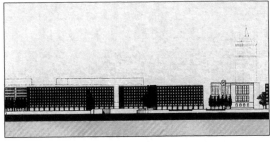

Fig. 40 Design proposal: view of Breite Straße
and Luststraße.

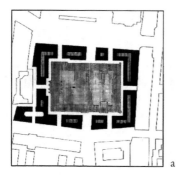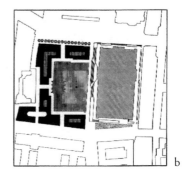

rebuilt due to ethical or other considerations, the negative space concept would still retain its viability. The open space in the shape of the castle's footprint is thus left as a void, a historical park within the dense urban structure. Conserving it as a space of memory would make the city's history part of its everyday reality (Fig. 42).

The urban planning concept for the reorganization of the Spreeinsel is based on ideas shaped by Schinkel in his Berlin plan, the concept of embedding solitary buildings into the overall urban structure. Schinkel's 1851 plan reinforced the general urban layout by carefully adding individual buildings and staging a diverse interplay of architectural highlights and general urban block development (Fig. 43). The proposed plan for the Spreeinsel functions along the same lines. Solitary buildings such as the Friedrichswerder Church, the State Council Building, the proposed restoration of the Alte Kommandantur [Old Commendantura], the Bauakademie, the Alte Münze [Old Mint Yard], the base of the Wilhelm I monument, and a few architectural gems inside the block act both as spatial and architectural highlights in an otherwise more or more less mundane urban fabric (Fig. 44).

The existing developments are complemented to become closed building blocks, thus creating a clear system of public street spaces, urban blocks, and greened inner courtyards (Fig. 45).

172

Fig. 41 The old castle as a courtyard (a: Building phase 1, b: Building phase 2).

a   b

The buildings of the State Council and the Foreign Ministry together form a diverse block with courtyards, squares, and passageways. The former Reichsbank [Imperial Bank] building is to be converted into the Ministry of the Interior. An added entrance volume with an indoor passageway connects the ensemble to Werderscher Markt, while Heinrich Gentz's Alte Münze will be restored and used as its reception building.

The character of the old Werderscher Markt should be restored. In addition to the church, another important element could be the construction of the Bauakademie, which could be used as the American Memorial Library. Here, too, the historic urban block development could lend itself for contemporary reuse, in this case in the form of a conference center.

The buildings on Werderscher Markt are rounded out by the block of the proposed media center, which also marks the end of the green corridor. The development around what would become Schloßplatz was to contain as dense an urban mix as possible: an arcaded ground floor with shops and cultural facilities facing the square, offices and medical practices on the floor above, and apartments atop.

The plan is an attempt not to redesign the center of Berlin by replacing existing buildings and structures with new ones or restoring old buildings. Instead, it aims to carefully complement and extend the fragmented and inconsistent building stock to

173

Fig. 42 Building construction and negative spaces (a: Berlin Palace, 1916, b: Place Royale, Paris (today Place des Vosges), detail of the Turgot plan (1734–1735)).

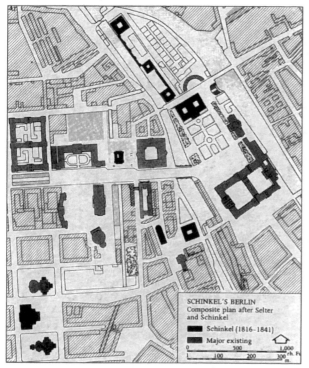

Fig. 43 Plan of Schinkel's design.

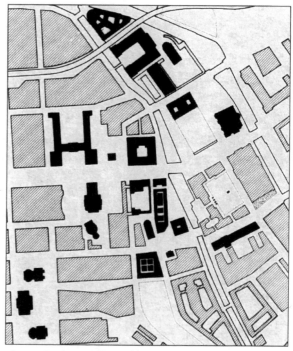

Fig. 44 Project: Perimeter blocks (gray) and freestanding buildings (black).

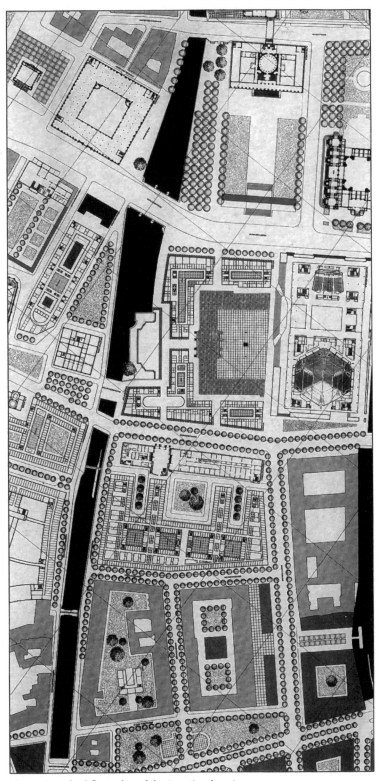

Fig. 45 Standard floor plan of the Spreeinsel project.

Fig. 46 Potsdamer Platz and Leipziger Platz at the time of the project.

create an overlain and diverse urban system. The strategy of seeing the city as a layering of foils is applied here in a subtle, less obvious way: The foremost focus is on the differentiated and flexible handling of each individual historical monument and unique urban situation. This means that the proposed structure is not uniform or exclusive, but instead dialectical and inclusive of different characters.

Project for the Potsdamer Platz and Leipziger Platz in Berlin (1991)

III. 105 Like the Spreeinsel, the area around Potsdamer Platz and Leipziger Platz is a site where the twentieth-century history of Berlin is reflected in an exemplary manner (Figs. 46 and 47). In the 1920s, the double-square ensemble was the busiest traffic hub in the entire Berlin metropolis. Thereafter, the area became a battlefield and, finally, a mine-laced no-man's-land. During the ensuing reconstruction, the ruins left by the war fell victim to a planning concept that upheld the ideal of the city as a landscape, manifest in the adjacent Kulturforum [Cultural Forum], an approach that deliberately negated the metropolitan tradition of the Potsdamer Platz and Leipziger Platz. Today, the area presents itself to observers as a place without history, an urban desert without a meaningful urban planning context.

With this in mind, the project for Potsdamer Platz and Leipziger Platz (Figs. 48–52) has two objectives: First and foremost is the need to once again define a clearly urban location, one with firmly defined spaces and a precise and orderly geometry. This includes addressing the historical aspects of the site in an effort to regain the historical continuity of the Potsdamer Platz and Leipziger Platz area. Secondly, a flexible and rational city structure must be created, one that takes into account the very real everyday needs of a contemporary city.

Based on the strategy of the city as a foil, the following concept has been developed (Figs. 53–55):

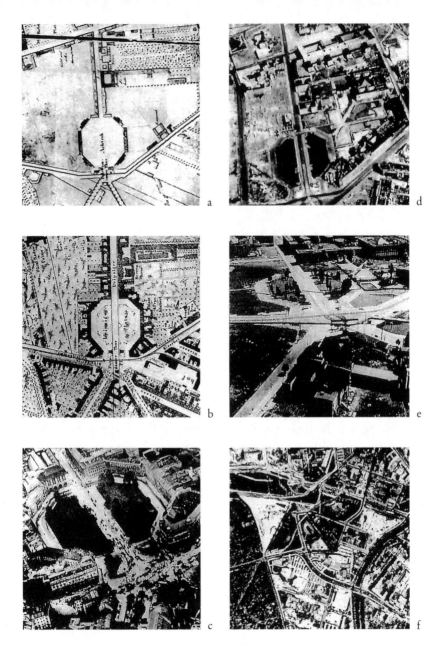

Fig. 47   Historical development of Potsdamer Platz and Leipziger Platz
(a: 1804, b: 1867, c: 1915, d: 1955, e: 1963, f: 1991).

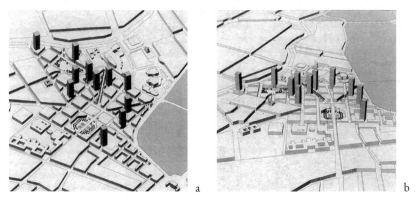

a

b

Fig. 48 Projected axonometric view (a: View from the northeast, b: View from the east).

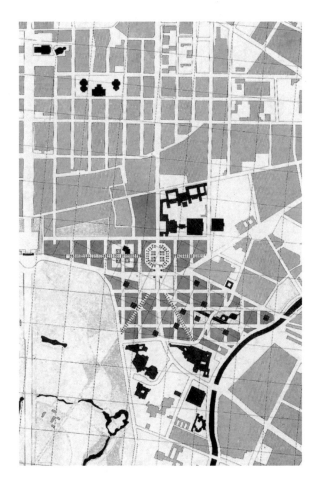

Fig. 49 Site plan.

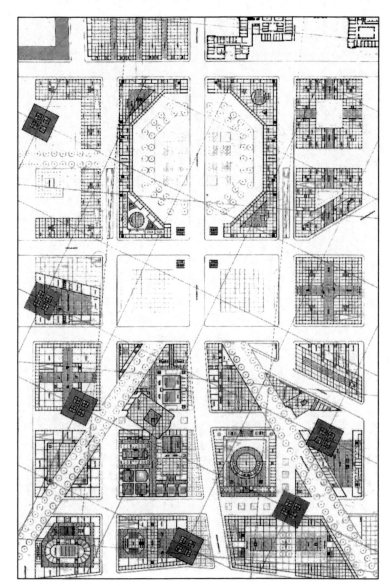
Fig. 50 Ground floor plan.

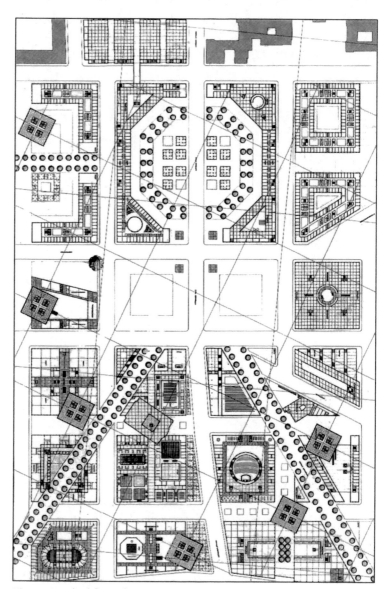

Fig. 51 Standard floor plan.

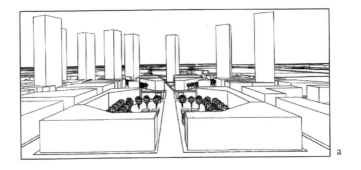

a

b

Urban structures   Various urban structures are relevant to the planning area. These are:

— Firstly, the historical grid layout of the Friedrichstadt district with its inherent urban block development along with the geometrically stringent dominance of Leipziger Platz.
— Secondly, the original parcellation of the developments located outside of Friedrichstadt, the coordinate network of which has retained its formative impact on the city.
— Thirdly, the postwar layout of street and traffic arteries between Kemperplatz and Leipziger Platz, which caused a de facto redistribution of the property situation.

Taking these historical structures into consideration is the very foundation of the new planning concept.

c

Layering By layering Friedrichstraße's block system with the current street and traffic network and further infusing it with a uniform grid of skyscrapers based on the historical coordinates of the former parcels of the Tiergarten, a dense, complexly structured, differentiated network of streets and building blocks of various forms, sizes, and significance emerges. This network takes into account both the existing property conditions and the highly varied use requirements.

Block and street patterns The differentiated block and street patterns stimulate maximum flexibility both in building development and in open spaces. The varying forms and sizes of the blocks, the spectrum of which ranges from standard urban blocks to double blocks to row and detached houses, provides a broad range of urban design and architectural alternatives. The same is true of the open spaces. From the central park to smaller squares, avenues (the old Potsdamer Straße), boulevards, pedestrian areas, passageways, traffic arteries, and symbolic squares and facilities (Potsdamer Platz and Leipziger Platz) —every conceivable type of urban open space is represented.

Typology The plan is a dense network of superimposed urban layers and building typologies. In order to define a typological order, a number of basic types can be identified:

183

Fig. 52 Projected views of Potsdamer Platz and Leipziger Platz (a: from Central Park, b: from Potsdamer Platz, c: from Leipziger Straße).

 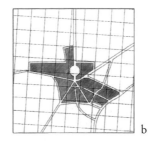 

Fig. 53 Basic block layer (a: Map of Berlin, 1985, b: Today's street layout,
c: Potential block structure).

 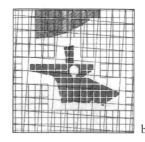 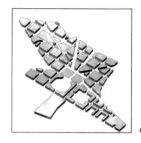

Fig. 54 Friedrichstadt layer (a: Latterscher Plan 1737, b: Friedrichstadt grid,
c: Layering the Friedrichstadt grid).

 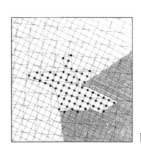 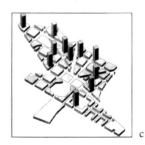

Fig. 55 Layer of historic land parcel: (a: Rhodenscher Plan 1772, b: Land parcel grid,
c: Second layering with land parcel grid).

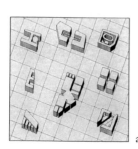 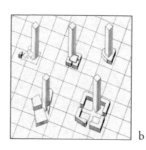 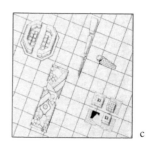

Fig. 56 Typologies (a: Block typology, b: Tower typology, c: Greenspace typology).

- *Block types* (Fig. 56) Rectangular block, H block, irregular block, inset block, interlocked block, compositional block
- *Street types* Urban street, traffic artery, avenue, boulevard, pedestrian area, passageway, gallery
- *Square types* Decorative plaza, square plaza, octagonal and triangular square, irregular square, street square, courtyard
- *Tower types* Tower in the park, tower in a block, tower with base, layered tower, double tower
- *Greenspace types* Central park, open space avenue, hedges, tree monument, tree grid, pocket park

Usage structures   The needs and requirements of a wide variety of uses can be met by the diverse building structures. Single buildings (Weinhaus Huth on the former Potsdamer Straße), existing historical structures (the Esplanade), super blocks with maximized office use, and blocks with complex mixed uses are all integral parts of the urban fabric.

Regulations   Neither a single architectural form nor an architectural language is predefined. The possibilities for architectural expression are subjective and depend on each respective task. This allows for utmost individuality in the selection of materials and style. Rules: a maximum height of 22 meters for blocks and 180 meters for towers. The tower grid and heights are binding, but exterior shape and materials remain undefined. The towers have uniform footprints in the dense network of blocks. The emergent conflict between tower and block structures is deliberate and stimulates the randomness that is necessary for a complex plan.

Art   Art is an integral part of the urban planning scheme, not an error of application. The structural layering leaves open a range of large to tiny areas that cannot be used for architecture. This is where art enters, at the interface between opportunity and "useless" space. The resources of art carry on the architectural and urban planning concept in extreme situations—with exaggeration or understatement.

The resulting randomness instills places with personality, introducing sculptures, unique objects, edges, and corners. Architecture, urban planning and use, history, and contemporary reality should be understood here as all being parts of a complex unity.

Finale: Humans, Culture, and Environment[1]

An architecture that starts out from a theme places humans at the center, since a human is more than a functional being, more than a "user"—as so often called today. Before all else, a human is a sensitive, spiritual being who wants to identify with their environment and who is in need of intellectual and emotional experiences. Why do such a large number of people visit the ancient temples of Greece and Italy, the Romanic and Gothic cathedrals of Germany and France, the palaces of Venice, the castles of the Loire, the fortresses of Scotland, or small medieval cities like Heidelberg or Rothenburg? They are looking for "the sublime", to use that suspect word, the grandiose, the fanciful, the romantic, or to put it in a single word, something outside the everyday. On the contrary, the functionalist Siedlungen of the 1920s, whose architecture is certainly on a high level, no longer form an element of attraction for the present generation. They are visited only by specialists, architects, and art historians for motives of study. If architecture wants to get back to being an experience, if it wants to enrich and not devastate the environment, then it must free itself from the straitjacket of functionalism and

186

remember its possibilities for conceptual and artistic expression. In this sense the thematization of architecture is at the same time a humanization of building, since it satisfies the demands of humankind, which go further than pure need, than the everyday, grasping them in their totality as spiritual and cultural beings.

1. Section heading by the editors of this book.

Process

The second chapter focuses on processes and the temporal dimension of urban form. First, Fumihiko Maki's systematic study of *Collective Form* is presented, followed by the thoughts of Alison and Peter Smithson on *Spatial Processes*. The two concepts share the assertion that the relationship between space and action is reciprocal: Not only does human agency shape space but urban form can also suggest, evoke, or trigger spatial processes.

Fumihiko Maki
Collective Form

I. Fumihiko Maki, *Investigations in Collective Form*, Special Publication of the School of Architecture (St. Louis: Washington University, 1964), 3–35.

II. Fumihiko Maki and Mark Mulligan (eds.), *Nurturing Dreams. Collected Essays on Architecture and the City* (Cambridge: MIT Press, 2008), 68–70, 72, 74, 76.

Collective Form: Three Paradigms

Beginning

I. 3 There is no more concerned observer of our changing society than the urban designer. Charged with giving form—with perceiving and contributing order—to agglomerates of building, highways, and green spaces in which people have increasingly come to work and live, they stand between technology and human need and seek to make the first a servant, for the second must be paramount in a civilized world.

For the moment, we are designers only, interested in technology and order, insofar as these may be divorced from the political, the economic. Of course, the progenitors of any formal idea include politics and economics. The reason, in fact, for searching for new formal concepts in contemporary cities lies in the magnitude of relatively recent change in those very problems. Our urban society is characterized by: (1) coexistence and conflict of amazingly heterogeneous institutions and individuals; (2) unprecedented rapid and extensive transformations in the physical structure of the society; (3) rapid communications methods, and (4) technological progress and its impact upon regional cultures.

The force of these contemporary urban characteristics makes it impossible to visualize urban form as did Roman military chiefs, or Renaissance architects Sangallo and Michelangelo; nor can we easily perceive a hierarchical order as did the original C.I.A.M. theorists in the quite recent past. We must now see our urban society as a dynamic field of interrelated forces. It is a set of mutually independent variables in a rapidly expanding infinite series. Any order introduced within the pattern of forces contributes to a state of dynamic equilibrium—an equilibrium which will change in character as time passes.

Our concern here is not, then, a "master plan", but a "master program", since the latter term includes a time dimension. Given a set of goals, the "master program" suggests several alternatives for achieving them, the use of one or another of which is decided by the passage of time and its effect on the ordering concept.

As a physical correlate of the master program, there are "master forms" which differ from buildings in that they, too, respond to the dictates of time.

Our problem is this: Do we have in urban design an adequate spatial language (an appropriate master form) with which we can create and organize space within the master program? Cities today tend to be visually and physically confused. They are monotonous patterns of static elements. They lack visual and physical character consonant with the functions and technology which compose them. They also lack elasticity and flexibility. Our cities must change as social and economic use dictate, and yet they must not be "temporary" in the worst visual sense.

We lack an adequate visual language to cope with the superhuman scale of modern highway systems and with views from airplanes. The visual and physical concepts at our disposal have to do with single buildings, and with dosed compositional means for organizing them.

The wealth of our architectural heritage is immense. One cursory look at architectural history is sufficient to find that the whole development is characterized by humankind's immense desire to make buildings grand and perfect. True, they have often mirrored the very strength of each civilization. They have produced the Pyramids, the Parthenon, the Gothic Cathedrals, and Seagram House. Today this is still a prevailing attitude among many architects—the creation of something new and splendid in order to outdo others.

Naturally, the theory of architecture has evolved through one issue as to how one can create perfect single buildings, whatever they are.

A striking fact against this phenomenon is that there is almost a complete absence of any coherent theory beyond the one of

194

single buildings. We have so long accustomed ourselves to conceiving of buildings as separate entities that today we suffer from an inadequacy of spatial languages to make meaningful environments.

This situation has prompted us to investigate the nature of "collective form". Collective form represents groups of buildings and quasi-buildings—the segments of our cities. Collective form is, however, not a collection of unrelated, separate buildings, but of buildings that have reasons to be together.

Cities, towns, and villages throughout the world do not lack in rich collections of collective form. Most of them have, however, simply evolved: they have not been designed. This provides a reason that so many professionals, both architects and planners, today often fail to make meaningful collective forms—meaningful as in giving the forms a forceful *raison d'être* in our society.

The following analysis evolves through two questions: first, how collective form has been developed in history; and second, what are its possible implications for our current thinking in architecture and urban design.

The investigation of collective form is extensive, but promising. The first step is to analyze structural principles involved in making collective form. We have established three major approaches (Fig. 1).

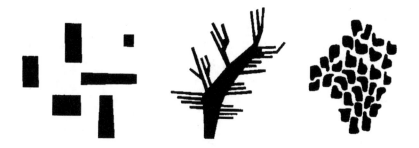

Fig. 1 Three approaches to collective form. From left to right: compositional form, megaform, and group form.

Compositional Form	Compositional Approach
Megastructure (Form)	Structural Approach
Group Form	Sequential Approach

The first of these, the compositional approach, is a historical one. The second two are new, and are efforts toward finding master forms which satisfy the demands of contemporary urban growth and change.

Compositional Form

The compositional approach is a commonly accepted and practiced concept in the past and at present. The elements which comprise a collective form are preconceived and predetermined separately. In other words, they are often individually tailored buildings. Then, proper functional, visual, and spatial (sometimes symbolic) relationships would be established on a two-dimension plane.

It is no surprise that this is the most understandable and used technique for architects in making collective form, because the process resembles the one of making a building out of given components. It is a natural extension of the architectural approach. It is a static approach, because the act of making a composition itself has a tendency to complete a formal statement.

Most contemporary large-scale urban designs fall into this category. Rockefeller Center, Chandigarh Government Center, and Brasília are good examples of compositional urban design (Figs. 2 and 3). In any case, the compositional approach is a familiar one, and it has received some treatment in works on architecture and planning. We will, therefore, let it stand on its own merit, and introduce two less well-known approaches.

Megastructure Form

The megastructure is a large frame in which all the functions of a city or part of a city are housed. It has been made possible by

196

Fig. 2 Compositional approach to architecture: Oscar Niemeyer's capital
complex for Brasília.

Fig. 3 Compositional form: the Horyuji Temple in Nara, Japan.

present-day technology. In a sense, it is a manmade feature of the landscape. It is like the great hill on which Italian towns were built.

Inherent in the megastructure concept, along with a certain static nature, is the suggestion that many and diverse functions may beneficially be concentrated in one place. A large frame implies some utility in combination and concentration of function.

Urban designers are attracted to the megastructure concept because it offers a legitimate way to order massive grouped functions. One need only look at work in the recent Museum of Modern Art show "Visionary Architecture" to sense the excitement generated among designers by megaform. While some of the ideas displayed in the show demonstrate structural virtuosity at the expense of human scale and human functional needs, others have a quality which suggests no divergence between compacted, economic function and human use.

That utility is sometimes only apparent. We frequently confuse the potential that technology offers with a kind of compulsion to "use it fully". Technological possibility can be useful only when it is the tool of civilized persons. Inhumane use of technological advance is all too frequently our curse. Optimum productivity does not depend on the mere concentration of activities and workers. As Percival and Paul Goodman say in *Communitas*:

We could centralize or decentralize, concentrate population or scatter it. If we want to continue the trend away from the country, we can do it; but if we want to combine town and country values in an agri-industrial way of life, we can do that. [...] It is just this relaxing of necessity, this extraordinary flexibility and freedom of choice of our techniques, that is baffling and frightening to people. [...] Technology is a sacred cow left strictly to (unknown) experts, as if the form of the industrial machine did not profoundly affect every person. [...] They think that it is more efficient to centralize, whereas it is usually more inefficient.[1]

Technology must not dictate choices to us in our cities. We must learn to select modes of action from among the possibilities technology presents in physical planning.

One of the most interesting developments on megaform has been made by Professor Kenzo Tange with MIT graduate students when he was a visiting professor there. In a series of three articles in the September 1960 issue of *Japan Architect*, Professor Tange presents a proposal for a mass human-scale form that includes a megaform, and discrete, rapidly changeable functional units which fit within the larger framework (Fig. 4).

> Professor Tange writes:
> Short-lived items are becoming more and more short-lived, and the cycle of change is shrinking at a corresponding rate. On the other hand, the accumulation of capital has made it possible to build in large-scale operations. Reformations of natural topography, dams, harbors, and highways are of a size and scope that involve long cycles of time, and these are the man-made works that tend to divide the overall system of the age. The two tendencies—toward shorter cycles and toward longer cycles—are both necessary to modern life and to humanity itself.[2]

Tange's megaform concept depends largely on the idea that change will occur less rapidly in some realms than it will in others, and that the designer will be able to ascertain which of the functions they are dealing with fall in the long cycle of change, and which in the shorter. The question is, can the designer successfully base their concept on the idea that—to give an example—transportation methods will change less rapidly than the idea of a desirable residence or retail outlet? Sometimes, the impact and momentum of technology become so great that a change occurs in the basic skeleton of social and physical structure. It is difficult to predict to which part of a

Fig. 4   A megastructure for a community of 25,000 by Kenzo Tange at the MIT
(with Pillorge, Halady, Niedernum, and Solomons).

pond a stone will be thrown and which way the ripples will spread. If the megaform becomes rapidly obsolete, as well it might, especially in those schemes which do not allow for two kinds of change cycle, it will be a great weight about the neck of urban society.

On the other hand, the ideal is not a system in which the physical structure of the city is at the mercy of unpredictable change. The ideal is a kind of master form which can move into ever new states of equilibrium and yet maintain visual consistency and a sense of continuing order in the long run. This suggests that the megastructure which is composed of several independent systems that can expand or contract with the least disturbance to others would be preferable to the one composed of a rigid hierarchical system. In other words, each system which makes up the whole maintains its identity and longevity without being affected by others while at the same time being engaged in dynamic contact with others. When the optimum relationship has been formed, an environmental control system can be made. The system that permits the greatest efficiency and flexibility with the smallest organizational structure is ideal. Two basic operations are necessary to establish this optimum control mechanism. One is to select proper independent functional systems and to give them optimum interdependency through the provision of physical joints at critical points (Figs. 5 and 6).

Although the megastructure concept presents the problems outlined above, it also has great promise for:

1. *Environmental engineering.* Megastructure development necessitates collaboration between the structural and civil engineer. Possibilities in large spans, space frames, lightweight skin structures, prestressed concrete, highway aesthetics, and earth forming will be developed far beyond their present level.

Fig. 6   An example of megaform: an agricultural city designed by Noriaki Kurokawa.

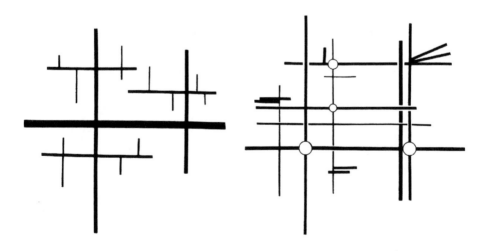

Fig. 5   Two types of megaform: From left to right: a hierarchical structure
and an open-ended structure.

Large-scale climatic control will be studied further. A new type of physical structure, environmental building, will emerge.

2. *Multifunctional structures.* We have, thus far, taken it for granted that buildings should be designed to fulfill one specific purpose. In spite of the fact that the concept of multifunctionalism must be approached with caution, it offers useful possibilities. Within the megaform structure, we can realize combinations such as those in Kurokawa's Agricultural City.

3. *Infrastructure as public investment.* Substantial public investment can be made in infrastructures (the skeleton of megastructures) in order to guide and stimulate public structures around them. This strategy can be further extended to a new three-dimensional concept of land use where public offices will maintain the ownership and upkeep for both horizontal and vertical circulation systems.

Group Form

Group form is the last of the three approaches of collective form. It is a form which evolves from a system of generative elements in space. Some of the basic ideas of group form can be recognized in historical examples of town buildings. Urban designers and architects have recently become interested in them because they appear to be useful and suggestive examples when making large-scale form. Medieval cities in Europe, towns in Greek Islands, villages in Northern Africa are a few examples. The spatial and massing qualities of these towns are worth consideration. Factors which determine the spatial organization of these towns are:

1. Consistent use of basic materials and construction methods as well as spontaneous, but minor, variations in physical expression.

2. Wise, and often dramatic, use of geography and topography.
3. Human scale preserved throughout the town. (This is frequently in contrast to superhuman land forms.)
4. Finally, sequential development of basic elements which predominantly include dwellings, open spaces between the houses, and the repetitive use of certain visual elements such as walls, gates, towers, waters, etc. The idea of sequential development has been recently elucidated by Prof. Roger Montgomery of Washington University, who sees the series of buildings or elements without apparent beginning or end as a contemporary compositional "theme" distinct from the dosed composition of forms which characterizes classic or axial "themes".

The sequential form in historical examples developed over a period of time much longer than that in which contemporary cities are being built and rebuilt. In this sense, then, the efforts of contemporary urban designers are quite different from their historical counterparts, and the forms which they consciously evolve in a short time span must differ accordingly. The lesson is, however, a useful one. A further inquiry of the basic elements and particularly of the relationship between the elements and groups reveals interesting principles involved in making collective form.

Throughout history, many Japanese villages have developed along major country roads (Fig. 7). Houses are generally U-shaped, and juxtaposed against one another perpendicular to the road—they are basically court-type row houses. The front part of the house is two stories high, and forms a tight continuous village façade together with other units. Behind it is an enclosed yard, which is used for domestic work, drying crops, making straw, etc. A barn is located at the other end of the house, and faces an open country field. There exists unquestionably a clear structural relationship between the village and the houses,

Fig. 7　An example of group form: a Japanese lineal village.

between village activities and individual family life, or between the movement of villagers and cows. Here the house unit is a generator of the village form, and vice versa. A unit can be added without changing the basic structure of the village. The depth and frontage of the unit, or the size of the court or barn may differ from unit to unit. But there is a prevailing understanding of basic structural principles in making the village.

Another example is Dutch housing of the sixteenth century. The Dutch have a reputation for living in communal units. Volunteer cooperation has long existed by limiting their personal liberty through common obedience to self-made laws. Their houses reflect this spirit. In *Towns and Buildings*, Steen Eiler Rasmussen tells us:

> A stone walled canal with building blocks above it on each side, covered with houses built closely together and separated from the canal by cobbled roadways. The narrow, gabled ends of the houses face the canal and behind the deep houses are gardens. [...] Outside the houses is a special area called, in Amsterdam, the *stoep*, which is partly a pavement and partly a sort of threshold of the house.[3]

The *stoep* is actually a part of the house, and the owner takes immense pride in maintaining it. It is also a social place, where neighbors exchange gossip and children play. By raising the ground floor of houses, it gives privacy to the resident even with large glass panes in front, which reduce the load on pilings under the house. There is again a unity between the existences of canals and of trees, of paved roadways and *stoeps*, and of large glass windows and rear gardens. This set of relationships has emerged through long experience and the wisdom of the people.

Forms in group form have their own built-in links, whether expressed or latent, so that they may grow in a system. They define basic environmental space which also partakes of the quality of systematic linkage. Group form and its space are indeed prototype elements, and they are prototypes because of implied system and linkage. The element and the growth pattern are reciprocal—both in design and in operation. The element suggests a manner of growth, and that, in turn, demands further development of the elements, in a kind of feedback process.

On the other hand, the element in megaform does not exist without a skeleton. The skeleton guides growth and the element depends on it. The element of group form is often the essence of collectivity, a unifying force, functionally, socially, and spatially. It is worth noting that group form generally evolves from the people of a society, rather than from their powerful leadership. It is the village, the dwelling group, and the bazaar which are group forms in the sense we are using this term, and not the palace complex, which is compositional in character.

Can we, then, create meaningful group forms in our society? The answer is not a simple one. It requires a new concept and attitude of design. It also requires the participation of cities and their social institutions.

Remarks by two modern architects cast light on this definition of group form. The distinction between form and design was given by Louis Kahn in a speech at the World Design Conference in Tokyo in 1960. Kahn said on that occasion:

> There is a need to distinguish *form* from *design*. Form implies what a building—whether it be a church, school, or house—would like to be, whereas the design is the circumstantial act evolving from this basic form, depending on site condition, budget limitation or client's idea, etc.[4]

As soon as a form is invented, it becomes the property of society. One might almost say that it was the property of society before its discovery. A design, on the other hand, belongs to its designer.

208

John Voelker, in his CIAM Team X report, comments on a similar subject. Referring to Oscar Hansen's and Jerzy Soltan's work in Poland, he said:

> In an open aesthetics, form is a master key not of any aesthetic significance in itself, though capable of reciprocating the constant change of life. Open aesthetic is the living extension of functionalism.[5]

Both Kahn's definition of *form* and Voelker's *open aesthetic* express their desire to produce a form that would be a catalytic agent which may become many forms rather than just a form for its own sake. While they are speaking on it still within architectural idiom, we are interested in examining the form in a much larger context—collectivity in our physical environment. Nonetheless, both statements are significant in assuming that such a form can be created by architects today.

It may be easy for someone to invent a geometric form and call it a group form because such forms have the characteristic of being multiplied in a sequential manner. This is, however, meaningless, unless the form derives from environmental needs. Geometry is only a tool of search for group form. One cannot seek group form in hexagons or circles. James Stirling says:

> The application of orthogonal proportion and the obvious use of basic geometrical elements appears to be diminishing, and instead something of the variability found in nature is attempted. *Dynamic cellularism* is an architecture comprising several elements, repetitive or varied. The assemblage of units is more in terms of growth and change than of mere addition, more akin to patterns of crystal formations or biological divisions than to the static rigidity of a structural grid. The form of assemblage is in contrast to the definitive architecture and the containing periphery of for example, a building such as [the] Unité.[6]

One finds the source of generative element in dynamic human terms, such as *gathering*, or *dispersal*, or *stop*. The human quality which determines form has to do with the way of life, movement, and relation of persons in society. If the function of urban design is the pattern of human activities as they express being alive in cities, then the functional patterns are crystallized activity patterns. Le Corbusier limits generative human qualities in urban architecture to *air*, *green*, and *sun*, while exponents of group form find a myriad of suggestive activities to add to that list.

The visual implications of such crystallized patterns of human activity become apparent. The way in which one activity changes to another as people move from work, to shopping, to dining, suggests the physical qualities which are used to express transformation in design rhythm, change, and contrast. Characteristic spaces may be named in accord with the way in which human groups use them, i.e., transitional space, inward space, outward space, and so forth. The addition of activities to physical qualities in a search for form determinants in the city suggests a new union between physical design and planning. The investigation of group form inevitably leads us to give our attention to regionalism in collective scale.

Until recently, our understanding of regional expressions had very much been confined to that of single buildings. In the age of mass communication and technological facility, regional differences throughout the world are becoming less well-defined. It is apparent that it is becoming less easy to find distinctive expressions in building techniques and resulting forms.

If materials and methods of construction or modes of transportation system are becoming ubiquitous in this world, perhaps their combination, especially in large urban complexes can reflect distinguishing characteristics of the people and the place in which they are structured and used according to their value hierarchy. Thus it may be possible to find regionalism more in collective scale, but less in single buildings. The primary regional character in urban landscape will probably be in the grain of the city. Both group form and megaform affect the urban milieu at precisely that level.

Homogenization of the environment is not, as many people feel, the inevitable result of mass technology and communication. These same forces can produce entirely new products. With modern communication systems one element (cultural product) will soon be transmitted to other regions, and vice versa. While each region is a set of similar elements, it can express its own characteristics from each of the elements. Here regionalism arises not only from indigenous elements or products, but rather from the manner in which such elements are evaluated and expressed. This suggests a concept of open regionalism, which is itself a dynamic process of selecting and integrating vital forces; however, these forces may conflict with inherent cultural values. Thus the genuine strength of different cultures can be tested and measured in this light. This is the thesis initially developed in collaboration with Prof. Roger Montgomery.

In group form, the possibility for creating grain elements, hence regional qualities, exists. The reciprocal relation between the generative elements and the system can produce strongly regional effects. In megaform, it is a large form that represents all the power of technique, and that may represent the best aspects of regional selectivity. In any event we predict that in the coming decades the investigation of regional expression in collective scale will become one of the most important and fascinating issues of architecture and planning.

Finally, these three approaches are models of thinking about possible ways to conceive large, complex forms. It is likely that in any final form of design, these three concepts will appear in combination.

Linkage in Collective Form
(Written in collaboration with Jerry Goldberg)

Introduction
Investigation of the collective form is important because it forces us to reexamine the entire theory and vocabulary of architecture, the one of single buildings. For instance, the components of the collective form, as conceived here, differ from the traditional elements as single structures:

1. *Wall*: any element which separates and modulates space horizontally. Walls are places where forces outward and inward interact, and the manner of the interactions defines the form and functions of the wall.
2. *Floor or Roof*: any element which separates and modulates space vertically. In a broad sense, *floor* includes underground, ground and water surfaces, and even floating elements in the air.
3. *Column*: architecturally a supporter of gravitational loads, but environmentally an element which transfers certain functions—people, goods, and other things.
4. *Unit*: a primary space which performs and contains some of the basic functions of human existence and of society.
5. *Link*: linking or dissolving linkage are invariant activities in making collective form out of either discrete or associate elements. In operational terms there are a number of linkages—physically connected link, implying link, built-in link, and so forth.

Collective form also requires a new dimension in conceiving construction methods and structural and mechanical systems. The aesthetics of collective form necessitate new definitions of scale and proportion of buildings. Above all, this entire essay questions the meaning of the very act of design in our society; it contains no answers, but seeks to ask the right questions and to draw out further discussion.

The Unity of Experience

Observation is the primary tool of urban designers. What they see in the city, they can relate to their own experience. Fact and observation are combined in order to comprehend new problems, and to provide new, three-dimensional solutions. The whole collection of articles on collective form is a means of ordering observation. What the exact categories of analysis are is not of great importance. They provide a framework within which we can present extremely important observable phenomena in cities. Only through seeing accurately can we locate the specific formal result of forces in the city—forces that sociologists, economists, and novelists have described in other terms.

We are fond of observing that our urban world is a complex one, that it changes with a rapidity beyond real comprehension, and finally, that it is a disjointed world. At times in our urban lives we relish all the diversity and disjointedness of cities and bask in the variety of them. Certainly, cities have been the locus of humankind's most creative moments in history because of the varied experience they afford us.

But when a plethora of stimuli begins to divert us from receptive consciousness, the city renders us insensible. Then, in our inability to order experience, we suffer the city, and long for some adequate means to comprehend it as a product of humans like ourselves—as the product of an intelligent, ordering force. If the scientist is frustrated when the order or pattern of phenomena is too fleeting to observe, or too complex to recognize with extant tools, so are city dwellers frustrated when they cannot find human order in their environment. At moments when they see only the results of mechanical and economic processes controlling the form and feel of their place, a feeling of estrangement, of not belonging, may arise.

If urban design is to fulfill its role, to make a contribution to the form of the city, it must do more than simply organize mechanical forces and create physical unity from diversity. It must recognize the meaning of the order it seeks to manufacture, a humanly significant spatial order.

Introduction to Linkage

Urban design is ever concerned with the question of making comprehensible links between discrete things. Furthermore, it is concerned with making an extremely large entity comprehensible by articulating its parts. The city is made of combinations of discrete forms and articulated large forms. It is collective form—the agglomerate of decisions (and rejections of decision) in the past concerning the way in which things fit together, or are linked. Linking, or disclosing linkage (articulating the large entity), are invariant activities in making collective form.

With regard to historical examples of collective form, we refer to the recent thinking of Aldo van Eyck. He finds in vernacular building a substantial clue to the natural process of human association in urban situations. Vernacular unit and link evolved together and appear at the end as a perfectly coordinated physical entity: a village or town. But one need not go to completely vernacular situations to discover examples of similar character. The builders of the cities we admire—cities that we sense are good environments—have generally been several generations of men and women working over decades, even centuries of time. We must perceive what they have done in our limited span of study. More importantly, we must build in our own environment in an abbreviated time.

One thing is certain. We have spent too little time observing the successes of our predecessors with an acute eye. Further, we probably do not approach particular parts of our cities with sufficient understanding to extrapolate what is useful from them in human terms. It is one thing to grunt ecstatically in the presence of a significant work. It is another to learn from it what it can offer for the future.

The specific subject of scrutiny here is linkage—in particular, the act of making linkage. In what follows, the business of putting things together is studied in a detailed fashion. First, historical examples provide examples of linkage. Each place, and each moment, had its own characteristic form of making coherent physical form. We are interested in how, and why, particular links were used. In the end, we are concerned, as designers, with making collective form. The examples that follow have been discovered in a framework of operational definitions. Looking at examples, we ask ourselves what the act of making a particular juncture among elements was, and how, theoretically, that act could be reproduced. This loosely operational framework was useful for purposes of analysis, but does not carry through the entire survey of material.

It is perhaps a mistake to insulate types of links from one another by categorizing them. The activity we are discussing is, after all, a singular one—that of making a comprehensible and humanly evocative urban environment. It is one of the primary theses of this study that once a link is established for any reason, it takes on a complicated secondary system of meanings and uses. See the discussion of the *stoep* in Amsterdam, for example, or of Bologna's arcades. One can see the medieval street bridges over the Via Ritorta in Perugia, an example of a link that began as a simple means of joining two buildings at their second story or perhaps reinforcing structurally weak walls. The bridges, which mediated between two buildings at the second level, also serve to define *overhead* in the street, and to reinforce it spatially as a pathway. The bridges serve all these functions because they are repetitive along the street. It is no longer important which is the primary kind of linkage and which the secondary.

What does this study of historical linkage suggest for the future? Certainly this: Whatever we use to determine the form of linkage in urban design must come from a body of largely untapped information about cities as we know them. We are involved in an investigation of the morphological resultants of forces present in cities. And this is certain: The primary motive is to make unity from diversity. We suggest, as the other side of that issue, that there is diversity in every unit situation of sufficient scale to admit more than one function or one point of view.

That we have not previously adequately identified form-giving forces is perhaps due to the fact that they seem to defy definition. At a particular scale of urban activity, they have more to do with movement through space than with a standard vision of the shape of a place. Thus we have been notably remiss in our ability to conceive of shapes for our paths of high-speed movement, or our commercial clusters, or power lines. Each of these things seems to defy relation to a human collective scale—their functional and social aspects seem diametrically opposed. Yet the Romans succeeded in making powerful symbols of their aqueducts and, in the United States, the TVA dams integrate functional and symbolic characteristics.

If a garage can serve as an architectural stop between the moving world of the highway and the static world of a town center or shopping precinct, it can, if handled as Louis Kahn suggests, become a symbol of the collective and human aspect of what occurs in the town or the shops. Garages, or rapid transit stations, can be conceived as links between the highway (or train) and pedestrian movement. If designed with sufficient understanding, each can serve as a defining wall, or perhaps a built mountain, for the activity each links to the world of the highway.

Another thing that seems indicated for the future is the realization of a wholly new concept of three-dimensional linkage. If we are successful at making unified and meaningful complexes of form and activity near the ground, we are notably unsuccessful at going up into the air with linked functions. A high-rise tower— for either apartments or offices—provides us with little integrated experience of its form, or of the excitement of rising through its many layers. Somehow, each deck of a tower or slab must be transparent to us, and each level of activity must be unique. Then, and only then, will we sense three-dimensional linkage. This type of linkage is necessary because we will be constructing more high buildings as land in our cities becomes scarcer. It is possible because our building techniques and our love of communication

216

makes it so. As early as 1913, Antonio Sant'Elia gave some indication of what the visual residue of such a three-dimensional linkage might be.

If we must learn to integrate our knowledge of short-range movement, movement through cities from point to point, so must we attach a more subtle time concept, one which deals with the constant cycle of decay in cities. An urban dwelling may last for 84 years, on average. If we allow all the old dwellings in a given area to become unsuitable for use at the same time, we are forced to declare extensive blight, clear hundreds of acres, and build new housing. There is no link between such a cleared and renewed area and the city around it. Persons who, by choice or force of economic circumstance, move into such developments feel isolation keenly enough that they cannot regard themselves as anything but *project* people. There is nothing less urban, nothing less productive of cosmopolitan mixture than raw renewal, which displaces, destroys, and replaces in such a mechanic way.

The cycle of decay can become a linking force in our cities. If recognized, it provides an opportunity to replace old structures in an old environment with new structures still in an old environment. Such diversity in age is itself a kind of linkage. It gives morphological demonstration of the ever-changing and diverse character of city life. It offers a new kind of choice to people in cities—the possibility that one can live in a historically significant place, but in a new house.

Our cities are fluid and mobile. It is difficult to conceive of some of them as places, in the real sense of that word. How can an entity with no discernible beginning or end be a place? It is certainly more apt to think of a particular part of a city as a place. If it were possible to articulate each of the parts of the city more adequately, to give qualities of edge and node to now formless agglomerates, we would have begun to make our large urban complexes at least understandable, if not easily visualized.

217

By the same argument, the rapidity with which the urban system expands suggests that there must be some means for linking newly established parts with parts not yet conceived. In short, there is a need for something that may be termed *open linkage*. Such an idea is inherent in the linkage of group form. Links become integral parts of both unit and system and suggest that system can be expanded indefinitely, and with variation.

Linkage is simply the glue of the city. It is the act by which we unite all the layers of activity and resulting physical form in the city. Insofar as linkage is successful, the city is a recognizable and humanly understandable entity. We are at home in it. We depend on understanding how two events within a city are combined to make a living sequence, and we depend on understanding how we can get from one place to another in the city. Each at its own level contributes to our ability to know and enjoy experience—social, temporal, and spatial linkage.

Time and Landscape:
Collective Form at Hillside Terrace

The Hillside Terrace project, a medium-density mixed-use devel- ɪɪ. 68
opment of apartments, shops, restaurants, and cultural facilities, took exactly 25 years from the first plans I drew in 1967 to the completion of its sixth phase in 1992 (Figs. 8 and 9). Although I have designed buildings and complexes far greater in physical scale over the past several decades, no other project has occupied my thoughts so continuously over time as Hillside Terrace has. The flow of time can be measured against its diverse buildings and their relationship to the city of Tokyo as it grew to envelop them. Changes in the project's architectural character, materiality, and expression from phase to phase also reflect shifts in my own

Fig. 8 Aerial view of the Daikanyama district, with buildings
of Hillside Terrace highlighted.

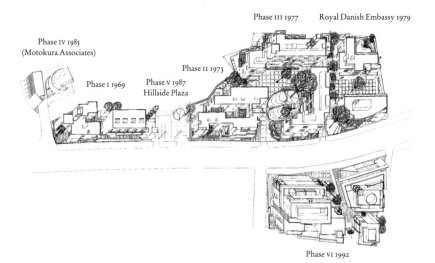

Phase IV 1985
(Motokura Associates)

Phase III 1977   Royal Danish Embassy 1979

Phase II 1973

Phase I 1969   Phase V 1987
Hillside Plaza

Phase VI 1992

consciousness with the passage of time. The opportunity to design Hillside Terrace—a commission I received almost immediately after setting up my architectural practice in Tokyo, was my first chance to confront the idea of modern architecture engaging, even creating, its urban context. Though I was unaware of it at that time, the project would bring me a deeper understanding of the *collective form* phenomenon that had fascinated me in my early years of architectural study, strengthening the notion that architecture and cities share a distinct relationship to time.

In the mid-1960s, the Daikanyama district still retained traces of the wooded hills for which the greater Musashino region was once known. After each rain, the air was heavily laden with earthy scents. Zelkova trees rose high over the low townscape. Downtown Tokyo, though geographically close, was still perceived as a distant place. It was in this context that my clients, the Asakura family, who for many generations had owned a 250-meter-long strip of land along Daikanyama's main road, asked me to design a number of apartments and shops to be built in separate phases. I realized that in designing a group of buildings, I could also generate exterior public spaces of a particular character.

220

Fig. 9   Axonometric site plan of Hillside Terrace.

Fig. 10   Entrance plaza from phase one.

Fig. 11   Courtyard from phase six.

Fig. 12   Creation of sense of depth through the layers of space, phase six.

The issue to be addressed in Hillside Terrace's first phase, which was located in the southernmost part of the property where the lot was relatively narrow, was the deployment of space along the street. The formal vocabulary was typical of modern urban design of the time and included such features as a corner plaza (Fig. 10), a small transparent lobby serving several ground-floor shops, a sunken garden, a raised pedestrian deck, and maisonette-style duplex apartments. More than any individual feature, however, what impressed most people about the project was its laconic, abstract geometrical character. A low, horizontally extended ensemble of white masses arranged along a fairly wide street was still a rare sight in Tokyo in 1969, and perhaps that added to the novelty of the landscape.

By the time I began work on the sixth and final phase some years later, in the late 1980s, Daikanyama had undergone a dramatic change in character. What had previously been a quiet residential neighborhood was quickly becoming a bustling mixed-use district—partly due to increased traffic and a rezoning of the district to eliminate the previous height restriction of ten meters and increase its floor area ratio. In response, the building mass in the sixth phase was treated in such a way as to create an overall impression of airiness (Figs. 11 and 12), as this development, with its greater height and volume, was apt otherwise to seem disproportionately large compared to earlier phases. A prominent eave line was created at a height of ten meters to echo the heights of previous phases across the street.

The challenge is the same whether the project in question is a single building or a complex of buildings: the creation of *topos* in the city through the medium of landscape. Looking back, I believe that the process that led from Hillside Terrace's first phase to the sixth suggests not only the changes in our notion of public space and the evolution of Modernism, but also what I would call the *landscape of time*.

223

A Modern Language for the Creation of Group Form
Although their architectural expression has varied in response to the times, the buildings of phases one through six share a consistent scale of massing, using a combination of staggered, cubical volumes, generally one and two stories tall, with apartment blocks frequently lifted above street level on transparent and/or recessed ground-floor volumes. Several unifying spatial elements, such as corner entrances and interior stairs echoing exterior topography, are repeated in different guises to create a sense of continuous townscape while allowing localized variations (Fig. 13). Within such an evolving framework, I have viewed each individual building design from the perspective of its urban presence and meaning—aiming to discover in this process a modern language for the creation of group form.

1. Paul Goodman and Percival Goodman, *Communitas: Means of Livelihood and Ways of Life*, revised 2nd ed. (New York: Alfred A. Knopf, 1960), 12–13.

2. Kenzo Tange, "Architecture and Urbanism", *Japan Architect*, October 1960, 12.

3. Steen Eiler Rasmussen. *Towns and Buildings* (Cambridge: MIT Press, 1951), 81, 91–92.

4. Louis Kahn, speech at the World Design Conference in Tokyo, 1960.

5. John Voelcker, "CIAM Team X Report", 1951.

6. James Stirling. "Regionalism and Modern Architecture", in *Architects' Year Book 8* (London: Elek Books, 1957), 65.

Fig. 13 Arcades along Yamate-dori street.

Alison Smithson and Peter Smithson
Spatial Processes

I.   Alison Smithson and Peter Smithson, *Italian Thoughts Followed Further*, manuscript (London: Alison and Peter Smithson Architects, 1997), 8–10, 14–15, 20, 24–25, 27–28, 33–34.
II. Alison Smithson and Peter Smithson, *Italian Thoughts* (London: Alison and Peter Smithson Architects, 1993), 58–61.

The Recovery of Parts of the Gothic Mind

I. 8 In the beginning, building on a leveled platform was an ordering (Fig. 1).[1]

In antiquity the Orders—the Doric, Ionic, Tuscan, Corinthian, Composite—seemed so perfect that they were regarded as a gift from the gods … a divine ordering.

There have been dozens of "orders"—ways of putting things together that seemed immutable in their time. Symmetry, reference to a center, serial addition along an axis, circle-drawn generation of forms—all were inventions.

In this century:

> to look "organic",
> to be planar, that is, to seem as if made of flat planes,
> to be regular, repetitive,
> to use cubic grids,
> to use number systems,
> to use proportional systems,

all have supported a recognizable ordering, codifiable in retrospect.[2]

Conglomerate Ordering

II. 58 Conglomerate ordering perhaps has to do with the recovery of parts of the gothic mind. A medieval city's ways are fundamentally different to those made after the Renaissance. Renaissance ways are theater. Medieval ways are fact.

In the *contado* of Siena is La Grancia di Cuna—a granary once in the holding of Santa Maria della Scala that one might say is a giant cupboard, an agricultural storehouse—a place of extraordinary presence, where an order of the rarest and yet the most ordinary kind is brought to the farmyard's directness: a place one

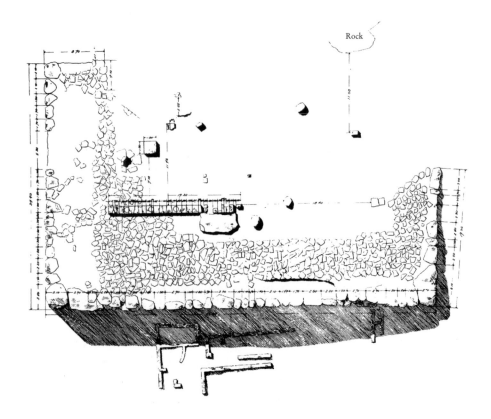

Fig. 1   Heraion Podium. Drawing: Charles Waldstein, 1902.

is almost afraid to visit for one knows that the end of its ongoing work will make it disappear.

La Grancia di Cuna has the capacity to absorb spontaneous additions, subtractions, and technical modifications which in no way disturb its sense of order: the small wooden sunshades hung from the walls by those living in the rooms behind to cover the residential windows, each different; the grain-blowing machinery which replaces the pack animals for which the central ramps were intended, machinery that is moved around to suit seasonal and day-to-day operations: every day changing yet every day the same, familiar and comforting.

Certainly, at La Grancia di Cuna it is possible to find oneself in a hidden, almost secret place; yet one is never afraid; an inner self reassures: "I can always find my way back to the central ramps which will take me down and out and even if the big door is locked, the sky above is open and I can shout and talk to the birds flying across the rectangle of sky, know what time of day it is by noting the shadows crossing the walls, feel the rain on my face."

In all, it is an experience not reducible to a simple geometric schema or even remotely communicable in two-dimensional images.

It is for this "naturalness", the feeling we experience of fabric being "ordered" when we do not understand the place at a glance or do not know the building, that we use the words *conglomerate ordering*. We may not be able to see where we are within the whole, yet are nevertheless able to navigate through our capacity to discern where the light is coming from, feel warmth and air on our skin, sense the density of the surrounding fabric, instinctively know that behind that wall are people, smell what once was here, sense where someone has been.

A fabric of conglomerate ordering harnesses all the senses: It can accept a certain roughness, it can operate at night, it can offer, especially, pleasures beyond those of the eyes.

The architects of the heroic period wanted straight façades, flat walls, level floors, ramps and not stairs, because these elements spoke for a revolution, like the height of Gothic, straightness best conveyed the revolutionary intent. But—to repeat—we are now in the fourth generation of that revolution. Machines and machine-organized processes are now everyday, yet we still think "straight": The horizon is datum, the vertical is plumb, both are "true", a statement of ethical and geometric soundness. Therefore, sitting in front of an evolved medieval building such as Santa Maria della Scala, trying to imagine a few simple starting lines to draw on paper which one could then relate, part by part, the mind collapses, lacking the usual supports of a horizontal floor, a level string course, a regularly spaced line of even windows, level rows of brickwork. The mind collapses because it has been trained to survey and to draw so as to make things fit, and the things that have to fit in our era are usually "square" to each other. Present-day building uses straight pieces of wood for good reason: Machines most easily and economically saw square, plane flat, extrude straight. So when we think about a building with floors that slope, ceilings that tilt or drop, walls that are set in and out, are battered or warped, we imagine a lump, in which, like a plum pudding, some ingredients are still recognizable, but most are an inextricable part of a general mass (Figs. 2–6).

The earliest years of ILAUD (International Laboratory of Architecture and Urban Design) visits to Siena were during the August Palio race. Following the events step by step, reading the I. 8 sociological interpretation of each one from Falassi's book[3] the night before, so as to feel that one would understand what one would be seeing the following day, awareness came that the territorial boundaries of the *contrade* shown on the famous map "decreed by the Princess Violante of Bavaria in 1729" are not marked in the streets (Figs. 7–8).

The two sides of the same street can be in a different contrada, but it remains the same street, each side similar to the other.

Fig. 2 Liquorice allsorts. Drawing: S. Smithson, 1983.

Fig. 3 La Grancia di Cuna In Val d'Arbia; access ramp courtyard.
Photo: Peter Smithson, August 1983.

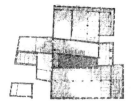

Third floor plan

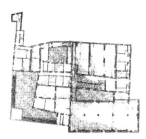

Second floor plan

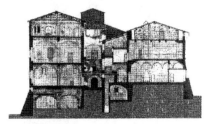

Section

First floor plan

Elevation

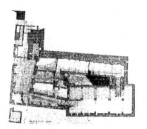

Ground floor plan

Fig. 4 La Grancia di Cuna, Val d'Arbia.
All drawings: G. Coscarella and F. C. Franchi, 1981.

Fig. 5 Sanatorium *Zonnestraal*, Hilversum: Bijvoet and Duicker, 1927:
"The straightness best carried the revolutionary intent." Photo: Peter Smithson, 1954.

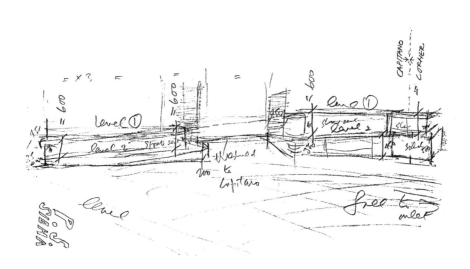

Fig. 6 Santa Marla della Scala: "Threshold to Capitano".
Sketch: Peter Smithson, August 1983.

For a Sienese, the fact that two contrade face each other across the street does not need an act of theater to announce it; it is known genetically, as it were, to those born and baptized into their contrada. During the Palio, the two sides of the street are alive with flags—each side with its own flag—as if in a medieval battle; but within days after the Palio has been run, the street reverts to its unmarked self.

Fig. 7 Siena, map of the contrade and their flags. Original map from a tourist shop.

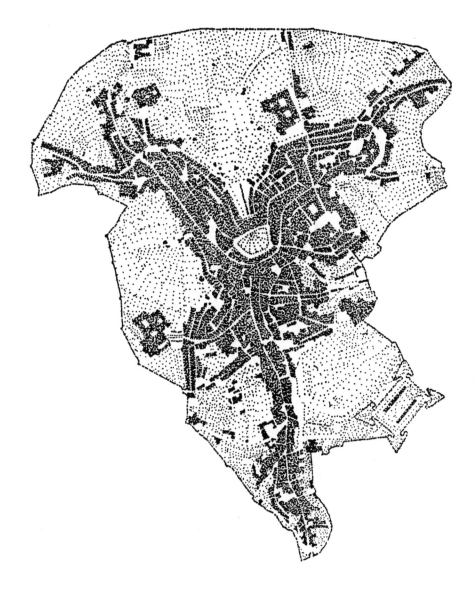

Fig. 8 Map of Siena, buildings following ridgelines. Drawing: ILA&DU document, 1980s.

Saturday, 14 August

7:30 pm. Set out to walk to Owls for Contrada dinner. Coincides with end of 5th trial run. When trying to bypass the crowds leaving the Campo, see (absolutely up against) disastrously injured horse being comforted (left hock, rear, almost completely severed). Later as the Owls are near the Giraffes, walk down to Piazza Provenzano. All quiet in stable yard, but small boys fascinated by bucket of water and blood. Gradually realize we've seen the Giraffes' horse (the injured horse from earlier). The whole Piazza (is) set out for dinner with the Captains' table backed onto the church forecourt. All is abandoned.

Men start dismantling the loudspeaker system, the lights, etc. They (the Giraffes) are out of the Palio. Everybody is very quiet. Some are quietly crying.

Monday, 16 August, the Palio

4:15 pm. The Giraffes paraded at the Palio with their flags furled, their drum covered in black, playing a slow beat. A page carried the remains of the horse on a pillow, the Captains' horse was saddled but unridden. At the final ceremony in front of the Palazzo (Municipale), their flag was not displayed, but held low, furled with black ribbon, throughout.

In Siena, the ordinary city streets and the interior street inside Santa Maria della Scala seem dark, airless, indifferent to us, unremitting; we feel we cannot escape.

It would seem that the Romantic movement's sensibility for "the prospect" has become a normal need in this century, the need to look out, to escape. Thus, looking out from the top floor at La Grancia di Cuna we can feel the possibility of further sensibilities growing in us, after the enlargements and constrictions of the Renaissance (Figs. 9–10).

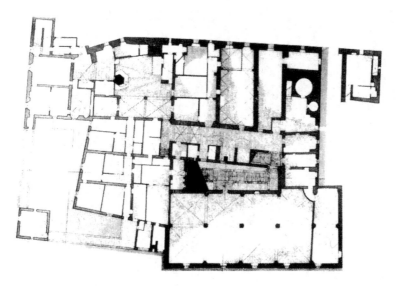

Fig. 9 La Grancia di Cuna, Val d'Arbia, floor plan.
Drawing: G. Coscarella and F. C. Franchi, 1981.

Fig. 10 View from the top floor of La Garcia di Cuna to the east.
Photo: Peter Smithson, August 1983.

Fig. 11 The bypass of St. Alban appears in this photo like an incision in the rocks below.

Fig. 12 The New York road system. Photo: Alison and Peter Smithson, 1960s.

In Siena it is easy to feel—as one bursts from the narrow city streets onto the beach of the Campo—that spatial experience is not only visual. All kinds of messages rush through one's body.

I. 10 The streets of Siena are facts, not theater. They are paths connecting this to that; narrow passages which nothing should obstruct. Entries to dwellings are therefore simply doors; flat holes in flat walls, with thresholds unmarked beyond the building face.

Widenings of the street serve the purpose of passage— following in all probability the openings of the original crossings of field paths, for the line of the track is the most persistent element of an urban fabric. It is our sudden understanding of this urban fact that one can regard as "a recovery of a part of the Gothic mind".

I. 9 We feel ready for another ordering that is in a way "Gothic", that is non-compositional, non-theatrical.

With the first experiences in the 1950s of American freeways— those of New York, Boston, and Los Angeles; with the realization that they are a geographical fact and that only in them did we have something capable of ordering a modern city; of providing a system of reference to relate to with all our senses. This is the moment in which one could say that Gothic sensibilities began to grow again (Figs. 11–12).

In medieval times, the relationship with the land—ranges of hills, rivers, the sea—was taken in with all the senses, which in turn created order in the placement of houses and pathways. This relationship is reestablished by the "geographic nature" of the freeways. One does not see them, one lives them, in the same way that one lives with the sea. They, too, have their seasons, their smells, their festivals. Our relationship to them is Gothic.

To recover parts of the Gothic mind means to be able to think in "big systems" and to have a sense of:

river
plain
basin
rail/road system
canal/water system
human arrangement
("Harrods is in Westminster")

and to build a sense of these systems into even the smallest parts of the things through which we architects act, such as doors and thresholds.

In the Middle Ages, the sense of the land, known through walking, riding, working it, permeated all acts of inhabitation.

Our sense of the land and the "big systems" we have built upon it—now known through car and air travel, through statistics, all kind of maps, old photographs, current photographic collages and aerial photographs, aerial mapping and computer modeling—can engage with a revived "Gothic" sensibility in new ways, can now permeate all our activities. Any doubts or difficulties we may have arisen from the absolute *material* nature of the "Gothic" together with the graphic nature of the new sources of information (Fig. 13).

PAST SKILLS ARE INACCESSIBLE

Because the machines, the mind, and the hand have changed. They lost the techniques, the sensibilities, and the skills they once had. Instead, they gained others. Especially inaccessible is the Gothic. The Gothic mind is of course not recoverable: Ordering meant something different, a different "logic".

The Binders

Traveling through the low countries by train, one is very conscious I. 24 of the cohesion effected by the common type of individual

242

Fig. 13   The Tiburtine Sybil's prophecy to Emperor Augustus.
Painting: unidentified Dutch painter, ca. 1480–1485.

Fig. 14   Holland from the air.
Photo: Peter Smithson, October 1995.

dwelling, gable to road, set like the teeth of a primitive comb, space slipping between the teeth, binding the land behind to the land in front.

In their earliest form, these houses stitch the land, the stored crops, the stock, the people, to the canal or access road and thus to the towns. A form of binding that is very different from that of the farmsteads in the Po valley, which, set apart in bigger units, punctuate the endless expanses of cultivated land.

Such were the kinds of spatial binding when land holding and the working of the land were dominant. The traveler would pass from one binding to the next and thus experience difference almost as the object of travel (Fig. 14).

TERRITORY AS A WORK OF ART

> The imprinting of territory is a fundamental act which establishes the style of an era. It is to the performance of this act that all our efforts—of investigation, of scientific inquiry, of testing, of language invention—must attend. It is the act through which a territory begins to be made into a conscious work of art.

Observable everywhere now in machine-dominated parts of the world, the old dense cities and towns have lost density, gained open space as new distribution roads plow through and gaps are opened for light and air and opportunity.

The inhabitants have left for the periphery. Riding in cars to work, to school, to church, to the hospital, to clinics and, above all, to shops in distant shopping malls; vast, sealed factories of selling including banks, bookshops, restaurants, and cinemas and flanked by petrol stations. In the periphery, the roads are the principal binding elements; living in the body memory of the inhabitants as the old field patterns did in the past.

The road, the way, is a dominant aspect of memory. The traveler from the outside experiences differences through the placing, the engineering, of roads. But it is a shallow difference.

A spatial process has been initiated but fails to find reciprocity in those things which are consequent.

When the working of the land was dominant, one ate and drank it, feeling seasons through this.

Now, what one eats and drinks is partly, even mostly, from far away, separated from the seasons of the place where it is consumed.

When we say that the spatial process initiated by roads fails to find a reciprocity in those things which are consequent, we mean simple things. The road is noisy; one must be protected from it. The need for secluded areas, for an aesthetic of seclusion, is greater: The current landscapes of Europe are sometimes empty of crops and animals and have to take on different shapes to become specific to this new mode of inhabitation, perhaps to compensate for the loss of specificity—of food or clothing, for example—elsewhere.

As the architects of the 1920s made housing the main focus of their effort, the focus of our efforts must now be on inventions for the space-between in the periphery. When one takes fences, field walls, roads, tracks, lines of trees, tree belts, or service lines as examples of binding devices to create specific territorial patterning, one takes easy examples (Figs. 15–20).

BUT THESE ARE NOT THE ONLY TREES

In Asturias, there are many plantations of the Australian tree, the eucalyptus, introduced in the last century. Planted close, it grows straight, for use as pit props in the mines and for making paper. The ubiquitousness of eucalyptus plantations is a strong territorial binder.

The mines are gradually being closed, but paper is now used extravagantly, so the eucalyptus remains a useful crop.

In these circumstances, should a new plantation tree and a new shaping of the plantation, good for paper perhaps, but essentially revealing the decline of the pits and the consequent reconsideration of the nature of the land which is now a principal asset of the province be considered?

Fig. 15   Fences as binders. Image from an American magazine from the 1950s.

Fig. 16 Tuscan agricultural landscape, road with trees.
Photo: from a postcard.

Fig. 17 Rural road near Etna, Sicily.
Photo: Peter Smithson, April 1992.

Fig. 18   Pipelines at Larderello, between Siena, Italy and the sea.
Photo: Peter Smithson, August, 1985.

Fig. 19   Line of trees at Cornell University.
Photo: Peter Smithson, February 1972.

Fig. 20   Street in Santa Monica with utility poles and palm trees.
Photo: Peter Smithson, November 1978.

Functional to Passage

To reiterate, as a crude antithesis: The urban ordering of the I. 27 Renaissance was an order of form, that of the Middle Ages an order of living arrangements. The street was functional to passage, the market square functional to market, the threshing floor functional to threshing, the sheepfold functional to the sheltering of sheep (Fig. 21).

The making of these places in a time of people with only hand tools was an enormous effort, such that every act had to yield the maximum advantage. Buildings for common use—the farm, the barn, the mill, the granary, the manor house, the bastion, the fort, the town walls, and the gates—needed therefore to be both themselves and part of the ordering of the territory around them; to offer places for use in the spaces contiguous to them, often before that use was fully comprehended. They had the capacity to charge the surrounding space with an energy that could join with other energies, influence the nature of things still to come, anticipate happenings. Buildings and outside places thus became natural to one another, needing only activity to complete the sense of entity (Fig. 22).

It would seem that the notion of a "spatial charge" that can influence the nature of happenings is not a thing which can make a place highly specific in the way that a machine needs to be highly specific. But few activities are specific in this way: For example,

250

Fig. 21 Case di Borgo. Drawing: D.G. Cavallero, 1985.

the marketplace is usually a flattish, well-protected space. But in Leiden, we find a market backing onto both sides of a canal and crossing two humped bridges over that canal to make a circuit of stalls. Stalls backed onto the water for the delivery of merchandise. The fronts of the stalls face the permanent shops, making—on market days—a street on both sides of the canal. The space, when empty of market, seems neither to lack it nor to suggest it. We do not feel a spatial charge specific to "market". The prime source of spatial charge here is, of course, the edge of the canal, for an edge, especially a water's edge, seems to pull everything into line with it: houses, people, market stalls, and vehicles. It has a magnetism of the strongest kind.[5]

The edge of the road exercises a similar magnetism: Houses face it, factories line up with it, trees follow it, whole communities are carried along. It is a direction as well as a source of connection. The road is our only accepted collectivity. We pay for it happily, we use it freely, our leisure activities are bound up with it. It has a literature, a mythology: "In our time, to walk away from the road is to walk away from the light."

To strengthen our fingerhold on the means to regenerate some parts of the Gothic mind, we have to learn to resist the magnetism of the edge. We have to learn to do without it, to make getting to some places more difficult.

251

Fig. 22   Donkey Haan in Midoun, Tunisia. Photo: Peter Smithson, August 1968.

Fig. 23 Photomontage with figures, Battlebridge Basin. Collage: Peter Smithson, 1972.

Fig. 24   Photomontage of Battlebridge Basin. View from the west, from the water, with reflections in the water. Collage: Peter Smithson, 1972.

Seeing the work of Jean Prouvé collected up in all its astonishing fecundity for the Centre Pompidou exhibition strikes me with a totally unexpected thought: The inventiveness, the generosity of idea is centered within the work itself; seen in its context each work or fragment seems neither to irradiate with its energy the rest of the building (if the work is only part of building), nor to enrich the context if it is a whole building. Prouvé buildings are ungenerous, seem to isolate themselves from their surroundings, sit uncomfortably, are not capable of joining. It is quite different with the airplane, which upon landing seems to sit naturally on the earth, be one with it, enriching it. It is not therefore an issue of the building being made of metal.

The Magnetism of the Edge

There seems to be a force field that pulls things parallel with an I. 33 edge: the edge of the road, the river, the canal, the harbor, in fact anything with a clearly defined edge. A child walking along the harbor follows along the edge as if held on course by magnetic tape.

It is of course a truism to say that any strong geometric form is surrounded by an invisible force field of a different shape for each form and the reason that certain forms cannot be adjacent to other forms is that their forces cause a clash (Figs. 23–25).

The force field of the water's edge seems particularly strong. Generally:

A dyke house is parallel to the dyke.   In the Netherlands, on the embankments of the old canals, there are small brick dyke houses. Frequently these dyke houses, because of age or the settling of the earth, lean at seemingly dangerous angles, yet still remain parallel to the canal (Figs. 26–27).

A canal house is parallel to the canal. A canal house that receives and sends goods seems most practical when parallel to the edge of the canal. When all the buildings line up with one another, no unsanitary kinks or heat loss occurs. The canal houses and the canal are parallel, people walk parallel to them, vehicles move in parallel, and even the reflections are parallel (Fig. 28).

The buildings on the dockside are parallel to the dock. Crane train tracks are parallel to the dock's edge, and the buildings seem to follow naturally.

The buildings along the harbor are parallel to the harbor's edge. Even in old fishing villages, the fishermen's houses line up with the harbor wall.

The buildings along the river are parallel to riverbanks. Boathouses, even the boat tents of regattas, are set parallel to the edge.

Buildings along the seashore follow the line of the sea. Where there is a straight shoreline, buildings and events set themselves parallel to it. Only rarely is the parallelism absolutely functional. It is the magnetism of the edge that holds things in parallel.

Roads and Responses

I. 14 *Urbanism's basic act is the initiation of a spatial process.* Royal Crescent, built in the late eighteenth century on the seafront at Brighton, faces south to the sea. It was the first such building to consciously absorb both the view and the sun.[6]

Fig. 25   Aerial photomontage, Battlebridge Basin. Collage: Peter Smithson, 1972.

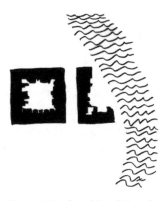

Fig. 26 North and South Parade, Bath. The first section built of classic Bath (1740–1748). Diagram: Peter Smithson, March 2000.

Fig. 27 Dyke house at Enkhausen, Holland. Photo: Peter Smithson, April 1990.

Fig. 28 Houses in Amsterdam, parallel to the canal. Photo: from a postcard.

Edinburgh made a decision to keep the valley between the Old Town and the New Town open (Fig. 29).

Both acts were indications of a spatial process. The draining of the North Loch in Edinburgh in the eighteenth century was the initiation of a special process from which a response flowed in the nineteenth century; the opening of the twentieth-century city for urban distribution roads was the initiation of a special process for which the response has yet to be invented. If the open space these roads create "lets in the sky", those things which come to the edge of this space should engage with that idea.[7]

The architecture of volume—the built event—has to "carry" with the volume its fragment of in-between space in the same way as in previous epochs it "carried" a fragment of the street or square, and, concomitantly, the spatial understanding of the new in-between space must have a foreshadowing of what it needs at the edges to carry its meaning further. The urban motorways, their sky, and what is drawn to them are all interlocked.

Sky

An urban space can never be considered a room, because it has a sky.

I. 20

The sense of spatial authority that the sky conveys can move us unimaginably; think how the Grand Canal lets the sky into Venice … through it, somehow, as the vaporetto moves along, we sense the course of the canal ahead … the city's nature and extent. We carry the sense of these fragments of sky with us. They are a large part of our sense of human-made order in the city.

What we experience in Edinburgh is the sky over the valley of what was once North Loch. Those things which have come to the edges of the valley—spiky, craggy things—seem to hold the edges against the sky. In a city which is "structured by the river", we experience something similar (Fig. 30).[8]

Fig. 29 Edinburgh, open space between the Old Town and the New Town.
Drawing: from a postcard.

Fig. 30 Sky over Princess Street in Edinburgh. Photo: Peter Smithson, April 1994.

In Edinburgh the Princess Street Gardens make a traditional
hole in the city, always open. Alongside the old city it was a
water/service hole; it is still a service hole: we arrive at low level
by train; a level above we can walk in the gardens; the hole lets
us see Edinburgh Castle; the hole has an architectural frame
around it and this frame is like a frame to a picture.

In the continuous band of sky revealed to us by the motorways
tracking through the city—through the things that come to it and
engage with its edges—a sky structure is revealed, holding the city
in a game of cat's cradle in the sky—an effect more complex than
that of the long sky views let into the city by Olmsted's Parkways
in the last century.

One of the building characteristics of the emergent conglomerate ordering[9] is that they speak to the sky ... we therefore have
an architectural ordering that can fix the connection between
building and sky.

The sky space above an urban motorway is, after all, something we experience in many different ways ... from being driven,
from driving, from walking the neighboring districts, from the
upper deck of a bus, from the high windows of an ambulance.

1. This is how the Doric order began.
2. If they are codifiable, are they dead?
3. Allen Dundes and Alessandro Falassi, *La Terra in Piazza* (Berkeley: University of California Press, 1975).
4. Extract from Peter Smithson's Palio diary, August 1982.
5. "Furthermore, temples that are to be built beside rivers, as in Egypt on both sides of the Nile, ought, as it seems, to face the river banks. Similarly, houses of the gods on the sides of public roads should be arranged so that the passers-by can have a view of them and pay their devotions face to face." (From *The Ten Books on Architecture*, Vitruvius, Book IV, Chapter V, Paragraph 2.)
6. Royal Crescent, 1798–1807.
7. Drainage of the North Loch began in 1759. Craig's plan for the New Town 1767; by 1781 St. Andrew's Square had effectively been built. Starks Report, which had absorbed the theory of the picturesque, 1814. (Dates from *The Making of Classical Edinburgh*, A. J. Youngson, Edinburgh University Press, 1966.)
8. See *To Establish a Territory*, ILA&DU (International Laboratory of Architecture and Urban Design) Yearbook 1985–86; *Italian Thoughts*, Sweden, 1993; and *Italienische Gedanken*, Vieweg, Braunschweig/Wiesbaden, 1996.
9. All faces are equally engaged with what lies before them; the roof is another face. See *Conglomerate Ordering*, ILA&UD (International Laboratory of Architecture & Urban Design), Year Book 1986–87, and see note above.

Place

The third chapter is devoted to two authors who
investigate material space from the angle of
its social-psychological dimension and human
characteristics. Both authors portray place
as a space with distinct character and contextual
meaning that is derived from cultural content.
Gordon Cullen describes the visual appropriation
and atmospheric experience of urban form in
The Art of Environment, and Lucius Burckhardt
presents *The Science of Walking*, a method of
understanding places and processes against the
backdrop of their cultural contexts.

Gordon Cullen
The Art of Environment

1. Gordon Cullen, *The Concise Townscape*, first paperback edition with new material (London: The Architectural Press, 1971), 7–12, 17–23, 29, 32–35, 44–45, 49–51, 182–187, 193–196.

I. 7 A city is more than the sum of its inhabitants. It has the power to generate a surplus of amenities, which is one reason why people like to live in communities rather than in isolation. Now turn to the visual impact which a city has on those who live in or visit it. I wish to show that an argument parallel to the one put forward above holds true for buildings: Bring people together and they create a collective surplus of enjoyment; bring buildings together and collectively they can give visual pleasure which none can give separately.

One building standing alone in the countryside is experienced as a work of architecture, but bring half a dozen buildings together and an art other than architecture is made possible. Several things begin to happen in the group which would be impossible for the isolated building. We may walk through and past the buildings, and as a corner is turned an unsuspected building is suddenly revealed. We may be surprised, even astonished—a reaction generated by the composition of the group and not by the individual building. Again, suppose that the buildings have been put together in a group so that one can get inside the group, then the space created between the buildings is seen to have a life of its own above and beyond the buildings which create it, and one's reaction is to say "I am inside IT" or "I am entering IT". Note also that in this group of half a dozen buildings there may be one which through reason of function does not conform. It may be a bank, a temple, or a church amongst houses. Suppose we are just looking at the temple by itself; it would stand in front of us and all its qualities—size, color, and intricacy—would be evident. But put the temple back amongst the small houses and immediately its size is made more real and more obvious by the comparison between the two scales. Instead of being a big temple it TOWERS. The difference in meaning between bigness and towering is the measure of the relationship.

267

In fact there is an *art of relationship*, just as there is an art of architecture. Its purpose is to take all the elements that create the environment: buildings, trees, nature, water, traffic, advertisements, and so on, and to weave them together in such a way that drama is produced. For a city is a dramatic event in the environment. Look at the research that is put into making a city work: demographers, sociologists, engineers, traffic experts, all cooperating to form the myriad factors into a workable, viable, and healthy organization. It is a tremendous human undertaking.

And yet ... if at the end of it all the city appears dull, uninteresting, and soulless, then it is not fulfilling itself. It has failed. The fire has been laid but nobody has put a match to it.

Firstly, we have to rid ourselves of the thought that the excitement and drama that we seek can be born automatically out of the scientific research and solutions arrived at by the technical human (or the technical half of the brain). We naturally accept these solutions, but are not entirely bound by them. In fact, we cannot be entirely bound by them, because the scientific solution is based on the best that can be made of the average: of averages of human behavior, averages of weather, factors of safety, and so on. And these averages do not give an inevitable result for any particular problem. They are, so to speak, wandering facts which may synchronize or, just as likely, may conflict with each other. The upshot is that a town could take one of several patterns and still operate with success, even equal success. Here then we discover a pliability in the scientific solution, and it is precisely in the *manipulation of this pliability* that the art of relationship is made possible. As will be seen, the aim is not to dictate the shape of the town or environment, but is a modest one: simply to *manipulate within the tolerances*.

This means that we can get no further help from the scientific attitude and that we must therefore turn to other values and other standards.

We turn to the *faculty of sight*, for it is almost entirely through vision that the environment is apprehended. If someone knocks at your door and you open it to let them in, it sometimes happens that a gust of wind comes in too, sweeping round the room, blowing the curtains and making a great fuss. Vision is somewhat the same; we often get more than we bargained for. Glance at the clock to see the time and you see the wallpaper, the clock's carved brown mahogany frame, the fly crawling over the glass, and its delicate, rapier-like pointers. Cézanne might have made a painting of it. In fact, of course, vision is not only useful but it evokes our memories and experiences, those responsive emotions inside us which have the power to disturb the mind when aroused. It is this unlooked-for surplus that we are dealing with, for clearly if the environment is going to produce an emotional reaction, with or without our volition, it is up to us to try to understand the three ways in which this happens.

1. Concerning OPTICS. Let us suppose that we are walking through a town: Here is a straight road, off which is a courtyard, at the far side of which another street leads out and bends slightly before reaching a monument. Not very unusual. We take this path and our first view is that of the street. Upon turning into the courtyard, the new view is revealed instantaneously at the point of turning, and this view remains with us while we walk across the courtyard. Leaving the courtyard, we enter the street beyond. Again a new view is suddenly revealed, although we are traveling at a uniform speed. Finally, as the road bends the monument swings into view. The significance of all this is that although the pedestrian walks through the town at a uniform speed, the scenery of towns is often revealed in a series of jerks or revelations. This we call SERIAL VISION.

Examine what this means. Our original aim is to manipulate the elements of the town so that an impact on the emotions is achieved. A long straight road has little impact because the initial view is soon digested and becomes monotonous. The human mind reacts to a contrast, to the difference between things, and when two pictures (the street and the courtyard) are in the mind at the same time, a vivid contrast is felt and the town becomes visible in a deeper sense. It comes alive through the drama of juxtaposition. Unless this happens, the town will slip past us, featureless and inert.

There is a further observation to be made concerning serial vision. Although from a scientific or commercial point of view the town may be a unity, from our optical viewpoint we have split it into two elements: the *existing view* and the *emerging view*. In the normal way, this is an accidental chain of events and whatever significance may arise out of the linking of views will be fortuitous. Suppose, however, that we take over this linking as a branch of the art of relationship; then we are finding a tool with which human imagination can begin to mold the city into a coherent drama. The process of manipulation has begun to turn the blind facts into a taut emotional situation.

2.   Concerning PLACE. This second point is concerned with our reactions to the position of our body in its environment. This is as simple as it appears to be. It means, for instance, that when you go into a room you utter to yourself the unspoken words "I am outside IT, I am entering IT, I am in the middle of IT". At this level of consciousness, we are dealing with a range of experience stemming from the major impacts of exposure and enclosure (which if taken to their morbid extremes result in the symptoms of agoraphobia and claustrophobia). Place a man on the edge of a 500-foot cliff and he will have a very lively sense of position; put him at the end of a deep cave and he will react to the fact of enclosure.

Since it is an instinctive and continuous habit of the body to relate itself to the environment, this sense of position cannot be ignored; it becomes a factor in the design of the environment (just as an additional source of light must be reckoned with by a photographer, however annoying it may be). I would go further and say that it should be exploited.

Here is an example. Suppose you are visiting one of the hill towns in the south of France. You climb laboriously up the winding road and eventually find yourself in a tiny village street at the summit. You feel thirsty and go to a nearby restaurant, your drink is served to you on a veranda, and as you go out to it you find to your exhilaration or horror that the veranda is cantilevered out over a thousand-foot drop. By this device of containment (street) and revelation (cantilever), the fact of height is dramatized and made real.

In a town we do not normally have such a dramatic situation to manipulate, but the principle still holds true. There is, for instance, a typical emotional reaction to being below the general ground level, and there is another resulting from being above it. There is a reaction to being hemmed in as in a tunnel and another to the wideness of the square. If, therefore, we design our towns from the point of view of the moving person (pedestrian or car-borne) it is easy to see how the whole city becomes a plastic experience, a journey through pressures and vacuums, a sequence of exposures and enclosures, of constraint and relief.

Arising out of this sense of identity or sympathy with the environment, this feeling of a person in street or square that they are in IT or entering IT or leaving IT, we discover that no sooner do we postulate a HERE than automatically we must create a THERE, for you cannot have one without the other. Some of the greatest townscape effects are created by a skillful relationship between the two. For example, in India, where this is being written: the approach from the Central Vista to the Rashtrapathi Bhawan[1] in New Delhi. There is an open-ended courtyard composed of the two Secretariat buildings and, at the end, the Rashtrapathi Bhawan. All this is raised above normal ground level, and the approach is by a ramp. At the top of the ramp and in front of the axis building is a tall screen of railings. This is the setting. Traveling through it from the Central Vista we see the two Secretariats in full, but the Rashtrapathi Bhawan is partially hidden by the ramp; only its upper part is visible. This effect of truncation serves to isolate and make remote. The building is withheld. We are Here and it is There. As we climb the ramp, the Rashtrapathi Bhawan is gradually revealed, the mystery culminates in fulfilment as it becomes immediate to us, standing on the same floor. But at this point the railing, the wrought-iron screen is inserted, which again creates a form of Here and There by means of the screened vista. A brilliant, if painfully conceived, sequence (see Fig. 5).[2]

3.   Concerning CONTENT. In this last category we turn to an examination of the fabric of towns: color, texture, scale, style, character, personality, and uniqueness. Accepting the fact that most towns are of old foundation, their fabric will show evidence of differing periods in architectural styles and also in the various accidents of layout. Many towns display this mixture of styles, materials, and scales.

Yet there exists at the back of our minds a feeling that if could we only start again we would get rid of this hodgepodge and make all new and fine and perfect. We would create an orderly scene with straight roads and with buildings that conformed in height and style. Given a free hand, that is what we might do ... create symmetry, balance, perfection, and conformity. After all, that is the popular conception of the purpose of town planning.

But what is this conformity? Let us approach it by a simile. Let us imagine a party in a private house, where are gathered together half a dozen people who are strangers to each other. The early part of the evening is passed in polite conversation on general subjects such as the weather and the current news. Cigarettes are passed and lights offered punctiliously. In fact, it is all an exhibition of manners, of how one ought to behave. It is also very boring. This is conformity. However, later on the ice begins to break and out of the straightjacket of orthodox manners and conformity real human beings begin to emerge. It is found that Miss X's sharp but good-natured wit is just the right foil to Major Y's somewhat simple exuberance. And so on. It begins to be fun. Conformity gives way to the agreement to differ within a recognized tolerance of behavior.

Conformity, from the point of view of the planner, is difficult to avoid—but to avoid it deliberately, by creating artificial diversions, is surely worse than the original boredom. Here, for instance, is a program to rehouse 5,000 people. They are all treated the same, they get the same kind of house. How *can* one differentiate? Yet if we start from a much wider point of view we will see that tropical housing differs from temperate zone housing, that buildings in a brick country differ from buildings in a stone country, that religion and social manners vary the buildings. And as the field of observation narrows, so our sensitivity to the local gods must grow sharper. There is too much insensitivity in the building of towns, too much reliance on the tank and the armored car where the telescopic rifle is wanted.

Within a commonly accepted framework—one that produces lucidity and not anarchy—we can manipulate the nuances of scale and style, of texture and color, and of character and individuality, juxtaposing them in order to create collective benefits. In fact, the environment thus resolves itself into not conformity but the interplay of This and That.

It is a matter of observation that in a successful contrast of colors not only do we experience the harmony released but, equally, the colors become more truly themselves. In a large landscape by Corot—I forget its name, a landscape of somber greens, almost a monochrome—there is a small figure in red. It is probably the reddest thing I have ever seen.

Statistics are abstracts: When they are plucked out of the completeness of life and converted into plans and the plans into buildings they will be lifeless. The result will be a three-dimensional diagram in which people are asked to live. In trying to colonize such a wasteland, to translate it from an environment for walking stomachs into a home for human beings, the difficulty lay in finding the point of application, in finding the gateway into the castle.

273

We discovered three gateways: that of motion, that of position, and that of content. By the exercise of vision it became apparent that motion was not one simple, measurable progression useful in planning, it was in fact two things, the Existing and the Revealed view. We discovered that human beings are constantly aware of their position in the environment, that they feel the need for a sense of place and that this sense of identity is coupled with an awareness of elsewhere. Conformity killed, whereas the agreement to differ gave life. In this way the void of statistics, of the diagram city, has been split into two parts, whether they be those of Serial Vision, Here and There, or This and That. All that remains is to join them together into a new pattern created by the warmth and power and vitality of human imagination so that we build the home of humankind. That is the theory of the game, the background. In fact, the most difficult part lies ahead, the Art of Playing. As in any other game there are recognized gambits and moves built up from experience and precedent. In the pages that follow an attempt is made to chart these moves under the three main heads as a series of cases.

New Delhi 1959

Casebook

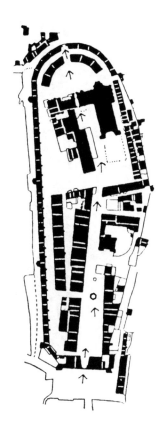

Serial Vision

I. 17   To walk from one end of the plan to another, at a uniform pace, will provide a
         sequence of revelations which are suggested in the serial drawings. Each arrow on
         the plan represents a drawing. The even progress of travel is illuminated by a series
         of sudden contrasts and so an impact is made on the eye, bringing the plan to life
         (like nudging a man who is falling asleep in church). My drawings bear no relation
         to the place itself; I chose it because it seemed an evocative plan. Note that the
         slightest deviation in alignment and quite small variations in projections or setbacks
         on the plan have a disproportionally powerful effect in the third dimension (Fig. 1).
         See visual sequence on following spread.

These three sequences—Oxford, Ipswich, and Westminster—try to recapture on
the limited and static medium of the printed page a little of the sense of discovery
and drama that we experience in moving through towns. Oxford: The cube, the
drum, and the cone create an unfolding drama of solid geometry (Fig. 2). This is
the unfolding of a mystery, the sense that as you press on more is revealed.

Ipswich: A modest archway performs the office of dividing the prospect into two things, the street you are in and the place beyond, into which you emerge so that you move out of one ambience into another (Fig. 3).

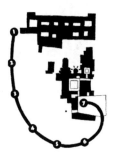

Westminster: The shifting interplay of towers, spires, and masts, all the intricacy of fresh alignments and grouping, the shafts of penetration and the sudden bunching of emphatic verticals into a dramatic knot—these are the rewards of the moving eye, but an eye which is open and not lazy (Fig. 4).

1

2

3

4

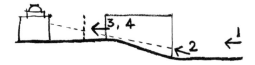

The sequence in New Delhi (read the photographs from top left to bottom right) emphasizes the role of levels and screening in serial vision, for here what could simply have been one picture reproduced four times, each view enlarging the center of the previous view and bringing us near the terminal building, turns out to be four separate and unique views (see description on p. 271–272) (Fig. 5).

Place

Possession
In a world of black and white, the roads are for movement and the buildings
for social and business purposes. Yet since most people do just what suits
them when it suits them, we find that the outdoors is colonized for social
and business purposes. Occupied territory, advantage, enclosure, focal point,
indoor landscape, and so on, are all forms of possession, as the following
pages show (Fig. 6).

Occupied Territory

Shade, shelter, amenity, and convenience are the usual causes of possession. The emphasizing of such places by some permanent indication serves to create an image of the various kinds of occupation in the town, so that instead of a completely streamlined and fluid outdoors, a more static and occupied environment is created, like the ones shown here where a periodic occupation (chatting after church?) is woven permanently into the town pattern by means of floorscape. The furniture of possession includes floorscape, posts, canopies, enclaves, focal points, and enclosures. Although the amount of possession may be small, its perpetuation in the furniture gives the town humanity and intricacy in just the same way that louvers on windows give texture and scale to a building even when the sun is not shining (Figs. 7–9).

Possession in Movement

But static possession is only one aspect of the human grip on the outdoors, and the next stage is to consider possession in movement. In the illustration above the church walk is a definite thing having a well-defined beginning and end with a well-defined character; and this may be possessed while moving through it just as surely as the village cross may be by a villager sitting on its steps (Fig. 10–11).

The Outdoor Room and Enclosure

In this section of the casebook we are concerned with the person's sense of position, their unspoken reaction to the environment, which might be expressed as "I am in IT or above IT or below IT, I am outside IT, I am enclosed, or I am exposed." These sensations are basically interlocked with human behavior, and their morbid expression is demonstrated in claustrophobia and agoraphobia. Enclosure or the outdoor room is, perhaps, the most powerful, the most obvious, of all the devices to instill this sense of position, of identity with the surroundings. It embodies the idea of HERENESS (which in the following pages will be seen also to include multiple enclosure, space, looking out, etc.). The two exits to the same square in Bordeaux, left page, provide an object lesson in how to preserve enclosure or how to let the sense of Hereness fade away into the remote distance. Above, a near-perfect example of the outdoor room with three-dimensional wallpaper (Figs. 12–14).

Defining Space

It is sometimes astonishing how fragile the means of establishing enclosure
or space can be. A wire stretched from wall to wall like a pencil stroke, a square
of canvas stretched out overhead. In Chandigarh I saw a bustee, or collection
of mud and thatch dwellings, arranged in the shade of three large trees alone
in the plain. The space thus enclosed by the three trees became the civic space
of the tiny community. In these pictures of the French Riviera, bottom, and
a restaurant at the Festival of Britain, top, we see how bamboo is used to establish
enclosure and space and how it achieves that evocative charm of containing
while revealing what is beyond (Figs. 15–16).

Looking Out of Enclosure
Having established the fact of Hereness, the feeling of identity with a place,
it is clear that this cannot exist of itself but must automatically create a sense
of Thereness, and it is in the manipulation of these two qualities that the spatial
drama of relationship is set up. These two examples demonstrate the primary
reaction; in the case of Bath, bottom, the view beyond comes as an extra dimension
and the trees inside the garden in Sweden, top, do not have the same kind of
wildness as the tree beyond the wall. It is There (Figs. 17–18).

Thereness

These two pictures try to isolate the quality of Thereness which is lyrical in
the sense that it is perpetually out of our reach, it is always There. The sea wall
at Aldeburgh, above, carries the shadows of houses, the shadows of warmth
and laughter. Beyond is the great emptiness. In the wild countryside of Scotland,
opposite, the distance is made personal to us by the extension outwards of
the roadside wall as a thin white line which, because of its meaning (possible
line of travel), projects us out into the wilderness (Figs. 19–20).

Here and There

The first category of relationships (pinpointing, change of level, vistas, narrows, closure, etc.) is concerned with the interplay between a known here and a known there. The second category [...] will be concerned with a known here and an unknown there.

In Nash's Regent's Park terrace, opposite, the dividing archway serves to give the single composition intricacy and growth. Judging by the inordinate height of the archway, we are meant to see out of the relatively modest courtyard up to the noble main façade. He is playing off one part of the composition against the other in order to intensify the total effect. My visualization, above, of Hawksmoor's plan for Cambridge includes this scene looking from Great St Mary's along a reformed Trinity Street. Here we are looking from Hawksmoor's great forum into another place whose individuality, direction, and character are unequivocally stated by the two monuments. By contrast, the street today winds quietly past the Senate House and unobtrusively folds itself away. This is not intended as a choice between the two but only to demonstrate the visual impact of Hawksmoor's scheme (Figs. 21–22).

Projection and Recession
This street in Rye demonstrates the charm of projection and recession. Instead of I. 44
the eye taking in the street in a single glance, as it would in a street with perfectly
straight façades, it is caught up in the intricacy of the meander, and the result is
a repose or dwelling of the mind that is wholly appropriate to the subject, which
is a street of houses and not a fluid traffic route (Fig. 23).

Incident

The value of incident in a street—tower, belfry, silhouette feature, vivid color, and so on—is to entrap the eye so that it does not slide out into the beyond with resulting boredom. The skillful disposition of incident gives point to the basic shapes of the street or place; it is a nudge. The pattern is there but in the preoccupation of life our attention must be drawn to it. I think that it is through the lack of incident that so many meticulously thought-out plans fail to come to life in three dimensions (Fig. 24).

Punctuation

If the vista seems like a complete sentence containing subject and predicate,
the use of the word punctuation may clarify those demarcations of the enclosed
phrase which this picture illustrates. In the continuing narrative of the street,
function and pattern change from place to place; this should be acknowledged
by some physical signal. The church, for instance, being a particular building,
interrupts the alignment of the street and so closes one phrase and conceals
the next, so that a pause is created (Fig. 25).

Narrows

The crowding together of buildings forms a pressure, an unavoidable nearness of detail, which is in direct contrast to the wide piazza, square, or promenade, and by the use of such narrowness it is possible to maintain enclosure without preventing the passage of vehicles and pedestrians. In this way the articulation of the city into clear and well-defined parts is made more possible. In its own right, narrowness has a definite effect on the pedestrian, inducing a sense of unaccustomed constriction and pressure (Fig. 26).

Anticipation

We now turn to those aspects of here and there in which the here is known but I. 49 the beyond is unknown, is infinite, mysterious, or is hidden inside a black maw. First among these cases is anticipation. This picture clearly arouses arouse one's curiosity as to what scene will meet our eyes upon reaching the end of the street (Fig. 27).

Infinity

There is a difference between sky and infinity. Sky is the stuff we see over the
rooftops, as in the picture in Pimlico, top left; infinity is a quite different thing.
There are, I think, two ways in which the solitude and vastness of the sky can
be made personal to us. Firstly, by the technique which served for truncation;
by cutting out the middle distance and juxtaposing the immediate here with
the sky, its more conventional overtones are somehow discarded and the deeper
qualities aroused, as these two pictures, top right and bottom, serve to remind us.
Secondly, we can consider the expected line of travel, the person's assessment of
where they can walk. To substitute sky for road produces a shock which changes
sky into infinity (Figs. 28–30).

Mystery
From the matter-of-fact pavement of the busy world we glimpse the unknown, the mystery of a city where anything could happen or exist, the noble or the sordid, genius or lunacy. This is not Withenshawe (Figs. 31–32).

Here and There

On a flat plain a house is built. It is an object standing up on the flat surface. Inside the house there are rooms, volumes of space, but from the outside these are not obvious. All we see is the object. Many houses built together form streets and squares. They enclose space and thus a new factor is added to the internal volumes or spaces: outside spaces. Whereas internal volumes, rooms, are justified in the purely functional sense of construction and shelter, there is no such forthright justification for external space/volume. It is accidental and marginal. Or is it?

In a purely materialistic world our environment would resemble a rock-strewn river, the rocks being buildings and the river being traffic passing them, vehicular and pedestrian. In fact, this conception of flow is false since people are by nature possessive. A group of people standing or chatting on the pavement colonize the spot and the passerby has to walk around them. Social life is not confined to the interior of buildings. Where people gather, in marketplace or forum, there will therefore be some expression of this to give identity to the activity. Marketplace, focal point, clearly defined promenade, and so on. In other words, the outside is articulated into spaces just as is the inside, but for its own reasons.

We can therefore postulate an environment which is articulated, as opposed to one which is simply a part of the earth's surface, over which ant-like people and vehicles are forever swarming and onto which buildings are plonked at random. Consequently, instead of a shapeless environment based on the principle of flow, we have an articulated environment resulting from the breaking-up of flow into action and rest, into corridor street and marketplace, alley and square (and all their minor devolutions).

The practical result of so articulating the town into identifiable parts is that no sooner do we create a HERE than we have to admit a THERE, and it is precisely in the manipulation of these two spatial concepts that a large part of urban drama arises. On the following pages of drawings are some points relevant to this use of space in urban scenery.

Here and There

Manmade enclosure, if only of the simplest kind, divides the environment into HERE and THERE. On this side of the arch, in Ludlow, we are in the present, uncomplicated, and direct world, our world. The other side is different, having in some small way a life of its own (a withholding). And just as the prow of a boat visible over a wall tells you of the proximity of the sea (vast, everlasting), so the church spire turns simple enclosure into the drama of Here and There (Fig. 33).

Section through
shopping street

shop awnings

Costers
barrows →

Inside Extends Out
The corollary of this is the expression of inside volumes externally. In the case
of the public house, the normal street façade is interrupted by the bulge which
expresses the function. Again, the section through the shopping street shows
how on one side, the left, we simply have shop windows, while on the right the
awnings and costers' barrows form an enclosure which transforms the whole
street from an arid inside/outside statement to a comprehensive and dramatic
linear market (Fig. 34).

Spatial Continuity
Similarly, but on a larger scale, this view of Greenwich market, produces
the effect of spatial continuity, a complex interlocking of volumes in which the
quality of light and materials denies the concept of outside and inside (Fig. 35).

Public and Private

Emphasizing this difference are the various qualities attached to parts
of the environment, qualities of character, scale, color, etc. In this case the
change is from a public Here (Victoria Street) to a private or precinctual
There (Westminster Cathedral) (Fig. 36).

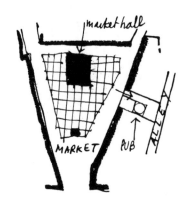

External and Internal

A different aspect of space is shown at Kingston market, above, where two similar spatial systems run side by side. First the Market Square, which is entered by circuitous small roads, widens out into the busy center, which is heightened by towers and statues. The sky is the dome of this outdoor room. Directly off the Market is the Wheatsheaf Inn, right, which also has a central busy area approached by a narrow corridor. This central area has its own sky, a glass dome. In summer the house is open from back to front and in walking through one is struck by this unity of space-sequence (Fig. 37–38).

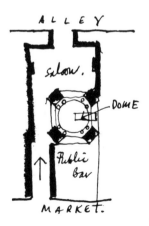

Space and Infinity
The effect of infinity is not normally apparent in sky seen over rooftops. But
if sky is suddenly seen where one might reasonably expect to walk, i.e., at ground
level, then there is an effect of infinity or shock (Fig. 39).

Captured Space
The carved frets reach out and grip space, the slender rail and posts enclose it, the pierced wall reveals it. Behind, the louvered openings reveal the next dim layer of internal space, and the windows complete it (Fig. 40).

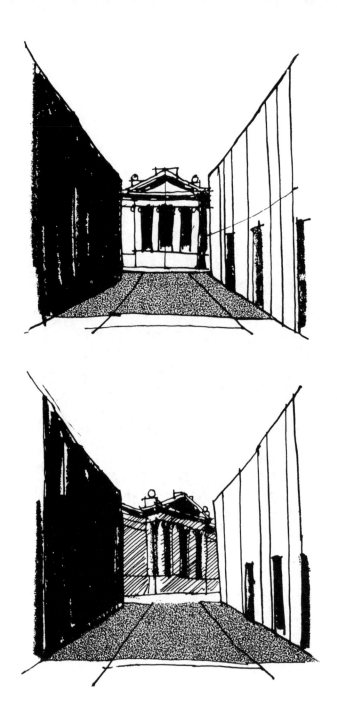

Deflection
Where a view is terminated by a building at right angles to the axis, then the
enclosed space is complete. But a change of angle in the terminal building,
as here in Edinburgh, creates a secondary space by implication. A space which
you cannot see but feel must be there, facing the building (Fig. 41).

Projection
Space, being occupiable, provokes colonization. This reaction may be exploited by placing space to achieve the desired results. In this view of the Bank of England, the lofty portico elevates the spirit more than a lofty solid building might (Fig. 42).

Functional Space

What better way of emphasizing an event in the street such as a theater than by giving this function its own space, which becomes alive and informed by sparkle and conversation and tension (Fig. 43).

Endpiece

I. 193 The message of this book is that there is a lot of fun and a lot of drama to be had from the environment. The reader may reply, "Yes, but you have combed the world for examples. Come and see where I live in the overspill housing of Liverpool or Manchester, in the new suburbs of Paris or the gridirons of American cities. See what you can make of that."

Agreed. But I have not combed the world just to make a picture book that can be picked up and put down. The examples are assembled for a purpose. The purpose is to expose the art of environment which, had it been understood and practiced, could have prevented the disasters mentioned. The reason for this book is to reach out to people like you to try to show you what you are missing and to try to implant a growth point of what could be.

Even if you lived in the prettiest of towns the message is still just as necessary: There is an art of environment. This is the central fact of TOWNSCAPE, but it has got lost along the way, and the environment gladiators have cast lots for it and divided it amongst themselves. On the one hand, it has devolved into cobbles and conservation, and on the other it has hived off into outrage and visual pollution. Neither of these, if I may be allowed to say so, is germane to the art of environment. And consequently, ten years later, it becomes necessary to start again. Now is the time to fashion a much more realistic tool. Thanks to the aforementioned gladiators the subject is now not unknown. But it is linked to constraints and exhortations. What is missing is the central power of generation. The art of putting the environment together has to be more clearly defined now, its rules stated and its typical products familiarized over a broad field of the lay population. This will be the subject of my next book.

There is an attitude of mind which recoils from the systematization of aesthetics, believing that the bird on the wing can never be the same when caught. There is another attitude which inclines to the view that unless you define your notes and establish a musical grammar you will never be able to play a tune—even a simple tune, let alone Mozart. This seems to me to be self-evident. At the risk of repetition let us get the field of activity defined.

A. The environment is put together in two ways. First, objectively, by means of common sense and logic based on the benevolent principles of health, amenity, convenience, and privacy. This may be compared to God creating the world as someone outside and above the thing created. The second way is not in opposition to this. It is a fulfillment of creation by employing the subjective values of those who will live in this created world. Without disrespect, this may be compared to God sending his son into the world to live as a human, find out what it is like, and redeem it. Both these attitudes are complementary. To take a simple analogy, commonweal lines of latitude which are parallel on the map diminish to vanishing points when observed by the individual. There is no moral distinction involved; both observations are true. The truth is where you are. In these studies we shall not be concerned with objective values, which appear to be thriving. But we shall be concerned with the subjective situation, which is disturbing.

What we are witnessing is the extreme difficulty of switching from one kind of truth to another, i.e., from the objective benevolence of the town hall to personal response and experience, especially when, in this mad world, there is usually so little time to adjust.

The main claim of TOWNSCAPE is that it has assisted in charting the structure of the subjective world. For unless it is charted, to what can you adjust? To opinions, to fashion, or to personal morality? How difficult it is to adjust to vagueness and what a waste of time.

B. But from what base do we set out? The only possible base surely is to set down the ways in which the human being warms to

314

their surroundings. To set down their affirmations. Not the grandiose views on Art or God or the Computer, but the normal affirmations about our own lives. It may help to observe human response to living itself. The baby is born, it has arrived, it is hungry, it cries, it sleeps. It is utterly helpless and utterly arrogant. Later, the growing child begins to discern things outside itself; some things are hot and others cold, sometimes it is light and sometimes dark, some big things move about singing. The youth grows up in the family and learns the dos and don'ts of family life. When not to ask questions or stay up late, how to get on the right side of Dad, and so on. Still later, as an adult, decides to make an own life, marries, and becomes responsible for the organization of their family.

Our response to the environment is very much the same and can be expressed in four affirmations:

1. Awareness of space: I am HERE, I am in this room, it is now.
2. Awareness of mood and character: They are THERE. That building is charming or ugly.
3. Awareness of a time structure: I understand BEHAVIOR. We walk about inside a web of perspective that opens before us and closes behind us.
4. Awareness of form: I ORGANIZE. I can manipulate SPACES and MOODS, knowing their BEHAVIOR, to produce the home of humans.

But what happens if we simply brush all this to one side and get down to a bit of designing?

Anti 1. There is then nothing to belong to, nothing but wasteland. Non-homes stretching to the horizon and a continuum of emptiness. The Expulsion from Eden.

Anti 2. There is nothing to communicate with. We turn this way and that, but all is faceless and mindless. Nobody laughs or weeps. We hold out a hand, but there is no response from the silent army.

Anti 3. An environment as ignorant and clumsy as a crashed gear change, scenery as catastrophic as the implications of a group home for girls.

Anti 4. Chips with everything. Shove in a couple of silver birches.

C.   Our first move in creating a system must surely be to organize the field so that phenomena can be filed logically in an Atlas of the environment. So far we have a column of affirmations on the left-hand side. Across the top we can set down the differing dimensions of the environment in which they operate. First there is the physical world of length, breadth, and height. Second is the dimension of time, and third is the dimension of ambience. From these two breakdowns, vertical and horizontal, we can construct a grid or elementary Atlas which, if the premises are sound, should be capable of immense growth.

Having arrived at the concept of an Atlas, we now consider the fourth affirmation, that concerned with organization or manipulation. If we consider the Atlas as a reference library of (visual) words then organization is the art of putting this word with that to make a lucid statement which is inherent in the particular design problem. And it is this glorious sense of communication that we all need. For God's sake, say something!

You can see that it is no more complicated than a cookbook: First you list your ingredients, then you describe how they behave in heat or water or whatever, and then you put them together and there it is, a loaf. The only difference between the two is that most people have a lust for eating which justifies the apparently inexhaustible supply of cookbooks, whereas the environment is, at the moment, a lust vacuum. It isn't really surprising. The dialogue stopped when they killed off the environmental virtues of Victorian architecture and substituted a lot of personal virtues such as truth, honesty, and self-expression. You can see where that's got us; everybody is bored stiff. We've lost our audience.

We have to join, separate, divide, conceal, reveal, concentrate, dilute, trap, liberate, delay, and accelerate. Throw the ball about, get those stiff muscles working. There is much to do.

Human life notwithstanding, there are few things more poignant than the stillbirth of an idea in the human brain. Suddenly in the rich humus of the mind an idea pushes up into the light of comprehension. The telephone rings—no we haven't got anthracite grains, only nuts. And the idea has gone. Quite often gone forever. The gods who threw the dice groan in frustration. Our world is continually throwing up concepts, ideas, and solutions, but a vast amount withers and dies while the rest recedes into the paper mountain. What is needed is a frame of reference in which these homeless ideas can be housed: an environmental equivalent to Shelter, the British organization that is privately tackling the housing problem. It is my view that there is an incredible waste of fertility and that this should be halted by the creation of a collecting, sorting, and retrieval agency. And so we end up with a box of concepts and a range of gambits, the whole being coordinated and internally self-justifying like a crystal. A weapon with which we can hack our way out of isolation and make contact with the educators, with the mass media, and so to the point of the story, the public.

1. The President's Residence,
   now Viceregal Lodge.
2. It was the cause of bitterness
   between Lutyens and Baker.

Lucius Burckhardt
The Science of Walking

I. Lucius Burckhardt, "Strollological Observations on Perception of the Environment and the Tasks Facing Our Generation", in Jesko Fezer and Martin Schmitz (eds.), *Lucius Burckhardt Writings. Rethinking Man-made Environments. Politics, Landscape & Design* (Vienna/New York: Springer, 2012), 239–248 (239, 242–248). First published as Lucius Burckhardt, "Promenadologische Betrachtungen über die Wahrnehmung der Umwelt und die Aufgaben unserer Generation", in Markus Ritter and Martin Schmitz (eds.), *Warum ist Landschaft schön? Die Spaziergangswissenschaft* (Berlin: Schmitz, 2006), 251–256.

II. Lucius Burckhardt, "Strollology—A New Science", in Markus Ritter and Martin Schmitz (eds.), *Why Is Landscape Beautiful? The Science of Strollology* (Basel: Birkhäuser, 2015), 288–294 (290). First published as Lucius Burckhardt, "Promenadologie—Eine neue Wissenschaft", in: *Passagen/Passages* no. 24, 1998, 3–5.

III. Lucius Burckhardt, "The Science of Strollology", in Markus Ritter and Martin Schmitz (eds.), *Why Is Landscape Beautiful? The Science of Strollology* (Basel: Birkhäuser, 2015), 231–266 (238–249). First published as Lucius Burckhardt, "Die Spaziergangswissenschaft", in Markus Ritter and Martin Schmitz (eds.), *Warum ist Landschaft schön? Die Spaziergangswissenschaft* (Berlin: Schmitz, 2006), 257–300.

IV. Lucius Burckhardt, "On the Design of Everyday Life", in Jesko Fezer and Martin Schmitz (eds.), *Lucius Burckhardt Writings. Rethinking Man-made Environments. Politics, Landscape & Design* (Vienna/New York: Springer, 2012), 142–152 (144–149, 152). First published as Lucius Burckhardt, "Design für den Alltag", in *Ästhetik im Alltag*, vol. 2, Offenbach, 1979.

V. Lucius Burckhardt, "Design Is Invisible", in Jesko Fezer and Martin Schmitz (eds.), *Lucius Burckhardt Writings. Rethinking Man-made Environments. Politics, Landscape & Design* (Vienna/New York: Springer, 2012), 153–165 (153–154). First published as Lucius Burckhardt, "Design ist unsichtbar", in Helmuth Gsöllpointner, Angela Hareiter, Laurids Ortner (eds.), *Design ist unsichtbar* (Vienna: Löcker, 1981).

VI. Lucius Burckhardt, "What Is Livability? On Quantifiable and Invisible Needs", in Jesko Fezer and Martin Schmitz (eds.), *Lucius Burckhardt Writings. Rethinking Man-made Environments. Politics, Landscape & Design* (Vienna/New York: Springer, 2012), 170–178 (174, 176). First published as Lucius Burckhardt, "Was ist Wohnlichkeit? —Messbare und unsichtbare Bedürfnisse", in *Wohnlichkeit in Städten*, SVG-Schriftenreihe, no. 80, Zurich, 1981.

VII. Lucius Burckhardt, "Urban Design and Its Significance for Residents", in Jesko Fezer and Martin Schmitz (eds.), *Lucius Burckhardt Writings. Rethinking Man-made Environments. Politics, Landscape & Design* (Vienna/New York: Springer, 2012), 115–122 (115–118, 121–122). First published as Lucius Burckhardt, "Die Stadtgestalt und ihre Bedeutung für die Bewohner", in Michael Andritzky, Peter Becker, Gerd Selle (eds.), *Labyrinth Stadt—Planung und Chaos im Städtebau* (Cologne: DuMont Schauberg 1975).

Strollology—The Science of Walking

I. 239 Aesthetic aspects of the environment have never before concerned people to the extent they do today. Never before were so many committees caught up in permit procedures; never before were such powerful organizations at work to protect the environment, the landscape, monuments, and a sense of local identity; never has it been so difficult to erect a new building in a historical location, or on a landscape that still bears traces of earlier gardens or agriculture. Yet despite all these safeguards, procedures, and rejected construction proposals, complaints about the "uglyfication" of the environment and the destruction of the landscape are growing louder by the day. My science, which is called strollology, attempts to analyze this phenomenon.

II. 290 Strollology is the science of walking. A brief introduction: The walk does not lead to a single, spectacular destination and then back again; and what we say from memory about the walk does not describe an individual image but synthesizes a string of impressions. Let us observe a classic walker as he leaves the city, passes through the suburbs and an agricultural zone, traverses a forest, crosses a bridge, climbs a hill, and then returns to the city after a detour through a deep valley. Once there, he says (depending on where he has been): the Jura is like this, the Vosges, the Vienna Woods, the Wetterau are like that. And what he describes is not a single place that actually exists, a place he has seen, but rather a synthesis of sequences of hill, valley, forest and agriculture. The walk is thus a chain, a string of pearls made up of more expressive and then less expressive passages that are ultimately synthesized in the mind's eye. Similarly, the walk in a city: one's memory—"Paris was like this"—does not describe the Eiffel Tower but rather a synthesis of the boulevards, squares, side streets and parks one has rushed through.

Strollology examines the sequences in which a person I. 239 perceives their surroundings. For it is not as if we find ourselves "beamed" all of a sudden to Piccadilly Circus or the Cancelleria; instead we find our way there, one way or another. We leave our hotel on the Via Nomentana or the Pincio, catch a bus or flag a cab—younger people go on foot. We check out the streets, cross squares, stroll along the Corso, perhaps take in the Palazzo Vidone, the Linotte, and St. Andrea della Valle, and are thus sufficiently prepared for the Cancelleria to also fall into place. A parachutist who happened to land among the endless cars parked in the narrow alley in front of the Cancelleria would gain a quite different impression of the architecture than we do.

The Destination and the Way[1]

The trip and the walk can have two different meanings: they can III. 238 either be the means to reach a destination, whereby the destination is of paramount importance; or they may be an end in themselves, undertaken for pleasure's sake or to gain knowledge through travel or, if undertaken on foot, for the simple enjoyment of stretching one's legs. Every trip has a little of both: a pilgrimage may initially appear to be focused exclusively on a destination, yet the journey itself is a powerful experience, not least owing to the devotional highlights found at different points along the route. Modern modes of transport tend to make the journey itself seem insignificant and abstract, for they focus only on the destination. The subway offers an abstract form of travel oriented purely to the target destination and likewise the now popular "non-stop quick hop" routes. Flight, which early pioneers imagined primarily as a trip, not simply as a means to reach a destination, is also now an extremely abstract means to arrive quickly at one's goal. This can be explained in strollological terms by the fact that the view of earth from an airplane cabin window is much less interesting than it was once imagined to be. I'd like to examine the extent to which our perception of landscape depends on the mode of transport used for a trip or a walk.

Walking: The Way Is as Important as the Goal²

The trip on foot, on horseback, or by horse and cart were the first modes available, as we know from historical memoirs. A whole world has been lost since those modes disappeared: the world of coachmen and inns, a world of encounters between nations, classes, and ranks, for every traveler, from the prince to the journeyman, had to rely on roadside inns. Contact with the localities traveled was indispensable, for food supplies and hay and oats for the horses had to be purchased en route from farmers, traders, or innkeepers.

When it comes to the landscape experience, traditional travel may be said to follow the "string of pearls" model.

I. 242 The experience of the landscape prior to the Golden Age of railroads was such that the way was as important as the goal. Perhaps a man would have left town on foot or on horseback via a brick city gate, seen strangers at their work, forded a river, entered a forest, or climbed a hill. He may have chosen another route back to his home town and then, in the evening, tired and weary, have described the landscape to his dear ones: that is how things are in Saint Germain or in the Jura near Besançon, and the forest of Fontainebleau is like this. Much of that which the stroller related at home he had never really seen, and much of that which he had seen was omitted from his account. The image he conjured was a collage of previous knowledge and fragments garnered along his way. The outcome was nevertheless certain knowledge—he now knew the forest of Fontainebleau.

Did he find it beautiful? Of course: for everything he saw of agriculture and natural growth on his travels was beautiful. Poetry since the days of Theocritus and Horace and the paintings of Neapolitan and Dutch Masters had prepared him for this beauty, had schooled his eye. And, moreover, he regarded this landscape with disinterest in Immanuel Kant's sense of the term, meaning he did not seek to derive any personal benefit from it. He was in search neither of mushrooms nor of a suitable place to till the soil.

The urban dweller's lack of familiarity with the rural landscape was precisely what enabled him to appreciate its aesthetic qualities and to perceive them as typical to this landscape.

Our perception registers the typical places and qualities, III. 239 filters out incidental aspects and accomplishes that feat of integration we attributed earlier to the walker. From the wealth of information that impacts the eye and all other senses, we select those bits we believe we have seen before or that can be subsumed in our previous knowledge; this and this alone makes them apt for recognition; and we store them in our memories, or record them in narratives and transcripts. Here, the feat of integration consists in our capacity to process fleeting sequences of heterogeneous impressions—the walker or traveler leaves a city, crosses an agricultural zone and comes upon a forest, where the trail leads them up hill and down valley, past a body of water and over a bridge—and to integrate these in a single image that we then hold to be "typical" of the area traveled.

Rail Travel and the Supremacy of Destination[3]

This perception of landscape accomplished by the integration of heterogeneous impressions stands in stark contrast to the perception of landscape fostered in the nineteenth century by a new mode of transport: the railroad. From the very start, rail travel was oriented to the destination. Its administration made this very clear, for anyone boarding a train requires a ticket to the chosen destination. The traveler must therefore know before starting a journey where they want to get off and spend some time. Only very few rail offers deviate from this model, for example, the Mystery Tour on special trains for short trips. Conventional rail vacation is extremely oriented on a fixed destination. The traveler spends a great deal of time choosing a resort, consulting brochures, travel agencies, colleagues, and neighbors, and ends up with great expectations of the landscape experience the resort is likely to provide.

Construction of railroads made certain resorts popular in the course of the nineteenth century and they provide clues to the railroad-related landscape experience, i.e. the experience rail travelers had of their destinations. Not all typical nineteenth-century railroad destinations can actually be reached by rail; often a short crossing by boat is necessary, or an ascent by mule, or with a porter. All the more evident it is, thus, that the destinations in question had extraordinary qualities. The destination had to guarantee with a single point that "typical" something accomplished during a walk by a feat of integration. The nineteenth-century guest takes up residence in a hotel room, throws back the curtains, looks though the window and—as long as the room booked is an expensive one—sees the ideal image of the typical Alps or the typical North Sea or the typical Mediterranean landscape. Ideally, the image framed by the window will be exactly the one already seen in the travel brochures. In the age of railroads and terminals, the landscape shrank to a postcard cliché: this is Ostend, and this Scheveningen, Interlaken, or the isle of Mont Saint-Michel. The stroll was reduced thus to the choice of a holiday destination, the purchase of a ticket, and the rental of a hotel room with a view to match the postcard.

I. 241

III. 240 These nineteenth-century destinations have now often lost their clientele; or they have won a quite different clientele. The large hotel blocks stand vacant at panoramic spots in the Alps or in the similarly extreme landscapes of northern Germany or Italy— on Helgoland, in Naples (where the size of the city and views of Mount Vesuvius and Capri ensure hotels a steady stream of visitors), or on Capri itself (where the joys of bathing have replaced delights for the eye); and likewise in France, at Mont Saint-Michel and Saint-Malo; the large panoramic hotels in Austria and Switzerland are literally vacant too, on the Semmering, the Rigigipfel (demolished), and Mount Furka (Hotel Furka has been demolished, the Furkablick turned into an art gallery). The Bélvèdere Rhône Glacier stood empty for many years while thousands of motorists whizzed by daily, or even made a stop. Alone the Hotel Giessbach has been revived, thanks to a group of nostalgic tourists. What does this mean? The construction of railroads and the cable cars that went with them meant the landscapes judged suitable for tourism were not explored on foot but merely perceived as an image. The tourist spent fourteen days or three weeks in a hotel—on a terrace or in a winter garden, often without ever leaving the building—and saw through the window a typical image already integrated by nature. This image had to be striking enough to constantly impart information. It must be mentioned too that perfectly beautiful weather was not yet so much in demand as it is today. In winter gardens with panoramic outlooks, we actually used to enjoy changes in the weather; and exposed places, such as the Furka or Helgoland, provided welcome shifts: dark clouds before the window soon ceding to a broad blue sky, or vice versa.

Automobility and Cruising without a Destination[4]

The aforementioned former destinations are no longer deserted, at least not if located on a roadside; but the hotel rooms are deserted. The motorcar has brought us a new mode of transport that, since it is steered individually and not bound to follow tracks, initially appeared to herald the revival of the walk. Someone who goes for a drive need not have a fixed destination in mind. They can set off, gaze through the window, integrate the things they see in a single landscape, as a walker does, and then change direction if dissatisfied by the impressions garnered, or park and while away some time if a certain spot on the string of pearls strikes them as especially remarkable. In many respects, however, a drive does not recreate the same conditions as the walk of yore. First, the scope of travel has greatly increased. While a walk on foot or a ride on horseback allows one to cross a village, river, valley, hills, etc. and integrate in one's mind eye and hence perceive the characteristics of a limited landscape, travel by car

326

facilitates access to much larger vistas. While the walker reports on the peculiarities of the nearby Habicht Forest, the motorist talks of Tuscany, Burgundy, and the Provence, just visited by car over Pentecost. We are accordingly now required to accomplish a more complex feat of integration: more heterogeneous impressions must be integrated in much more abstract ideal landscapes. Anyone traveling through Burgundy sees the big cities, highways, factories, ugly settlements, and yes, also the vineyards, wine-growing villages, and Romanesque or Gothic churches they had reckoned with. But what constitutes "typical Burgundy" today? The feat of integration is too demanding and the subsumption of all one sees in the single image learned of in school impossible. So our motorized tourist returns home downhearted and tells their friends that Burgundy, too, is no longer what it used to be.

Evidently, the improved accessibility of more remote areas and the difficulty of successfully integrating all one's impressions of them have fostered the need for a new type of landscape perception, one that we see as a kind of abstraction. The tourist travels namely to several similar points. This is also a reason they drive past the old "panoramic hotels". Today, the Rhône Glacier alone is never touted; only the "Five Glaciers Trip". The Swiss mail truck company now offers a "Passes Trip" as well as the "Three Countries Trip". The latter starts in Grison Canton and covers a bit of South Tyrol and a slice of Austria. What information does such a trip convey, above and beyond the day-tripper's sense of pride at having visited five glaciers, three mountain passes, or three countries?

Obviously, the tourist is in search of the ideal image of the glacier, in search of the ultimate, essential glacialness of glaciers, which can apparently be identified only after viewing several samples. Similarly, the "Three Countries Trip" tends to abstraction insofar as one pays for cigarettes here in francs and there in lira or shillings; but Alps are Alps from wherever you look at them.

The increase in motorists and the construction of freeways have challenged the notion that a drive is a kind of motorized walk. The idea that one is free to choose one's route is now largely rhetorical; in practice, a trip by car requires some planning and relatively long stretches of it cannot be easily modified or interrupted. The crisscrossing local road system is now overlaid by the linear system of freeways. Driving from one hotel to the next is now history, rendered redundant by new offers: the tourist location is touted only as the "base camp" from where one embarks on brief excursions. The thousands of tourists who drive by the Hotel Furkablick or the Rhône Glacier each summer spend the night at one of the "starting blocks" on a major road through the Alps, in Interlaken or Montreux, Merano or Innsbruck. The destination and the stretch of road beyond it are touted as a single package deal: a tourist location no longer advertises its own qualities but explains rather, how convenient a springboard it is for further travel. However, given the severe congestion prevalent on road networks in tourist areas, this form of vacation too will soon be history.

The Contemporary Crisis of Classic Perception[5]

We read the walk as a sequence, as a string of pearls that demands a feat of integration, namely to produce an image of the typical landscape. But this feat of integration in its original form was based initially on yet another sequence, namely the transition from the city to the countryside. The landscape was invented by urban dwellers. Urban societies that necessarily still source food in the countryside but whose only connection with it is their power and money—and whose food hence arrives in the city in the form of tributes, taxes, interest, rent, or commodities—tend to develop an aesthetics of landscape, because the urban dweller so disconnected from agricultural production leaves the city to go for a walk and sees the countryside only in aesthetic terms or, as Kant puts it, without interest. The urbanite has namely no vested interest, no direct stake in the production process, and so potato or sunflower fields do not bring investments and yields to mind; nor are poppies and cornflowers harmful weeds, in their eyes, but seem to be, like everything else, a natural part of the landscape. Even the country folk, so alien yet so likeable—those "happy people of the fields"—are part of the landscape, are what painters call staffage or props. To transform phenomena into an aesthetic image a border must be crossed, in this case the city limits marked by a gate. In analogy, although sociologically more problematic, one could imagine the farmer entering the city and regarding buildings there likewise "without interest".

The contrast, both aesthetic and economic, between the city and the countryside thus underpins the basic pattern of classic perception as shaped by the walk. The economic prerequisite is a lack of vested interest, the purely indirect relationship to income or profit generated by agricultural activity. Even if the occasional walker happens to own or lease a plot of land, or make purchases, in the role of walker they join the ranks of the "disinterested urban dwellers". The impact of the look of the landscape, for its part, is determined by the existence (or not) of distinctive city limits. There has to be a point, a border, at which aesthetic perception is switched on or switched off. This is the reason classic perception as shaped by the walk is now in crisis and must be redefined.

Today's walker, who is also a consumer of TV, radio, and newspapers, participates or, more precisely, is implicated in agricultural production and in the current condition of fallow land. Everyone has heard that the forests are dying and so the sight of a scrawny or perhaps withered tree is a rude reminder for the urban consumer of heating oil: it fuels a personal share in the guilt. On the other hand, a walker can observe today that the "happy people of the fields" are up to something other than merrily binding ears of corn. The urban dweller eyes with suspicion the mysterious sacks and containers stacked up by the stables and likewise the strange vehicles spreading powders or liquids on the fields. Are these fertilizers or poisons? Will our bodies absorb them along with our food and drinking water? Here, the culprit becomes the victim, the injured party the aggressor; we urban dwellers feel guilty about our part in killing off the forest yet are simultaneously outraged to see our essential raw materials being ruined by chemicals—and feel powerless to stop it happening. And what about the cattle, now that they no longer stand around picturesquely in a clearing? True, we cannot see them, but we rightly presume them to be on the far side of those extremely long walls from behind which trucks appear, laden with dung and headed for the fields, fields where vegetation is sparse, not because of a lack of dung but because of its sheer abundance. The walker who sees all this and necessarily gives it some thought due to being confronted with it time after time daily is no longer quite the disinterested observer. But what then?

The second component of the crisis of our perception of the landscape relates to the suburbs. We move nowadays in a continuum that we call the metropolis. By that we mean this mixture of buildings and green spaces that now sprawls across what used to be the city or used to be the countryside. We know the following statement provokes protest, but we make it anyhow: "Never before have our cities been as green as they are today." Not a single administrative building, not a single pedestrian zone has failed to render its limited space unusable by planting rampant vegetation purchased from nurseries. We will return later to the fact that the very ubiquity of urban greenery can render actual gardens invisible. Changes in the former countryside are easier to see. No rural town is at peace until it too, like the city, has a few low high-rise buildings. And even in villages, at the least the local council offices are expanded so that one could easily take them for Deutsche Bank. And none of this happens, let us emphasize, without the requisite dwarf shrubs and steppe grasses being planted in former farmland, where they struggle unsuccessfully to assert themselves in the face of non-native sunflowers and giant hogweed. And so we must ask ourselves once again: Is our image

330

of landscape in crisis simply because a distinct border between the countryside and the city no longer exists?

Here we must touch upon a third point that we will not discuss conclusively, however: the confusion of the landscape and nature. Such confusion is a latent companion every time we look at or try to represent the landscape. The urban dweller walking in the countryside takes pleasure in signs of different types of agricultural processing or non-processing. The classic landscape paintings of the Italian and Dutch painters show both: the interventions made by the farmer-landowner as well as unspoiled nature, here symbolized perhaps by the portrayal of old, half-dead veteran trees that are surely not destined to land in a carpentry workshop or on a fire. Both options are obviously well worth considering: using a thing—or letting it lie fallow.

In this respect too, we are currently experiencing momentous change: use is intensifying and more land is being left fallow. The economic reasons for this need hardly be explained here. Also understandable is the aesthetic phenomenon that ensues from this development, namely, that the denser and more homogeneous agricultural use becomes, the more the walker loses aesthetic interest in it. We don't pull on our hiking boots in order to see endless fields of grain and poultry factories. In the future, we'll more likely head for fallow land; but pitfalls are in store there, too. Any land neglected by its users, be they farmers, the Bundeswehr [German Federal Armed Forces], or whoever, becomes unstable. That which we witness, glad or incredulous—invasive weeds, the prickly jungle of thistles, then the emergence of the first alder thickets and, finally, after a few years, the inaccessibility of these areas—has still to be discussed. For now, at least, the matter is on the agenda.

Making Things Visible
Faced with this crisis of the perception of landscape, we take two divergent approaches, both of which are an attempt to use something visible to satisfy our longing for the natural.

331

The one tendency is to seek naturalness in the extreme landscape. Only a location in which we are not implicated can be perceived aesthetically. Just as a search began in the eighteenth century for the last blank spots on the map, so today the search is on for the last unspoiled corners of the world. It is clear, however, that the latter are not only not uninhabited but also doubtless given over in part to tourism.

Perhaps such unspoiled and unexploited areas actually do still exist, or even tribes of people who have never yet seen a tourist. Yet they are not within our reach. It is unnecessary however for such unspoiled unexploited places to exist in the here and now, if they happen to exist within a specially adopted system of signs. And the extreme landscape provides such signs. While, historically, the landscape experience was initially satisfied by elements of the charming landscape and then eventually, in the eighteenth century, took on elements of the, in Burke's sense, "sublime" landscape, today we seek the very opposite, or at least the opposite of "charming". Some travel agencies specialize in trips of this sort: Ireland, Iceland, hikes in the northern tundra and steppes, cruises between cliffs and icebergs with a view of spartan fishing villages, or treks by camel or mule through the desert, the Atlas Mountains, or the Himalayas, whereby the ideal of diversity still alive and kicking in the minds of certain landscape designers cedes dramatically to the lure of solitary expanses.

Travel agencies cannot convey the adventurous landscape of a jungle trek but cigarette advertising can at least give it a good try: a Jeep hauled onto a raft, the faithful dog, boots, a slouching hat, a bottle of whiskey and, of course, a cigarette. This so trammeled system of signs beyond the conventionally sublime—trans-sublimity, we might call it— now serves to communicate to today's traveler (the one with a guilty conscience thanks to environmental propaganda) what was previously the situation of the disinterested observer, namely of one not implicated in what is happening around them, and who is thus able to perceive it in aesthetic terms.

The other, likewise commercially (although in a different line of business) mediated system of signs is that of ecology. Ecology is invisible. It is a scientific construct that first requires an operable definition of goals and thereafter must be proven by scientific means. But this is of little concern to the urban dweller stricken by a guilty conscience. This person wants to see ecology in simple, legible terms—and immediately. This is why landscape nurseries now offer organic vegetation alongside their dwarf shrubs and large-petal tulips. Of course, the organic flower meadows that the urban gardener plants are not really organic. You can tell that alone from the fact they need full-time care. For they are nothing less than interrupted successions, transition states artificially brought to a halt between care and the absence of care, between the urban lawn mowed weekly and the wasteland full of scrub. After all, even the "real" alpine flower meadow, on which commercial mixed-seed bags are modeled, used to be intensively exploited as part of a rigid scheme of farming, and its urban counterpart must likewise be coddled with fertilizers and novel means of loosening or aerating the soil. But the image thus produced brings relief to the troubled conscience of any urban dweller no longer able to take much pleasure in the disposable flora on offer in conventional city nurseries.

Object and Context

I. 245 And now I wish to describe why and to what extent our generation is the first to find itself in a novel situation vis-à-vis the object observed, be it a building or a landscape. And the explanation is once again strollological. It is not objects themselves that have changed, but the context. I'll name here some of the changes.

One actually does arrive in front of many an interesting building in much the same way as our parachutist, but from below now, from the subway. I have traveled from the Gare de l'Est to the Louvre metro station and find myself now in the Rue de Rivoli. Where am I? What is that? And how rapidly the picture changes: now I am in the courtyard of the Louvre or in the Tuileries Garden. Without my prior knowledge, my city map, or my travel guide, I am at a loss.

I park my car and head for the city forest. Gas stations, factories (abandoned ones mostly), a second-hand rubber dealer with a stock of old tires, a farmer on a tractor who is spraying his field with a white powder or vapor and, finally, trees. Are they valiant warriors, bowed by the tide of time, or is the forest here dying? And if so, whose fault may that be? Possibly mine, it is said, insofar as I drive a car and have a centrally heated home. And who drinks the water from beneath the sprayed field? Again, I do. So I am implicated in what is happening around me, after all, and by no means alien or disinterested, as Kant would have it.

Another example: let's say I go to the park, back to the Tuileries Garden. In historic times, one used to cross the built-up city, the city in which every last square meter was exploited and the king used his great wealth to plant a green oasis, the Tuileries Garden. So I walk through the "stone city",[6] cut through the palace, and find myself gazing in delight upon this precious public park. Yet since the nineteenth century, the Tuileries Garden has come to present a quite different aspect: we arrive now from the Champs Elysées, cut through the grounds that were laid out for the World Exhibition, search between the Seine and the Place de la Concorde for a way to reach the entrance and ultimately find ourselves in a place not so very unlike the previous grounds. The experience of "I am now setting foot in the park" has been lost.

And now let us leave these anyhow still classical situations and take a look around those infinite zones we might best describe as "metropolises". These are the zones in which the city strives to be the countryside and where everybody, whether building a home or a factory, surrounds themselves with as much greenery as possible. The same is true of the zones in which the countryside aspires to be urban and every small town mayor is in search of an investor prepared to make a gift of a tower block or, at the least, of a railroad station with an underground section, a pedestrian level, and a multistory

Fig. 1 "I am a country chapel", yesterday and today.
Drawing: Lucius Burckhardt, 1996.

parking lot. And now, my discovery: in those zones of our environment inhabited or visited by the majority, the strollological context that fosters understanding of what we see has completely disintegrated.

We are therefore the first generation of people for whom the aesthetic experience does not occur automatically. Instead, the place itself must explain its aesthetic intent. When we create a park, the park can no longer rely on the fact that we proceed from the town and through a gate to a green space and hence know we are visiting the park. Rather, the park must now substantiate by means of its interior design the extent to which it contrasts with its surroundings. So, without us even taking a single step, it must give us the strollological explanation: "You have come from the city to the park."

The same holds true for architecture. Architecture can no longer rely on us grasping its greater significance thanks to location alone and so must assert its singularity by deviating slightly from the stylistic ideal. For instance, a new bank must now introduce a slightly different nuance to the banking district. Now, an acclimatized suburban cube that has been incorporated in a partly green, partly concrete-braced artificial plane must fall back on a conveniently ambivalent statement: I am in the suburbs but I am resolutely urban; I am a bank, but a bank like no other … (Fig 1).

To reiterate: we are the first generation to have to construct a new aesthetic, a strollological aesthetic. Strollological, for the simple reason that the way or route to a place can no longer be taken for granted, but must be reproduced in, or represented by, the object itself. The multilayered message that a building, garden, or cultivated landscape must deliver can no longer depend only on an architect's flash of genius. It is not enough for the enterprising architect to say: "Where there is no place, I will create a place myself." There are plenty such aesthetic cactuses dotted about already and, indeed, it is they which have contributed so decisively to the much lamented deterioration of the natural environment (Fig. 2). What is required here, rather, is design intelligence, intelligence that conveys a dual message: information about the context as well as about the object in question.

Fig. 2 "This much one can say: Our buildings work wherever one puts them!"
Drawing: Lucius Burckhardt, 1996.

Design is Invisible

My intention here is to identify the organizational context of IV. 142 designed or planned systems, which is to say, the rules that govern usage and actually comprise our environment—in other words, to correlate the invisible part of our lives with its planned, visible, physical dimension.

To make that perhaps a little less abstract, I'll tell you first about something I have observed. I usually spend my vacation on a farm where the mailman used to stop by each day. He never knocked on the door, just opened the door so loudly that one could tell he was in the house. He then put the mail on the table, and waited expectantly for someone to come talk to him a while. Then he went to the next farm. Then the post office decreed that farms should install a mailbox on the road, in order to save the mailman's time: a beautiful design task. We therefore acquired a mailbox, a yellow one trimmed in black, with very distinguished-looking metal moldings flat enough to let the rain pour in, and we installed it. After that, we noticed that our farmer and all the farmers in the area no longer had any information, as the dissemination of information in rural areas does not take place through letters. Namely, neighbors do not write to one another; they tell their stories to the mailman, who passes them on at the next farm. The post office actually had no idea of how it conveyed news. It believed it transported letters containing news. In reality however, an invisible system was at work, which actually conveyed news in a most appropriate way. We who are interested in visual culture have partly forgotten to reference the organizational and social dimension, as well as other dimensions that we will address later.

We can perceive the world as a realm of objects and divide these, for example, into houses, streets, traffic lights, kiosks, coffee makers, washing-up bowls, tableware, or table linen. Such classification is not without consequences: it leads namely to that concept of design which isolates a certain device—a coffee maker, let's say—acknowledges its external parameters, and sets itself the goal of making a better or more attractive one; that is, of producing the type of thing likely to have been described in the 1950s as "good form".[7]

But we can divide the world up in other ways too—and, if I have understood *A Pattern Language*[8] correctly, that is what Christopher Alexander strives to do. He does not isolate a house, a street, or a newsstand in order to perfect its design and construction; instead, he distinguishes an integral composite, such as VI. 174 the street corner, from other urban composites. The street corner, seen as an integral composite, is a combination of intersection, bus stop, newsstand, and crosswalk. These are the visible elements of the street corner, and they are complemented by invisible, organizational factors: the bus timetable, traffic light sequences, and the newsstand's opening times. For the newsstand V. 154 thrives on the fact that my bus has not yet arrived, and so I buy a newspaper; and the bus happens to stop here, because this is an intersection where passengers can change to other lines. If the VI. 174 newsstand is still closed when I am waiting for my bus to work, the street corner subsystem fails to function: it lacks an element of livability.

V. 154 This way of dividing up our environment also triggers a design impulse—yet one that takes account of the system's invisible components. What we need, perhaps, so that I won't miss my bus while scrabbling for change, or because the newsagent is serving another customer, is a simplified method of paying for a newspaper. Some people instantly dream up a new invention—an automatic magazine dispenser with an electric hum—while we imagine somehow intervening in the system: selling magazines for a round sum, or introducing a subscription card that we can simply flash at the newsagent—in any case, some kind of ruling to tackle magazine distribution and the institution of "the morning VI. 176 paper". [...] Our personal environment does not consist only of all that is physically present, which is to say, of built structures,

339

stones, bricks, grass, trees, and parking lots. More importantly, our environment must provide food for thought, so that our imaginations can build a world for us that we sense is right for us, and can accept.

On the Design of Everyday Life

Kevin Lynch introduced in the 1960s a remarkable new approach to the architectural field, one that could be read in two ways. In *The Image of the City*,[9] he asks: "How do people actually see their city" and "What do they see of the city?" Lynch observed that people do not see urban planners and architects' input in the city. When someone asks the way to the railroad station, they are not told in reply: "You must go to the beautiful house designed by Le Corbusier, then take a right, then comes a building designed by Mies van der Rohe, then you go straight ahead, and you'll be at the station!" They are told rather, "You must go as far as this road sign then, if no one is looking, you just cut through the flower bed, go past the tobacconist's, and right behind that is the best way to the station!" So people see the city from their everyday perspectives: Where is the short cut? Where can I buy cigarettes? Where is there a slot machine? And so forth …

Lynch's theory was understood in a dual sense, or misunderstood, whereby one cannot be too sure whether or not Lynch misunderstood himself—if that is possible. For he, or at least his successors, called for the construction of expressive buildings by which people could orientate themselves, whereby actual observations suggest people are orientated not to forms per se but to forms plus usages, which is to say, to everyday signs rather than aesthetic signs.

Herbert J. Gans's book *The Levittowners*[10] was also published in the 1960s. The author asked himself why people live in or buy houses in Levittown, in those monotonous settlements made up of detached houses that are built in a strange, old-fashioned colonial style, with terrible lawns out front that one is not allowed to use, and so forth. So these detached family homes have everything the architect or initiated layman abhors—yet they sell like hot cakes. Mr. Levitt & Sons are doing good business, and the buyers are satisfied. Herbert J. Gans also bought such a house, spent two years there, studied the phenomenon, and ascertained that the people's environment there is not the visible environment; rather, the Levitts succeeded in creating an invisible social environment that perfectly suited a certain class of income and social standing. Such people find there what they need, namely families of the same age, who have children who also want to go to schools that lead to university, and who also belong to certain churches of certain denominations, churches that offer a social as well as an ecclesiastical perspective; families in similar professional positions. Levitt pitches people's environment correctly, because his plans are based on a classification system in which the house itself, its lawn, its garden, its driveway and all the things we find so horrible, rank very near the bottom, whereas invisible factors rate very highly.

Finally, let me name a very different discovery made by Ivan Illich, namely that properties with a social character are inherent to objects. Illich expresses this thus, in his striking manner: "Everything that moves faster than 20 kilometers per hour is undemocratic." I do not agree with that. I think the railroad—it is democratic—should have a special permit. Yet we must take advantage of the discovery itself. There are objects that create liberties, and there are objects that create dependencies; there are objects that foster social relations, and there are objects that foster isolation.

What we are looking for here, is—to use my term of choice— an integrated or integrative theory of design or planning; one that incorporates regulatory systems as well as the visible dimension of our environment. Until now, architects and designers have said: Spaces regulate life—regulate where entrances are, what shape rooms are, and how objects look. Then there is a profession that says: laws regulate life. And then along come the sociologists and say: no, behavioral patterns and systems of relationship regulate life. And since these professions go about their business so perfectly in parallel, the architects build their buildings; they build schools, and rave on the opening day about how this school will be a community center, a hub of the neighborhood; and they never suspect (or perhaps already suspect), that it will never become a community center, not because any architectural failing precludes this possibility but because the janitor locks up at 8 p.m.—which is good for business of course, for the construction of a community center can be commissioned next. Traffic is approached in a similar manner, namely as an isolated phenomenon. It is calculated how many people will move to an area. A basic presumption is that growth will be continuous. It is then calculated how many people have a car nowadays, and how long it will take until the last baby also has a car. The road width is then adjusted accordingly. Here, the English term "self-fulfilling prophecies" should be taken quite literally: the roads will full-fill, i.e. will fill until they are full, because once roads have been built, they are used, naturally, for this kind of extrapolation, of course, forces people to use a car to get around. That other possibilities exist, that one might move beyond full capacity calculations, for example by introducing staggered work schedules and the like, can never be grasped—simply because the expert in this field is not available.

Now the built, physical world certainly has defining properties. There is a saying in German: "One can't walk through a wall." Therefore a door must exist. But hidden doors and non-doors exist too, namely laws and prohibitions. And walls are not as important as dos and don'ts are. The tram stop I use each day is organized in such a way that I miss the tram whenever I use the crosswalk with traffic signals that leads to the tram stop, because the tram can drive off the exact same moment the cars do. And I cannot board the tram at that moment, because the cars do not stop for me when they have a green light. So, if I don't want to miss my tram, I have to jump over the flowerbed that lies outside the traffic signal zone. What is decisive here is not the physical access point per se but rather, the regulation. A tram stop is thus an integrated system comprising design, laws, and regulations—and it obviously cannot find its designer.

I would like now to speak about an important aspect of non-physical organization, about time. Time and temporal rhythms, timetables and transport schedules: these are the things that govern our lives. I was recently sent a book from France, Anne Cauquelin's *La ville la nuit*.[11] Can one write a book about the night? The night is a natural phenomenon of course, yet since electric light was invented we can light up the night, at least as far as we need to. But, says Anne Cauquelin, the night is an institution. It is determined, not by the fact that nature creates darkness and light, but by rules. When are lights turned on? When are they turned off? In consequence, public transport ceases to operate at a particular time for example, and bars close—hence, infrastructure is not used to full capacity, and our freedom to do as we like is restricted: the freedom, for example, to spend an evening having a drink with friends, then return home by public transport with alcohol in our blood. We cannot do so, because public transport does not run after midnight. In Hamburg's City Nord district, or in the city of London, there are restaurants that close in the evenings; other restaurants in more outlying districts open only in the evenings, because people in the evening go to other places than they do at midday. The institution of night necessitates a dual infrastructure.

Let us stick for a while with this issue of time and temporal rhythms. The history of labor struggles, of safety at work, and of the acceptability of labor also includes the struggle for a shorter working week. But one gets the impression that those responsible on both fronts in this struggle, or on its three fronts—the state, the employers, and the unions—do not think the temporal rhythm concept through to its end. Their hitherto legitimate struggle therefore enters a new phase, for we are obliged now to consider how to use leisure time. I'm not talking here—and I should stress this three times over—about the problem of leisure per se. That does not exist in any case. Everyone is convinced that everyone else has problems with leisure, but no one believes themselves to. If only everyone would admit this once and for all, it would put a stop, not only to all this talk of the problems with leisure but also to the leisure facilities that are built in order that other people spend their leisure time properly.

So, that is not my issue here. Rather, I am concerned with the issue of how these temporal rhythms determine our lives, namely the daily rhythm, the weekly rhythm, hence also the weekend, the annual rhythm, vacation time, and the rhythm of life—at what age do we embark on our working lives, and at what age do we retire? We really ought to know more about the consequences these rhythms have, as well as about how life can be organized under the conditions imposed by temporal rhythms. I consider this really an issue when it comes to designing our lives. It is moreover, also a visible problem: the daily rhythm leads to congestion on our roads, the annual rhythms to congestion in our tourist resorts, etc. In France at the moment, the planners' watchword is "desynchronization", by which they mean that the masses' working day, and likewise their weekend and vacation schedules, should not follow a uniform temporal rhythm. It is hoped that desynchronization will render redundant the famous July announcements that tell us on certain Friday evenings and Saturday mornings that roads from Paris to the South have become impassable. Of course, this is functionalism once again: traffic becomes jammed, and so organization is called for; yet this is far from being a redesign of the problem.

So, we evidently live in systems that are partly visible but also contain some invisible reference systems, regulatory systems, or temporal rhythms. The transitions between these systems are a type of invisible door, namely the rules that facilitate or assure this transition. At some point our work is done and we may go home. The next question might be whether we can still go shopping, whether our working day, our company's closing time corresponds to the stores' closing time. Some stores close a little later than our company, if we are lucky, and perhaps we can make it to the post offce too, although, naturally, it is too late to go to any other offce. These institutional doors govern how we organize our everyday lives. It is evident therefore, that we are surrounded by an invisible functional system of sorts, which is integrated in the social system comprised of our participation in working life, in our circle of friends, and in hierarchies.

And now, the final question: Who actually designs this environment by combining the organizational aspect and the visible aspect? Who has even a clue as to who designs what, and as to who determines the regulatory aspects of our environment? Allow me therefore to reiterate the provocative challenge: be an integrated designer! For only then will you be a true designer of everyday life or an architect of everyday life.

Urban Design and Its Significance for Residents

VII. 115 People would be hard put to come up with a word to match our German word *Gestalt*.[12] It says a great deal, and veils even more. Its implicit assertion that "the whole is greater than the sum of its parts", is fruitful; yet it fails to convey that to make a whole of various parts is not a natural process but a social act, an act which reflects history, culture, hegemony, and education.

How modern this concept of the city as a conscious design, as a planned object, or cityscape is, and how tightly interwoven it is with our—possibly Romantic—way of seeing, becomes evident when we try to glean from the historical travelogues of Montaigne, Felix Platter, or even of such a late author as Madame de Staël, something of the appearance of the cities they visited. We learn the name of the city as well as that of the river on which it stands—both are traced back to their Latin roots perhaps—then we learn about the churches. Some Roman antiquities are sure to be mentioned and, before we know it, we are on nodding terms with several more or less famous personalities. The cityscape corresponds to the pictograms of an artist such as Matthäus

345

Merian. His etchings appear to render urban form visible; in reality they collate information about the actual location, fortifications, major churches, and curiosities of a place. Baedeker takes a very different angle: human beings vanish, except when in the guise of the typical *Volk*, or commoners. Buildings and streets, especially historic ones, acquire importance. It is they, taken as a whole, which constitute the picturesque and photogenic city—which admittedly encompasses only the inner city. Actual residential areas, villa districts, and social housing projects, to say nothing of supermarkets, are not yet an object of "urban design", or part of the cityscape as such, even today.

The cityscape as seen by the city resident is a construct too, which is to say, an image engendered by learning processes that unfold in a social setting. The resident's city differs from that of the tourist presumably inasmuch as the resident processes a greater amount of information to a lesser degree of picturesqueness. The resident has a more precise knowledge of the city than the visitor, but feels no need to distill this knowledge into a souvenir image. It is more likely that familiar features—the street they live on, the workplace, local shops, Sunday excursions—are fixed in the mind's eye solely for the purpose of getting about the place, in a skeleton framework whose extreme form is the subway map. A series of research projects on this theme have shown that residents take their bearings from features of relevance to them personally, i.e. those that foster or prohibit activities. Conspicuous landmarks that play no part in the personal sphere are registered consciously, only when no other pointers are available.

Beyond this personal experience of the environment, a resident's cityscape is no different than that of the tourist. They describe their city by drawing on those very clichés established by the local tour guide or tourism office. The familiar hometown, which one tends a priori to regard as nothing out of the ordinary, is imbued with flair thanks to foreign forces, and to the slogans coined to market it: "The City of Gorgeous Gables", for example, or "The Ruhr District's Showcase". A resident adopts such slogans, even if they have no personal experience of the feature in question but have heard simply that other people set great store by it.

This leads to an important insight. Residents observing parts of the city are unsure how to interpret them whenever coming across phenomena that have no relevance to their own life, which is to say, no social relevance. Picturesqueness alone, combined with existential irrelevance, is not conducive to legibility. Such parts of the city or architectural structures are read more easily in terms of secondary characteristics, which are more indicative of the social background. A residential street lined—from the connoisseur's viewpoint—with striking nineteenth-century buildings, let's say, is judged by any passerby one cares to ask, in terms either of the make of cars parked in front of the buildings, or the matter of how well-kept, neglected, or full of trash the front yards may be. And it is such secondary characteristics, in fact, which tell us something about the street's current social significance.

For any city resident unbiased by knowledge of art history the objects in question are significant, not as architectural monuments but as institutions. The city resident's visible environment is therefore only of secondary importance; the invisible circumstances that shape the environment are of much greater relevance. What types of people live here? How high is the rent? Who owns the house? What are the house rules? Are children allowed to make noise? Are the local shops affordable? Will the street be considered a good address when I apply for a job? This sort of information outweighs by far the fact that the street was built around 1880, or that its style reflects English Neo-Gothic of the 1840s, which derived in turn from certain Tudor revivals in eighteenth-century English castles. Given this primacy of the "invisible" dimension, the apparently contradictory insights acquired through primarily sociological research (such as that of Herbert J. Gans),[13] and primarily cognitive research (in Kevin Lynch's sense of the term),[14] seem to me to lead to the same results.

If we acknowledge, in consequence, that the city resident's environment is first and foremost a social environment, and that urban design has a role to play only insofar as it conveys social information, and hence a sense of social belonging, [...] the question arises as to why anyone ever strives to create good architecture? Or, in other words: What is design? Architectural and social significance have coincided at certain moments in history, perhaps purely by fluke. Such good fortune in any event allows us a brief glimpse of Paradise; what becomes visible is the ideal of a society rid of conflict and living in harmony with its self-built environment; without history, certainly, but happy (perhaps). In our constantly shifting society, such buildings immediately become monuments; they become historical because history refutes the supposedly happy moment, and exposes its contradictory foundations. So buildings of the past, thanks to their design and fragmented condition, make us aware of the shifts in power relations that lie behind us, and of those that lie ahead.

To recapitulate briefly: urban design as such does not exist; rather, it is a construct, the outcome of how we have learned to interpret whatever we see. For the eye schooled in art history, visible elements merge in a certain design; for the average city resident, social relations constitute the environment. The latter primarily reads their own environment not in terms of architecture but in terms of the secondary characteristics that inform about the current use and ranking of streets and neighborhoods.

To design the city is therefore primarily a matter, not simply of caring for buildings but of creating an urban environment that fosters a strong sense of community.

348

1. Section heading by the editors of this book.

2. Section heading by the editors of this book.

3. Section heading by the editors of this book.

4. Section heading by the editors of this book.

5. Section heading by the editors of this book.

6. A reference to Werner Hegemann's book *Das steinerne Berlin* [Berlin of Stone] (Berlin: Kiepenheuer, 1930).

7. Max Bill's book *Die Gute Form* (1957) decisively shaped the criteria propounded at the time for functional yet aesthetically pleasing "timeless" design. The German Ministry of Economics and Technology awarded the "Federal Prize for Good Form" for the first time in 1969. Since 2006, it has been presented annually under the name "Design Award of the Federal Republic of Germany".

8. Christopher Alexander: *A Pattern Language. Towns, Buildings, Construction* (New York: Oxford University Press , 1977).

9. Kevin Lynch, *The Image of the City* (Cambridge, MA: MIT Press, 1960).

10. Herbert J. Gans, *The Levittowners: Ways of Life and Politics in a New Suburban Community* (New York: Routledge & Kegan Paul, 1960/ New York: Random House, 1967).

11. Anne Cauquelin, *La ville la nuit* (Paris: Presse Universitaires de France, 1977).

12. The German word *Gestalt* has several meanings, among which number design, form, guise, cast, and stature.

13. Herbert J. Gans, *The Levittowners: Ways of Life and Politics in a New Suburban Community* (New York: Routledge & Kegan Paul, 1960/ New York: Random House, 1967). For more on Gans and Lynch, see also the paper "On the Design of Everyday Life".

14. Kevin Lynch, *The Image of the City* (Cambridge, MA: MIT Press, 1960).

Things

The fourth chapter is dedicated to theories that
extend societal agency to non-human actors.
First, in *Agency of Things*, Bruno Latour examines
the political performance of objects and urban
spaces, and claims that any material form should
be understood as social assembly in which human
and non-human actors both perform. In *Urbanity
of Things*, Manuel de Solà-Morales defines
urban form as the density of specific elements and
episodes that relate people to things and uses the
term "skin of the city" to describe the accumulation
of all things through which we can experience
and shape the city.

Bruno Latour
Agency of Things

I. Bruno Latour, *Reassembling the Social. An Introduction to Actor-Network-Theory* (Oxford: Oxford University Press, 2005), 64–65, 71–74.

II. Bruno Latour, "From Realpolitik to Dingpolitik or How to Make Things Public", in: Bruno Latour and Peter Weibel, *Making Things Public—Atmospheres of Democracy*, exhibition catalogue (Cambridge, MA: MIT Press, 2005), 4–31.

The starting point of this thesis is the difference between "social" as in "social ties" and "social" as in "associations"—bearing in mind that the second meaning is closer to the original etymology. Most often in social sciences, "social" designates a specific *type of link*, distinct from "material", "biological", "psychological", and "economic" connections. I argue that the definition of the term is different: it doesn't designate a static link, but rather is the name of a *movement*, a displacement, a transformation, a translation, an enrollment. It is an association between entities which are in no way recognizable as being social in the ordinary manner, except during the brief moment when they are reshuffled. Thus, social will be interpreted here as the name of a type of momentary association which is characterized by the way it gathers people, objects, and other elements together into new shapes.[1]

Taking the first definition, *action* is limited a priori to what "intentional", "meaningful" humans do. Thus, it is hard to see how a hammer, a basket, a doorstop, a cat, a rug, a mug, a list, or a tag could *act*. They might exist in the domain of "material" "causal" relations, but not in the "reflexive" "symbolic" domain of social relations. By contrast, if we stick to our alternative definition of the social and start from the controversies about actors and agencies, then *any thing* that modifies a state of affairs by making a difference is an actor—or, if it has no figuration yet, an actant. Thus, the questions to ask about any agent are simply the following: Does it make a difference in the course of some other agent's action or not? Is there some trial that allows someone to detect this difference?

The rather common-sense answer should be a resounding "yes". If you can, with a straight face, maintain that hitting a nail with and without a hammer, boiling water with and without a kettle, fetching provisions with or without a basket, walking in the street with or without clothes, zapping a TV with or without a

355

remote, slowing down a car whether there is a speed bump or not, keeping track of your inventory with or without a list, or running a company with or without bookkeeping are exactly the same activities, that the introduction of these mundane implements change "nothing important" to the realization of the tasks, then you are ready to migrate to the Far Land of the Social and disappear from this lowly one. For all other members of society, it does make a difference and so these implements, according to our definition, are actors or, more precisely, participants in the course of action waiting to be given a figuration.

This, of course, does not mean that these participants "determine" the action, that baskets "cause" the fetching of provisions or that hammers "impose" the hitting of the nail. Such a reversal in the direction of influence would be simply a way to transform objects into the causes whose effects would be transported through human action now limited to a trail of mere intermediaries. Rather, it means that there may exist many metaphysical shades between full causality and sheer inexistence. In addition to "determining" and serving as a "backdrop for human action", things might authorize, allow, afford, encourage, permit, suggest, influence, block, render possible, forbid, and so on.[2] Our project, Actor–Network–Theory (ANT) is not the empty claim that objects do things "instead" of human actors: it simply says that no science of the social can even begin if the question of who and what participates in the action is not first of all thoroughly explored, even though this might mean permitting elements that, for lack of a better term, we would call *non-human*. This expression, like all the others chosen by ANT is meaningless in itself. It does not designate a domain of reality. It does not designate little goblins with red hats acting at atomic levels, only that the analyst should be prepared to look in order to account for the durability and extension of any interaction.[3] The goal of ANT is simply to extend the list and modify the shapes and figures of those assembled as participants and to design a way to make them act as a durable whole.

356

For sociologists focusing on associations, what is new is not the multiplicity of objects a course of action mobilizes along its trail—no one ever denied they were there by the thousands; what is new is that objects are suddenly highlighted not only as being full-blown actors, but also as being what explains the contrasted landscape we started with, the overarching powers of society, the huge asymmetries, the crushing exercise of power. This is the surprise from which sociologists of associations wish to start instead of considering, as do most of their colleagues, that the question is obviously closed and that objects do nothing, at least nothing comparable or even *connectable* to human social action, and that if they can sometimes "express" power relations, "symbolize" social hierarchies, "reinforce" social inequalities, "transport" social power, "objectify" inequality, and "reify" gender relations, they cannot be at the origin of social activity.

This, for me, has always been a great surprise: How is it that, in spite of this massive and ubiquitous phenomenon, sociology remains "without object"? It is even more startling when you realize that this discipline emerged a full century after the Industrial Revolution and has been evolving in parallel with the largest and most intensive technical developments since the Neolithic. Not only that, but how to explain that so many social scientists pride themselves in considering "social meaning" instead of "mere" material relations, "symbolic dimension" instead of "brute causality"? Much like sex during the Victorian period, objects are discussed nowhere and felt everywhere. They exist, naturally, but they are never given a thought, a social thought. Like humble servants, they live on the margins of the social doing most of the work but never allowed to be represented as such. There seems to be no way, no conduit, no entry point for them to be knitted together with the same wool as the rest of the social ties. The more radical thinkers want to attract attention to humans in the margins and at the periphery, the less they speak of objects. As if a damning curse had been cast onto things, they remain asleep like the servants

357

of some enchanted castle. Yet, as soon as they are freed from the spell, they start shuddering, stretching, and muttering. They begin to swarm in all directions, shaking the human actors, waking them out of their dogmatic sleep. Would it be too childish to say that ANT played the role of the Prince Charming's kiss tenderly touching Sleeping Beauty's lips? At any rate, it is because it was an object-oriented sociology for object-oriented humans that this school of thought was noticed in the first place—and that it makes sense to write an introduction to it.

From Realpolitik to Dingpolitik
or How to Make Things Public

Some conjunctions of planets are so ominous, astrologers used to II. 4 say, that it seems safer to stay at home in bed and wait until Heaven sends a more auspicious message. It's probably the same with political conjunctions. They are presently so hopeless that it seems prudent to stay as far away as possible from anything political and to wait for the passing away of all the present leaders, terrorists, commentators, and buffoons who strut about the public stage.

Astrology, however, is as precarious an art as political science; behind the nefarious conjunctions of hapless stars, other much dimmer alignments might be worth pondering. With the political period triggering such desperation, the time seems right to shift our attention to other ways of considering public matters. And "matters" are precisely what might be put center stage. Yes, public *matters*, but how?

While the German Reich has given us two world wars, the German language has provided us with the word *Realpolitik* to describe a positive, materialist, no-nonsense, interest only, matter-of-fact way of dealing with naked power relations. Although this "reality", at the time of Bismarck, might have appeared as a welcome change after the cruel idealisms it aimed to replace, it strikes us now as deeply *unrealistic*. In general, to invoke "realism" when talking about politics is something one should not do without trembling and shaking (Fig. 1). The beautiful word "reality" has been damned by the too many crimes committed in its name.

What Is the Res of Res Publica?

By the German neologism *Dingpolitik*, we wish to designate a risky and tentative set of experiments in probing just what it could mean for political thought to turn "things" around and to become slightly more *realistic* than has been attempted up to now. A few years ago, computer scientists invented the marvelous expression of "object-oriented" software to describe a new way to program their computers. We wish to use this metaphor to ask the question: "What would an *object-oriented* democracy look like?"

The general hypothesis is so simple that it might sound trivial—but being trivial might be part of what it is to become a "realist" in politics. We might be more connected to each other by our worries, our matters of concern, and the issues we care for than by any other set of values, opinions, attitudes, or principles. The experiment is certainly easy to make. Just go in your head over any set of contemporary issues: the entry of Turkey into the European Union, the Islamic veil in France, the spread of genetically modified organisms in Brazil, the pollution of the river near your home, the breaking down of Greenland's glaciers, the diminishing return of your pension funds, the closing of your daughter's factory, the repairs to be made in your apartment, the rise and fall of stock options, the latest beheading by fanatics in Falluja, the last American election. For every one of these objects, you see spewing out of them a different set of passions, indignations, opinions, as well as a different set of interested parties and different ways of carrying out their partial resolution.

359

Fig. 1 Clinton's cat Socks, or the degree zero of politics, Little Rock,
Arkansas, 1992. Chelsea Clinton's cat Socks gets the attention of
photographers on the sidewalk outside the fenced Arkansas Governor's
Mansion in Little Rock. Socks strolled about a two-block area with
photographers in tow. President-elect Bill Clinton was working on his
transition and preparing for a trip to Washington and a meeting with
President George H. W. Bush. Photo: Greg Gibson.

It's clear that each object—each issue—generates a different pattern of emotions and disruptions, of disagreements and agreements. There might be no continuity, no coherence in our opinions, but there is a hidden continuity and a hidden coherence in what we are attached to. Each object gathers around itself a different assembly of relevant parties. Each object triggers new occasions to passionately differ and dispute. Each object may also offer new ways of achieving closure without having to agree on much else. In other words, objects—taken as so many issues—bind all of us in ways that map out a public space profoundly different from what is usually recognized under the label of "the political" (Fig. 2). It is this space, this hidden geography, that we wish to explore here.

It's not unfair to say that political philosophy has often been the victim of a strong object avoidance tendency. From Hobbes to Rawls, from Rousseau to Habermas, many procedures have been devised to assemble the relevant parties, to authorize them to contract, to check their degree of representativity, to discover the ideal speech conditions, to detect the legitimate closure, to write the good constitution. But when it comes down to *what* is at issue, namely the object of concern that brings them together, not a word is uttered. In a strange way, political science is mute just at the moment when the objects of concern should be brought in and made to speak up loudly. Contrary to what the powerful etymology of their most cherished word should imply, their *res publica* does not seem to be loaded with too many *things*. Procedures to authorize and legitimize are important, but it's only half of what is needed to assemble. The other half lies in the issues themselves, in the *matters* that matter, in the *res* that creates a *public* around it. They need to be represented, authorized, legitimated, and brought to bear inside the relevant assembly.

What we call an "object-oriented democracy" tries to redress this bias in much of political philosophy, that is, to bring

361

together two different meanings of the word *representation* that have been kept separate in theory although they have remained always mixed in practice. The first one, so well known in schools of law and political science, designates the ways to gather the legitimate people around some issue. In this case, a representation is said to be faithful if the right procedures have been followed. The second one, well known in science and in technology, presents or rather *represents* what is the object of concern to the eyes and ears of those who have been assembled around it. In this case, a representation is said to be good if the matters at hand have been accurately portrayed. Realism implies that the same degree of attention be given to the two aspects of what it is to represent an issue. The first question draws a sort of place, sometimes a circle, which might be called an assembly, a gathering, a meeting, a council; the second question brings *into* this newly created locus a topic, a concern, an issue, a *topos*. But the two have to be taken together: *Who* is to be concerned; *What* is to be considered?

When Thomas Hobbes instructed his engraver on how to sketch the famous frontispiece for *Leviathan*, he had his mind full of optical metaphors and illusion machines he had seen in his travels through Europe.[4] A third meaning of this ambiguous and ubiquitous word "representation", the one with which artists are most familiar, had to be called for to solve, this time visually, the problem of the composition of the "Body Politic". Up to now it has remained a puzzle: How to represent, and through which medium, the sites where people meet to discuss their matters of concern? It's precisely what we are tackling here.[5] Shapin and Schaffer might have renewed Hobbes's problem even more tellingly when they redrew his monster for *their* frontispiece and equipped his left arm not with the Bishop's crosier but with Boyle's air pump.[6] From now on, the powers of science are just as important to consider: How do they assemble, and around which matters of concern?

362

Fig. 2 Presidential hopefuls US Vice President Al Gore and former US Senator Bill Bradley listen to a question on 17 December 1999 during an ABC TV Nightline town hall meeting moderated by Ted Koppel at Daniel Webster College in Nashua, New Hampshire. Photo: Luke Frazza.

Fig. 3   Ambrogio Lorenzetti, *The Effects of the Good Government*, 1338–1339, fresco (detail), Palazzo Pubblico, Siena, Sala dei Nove. Photo: Lensini Siena.

But in addition to the visual puzzle of assembling composite bodies, another puzzle should strike us in those engravings. A simple look at them clearly proves that the "Body Politic" is not only made of people! It is thick with things: clothes, a huge sword, immense castles, large cultivated fields, crowns, ships, cities, and an immensely complex technology of gathering, meeting, cohabiting, enlarging, reducing, and focusing. In addition to the throng of little people summed up in the crowned head of the Leviathan, there are objects everywhere.

To be crowded with objects that nonetheless are not really integrated into our definition of politics is even more tellingly visible in the famous fresco painted by Lorenzetti in Siena's city hall (Fig. 3).[7] Many scholars have deciphered for us the complex meaning of the emblems representing the Good and the Bad Government, and have traced their complex genealogy. But what is most striking for a contemporary eye is the massive presence of cities, landscapes, animals, merchants, dancers, and the ubiquitous rendering of light and space. The Bad Government is not simply illustrated by the devilish figure of Discordia but also through the dark light, the destroyed city, the ravaged landscape, and the suffocating people. The Good Government is not simply personified by the various emblems of Virtue and Concordia but also through the transparency of light, its well-kept architecture, its well-tended landscape, its diversity of animals, the ease of its commercial relations, its thriving arts. Far from being simply a décor for the emblems, the fresco requests us to become attentive to a subtle ecology of Good and Bad Government. And modern visitors, attuned to the new issues of bad air, hazy lights, destroyed ecosystems, ruined architecture, abandoned industry, and delocalized trades are certainly ready to include in their definition of politics a whole new ecology loaded with things.[8] Where has political philosophy turned its distracted gaze while so many objects were drawn under its very nose?

Peter Sloterdijk recently proposed a fable.[9] He imagined that the US Air Force should have added to its military paraphernalia a "pneumatic parliament" that could be parachuted at the rear of the front, just after the liberating forces of the Good had defeated the forces of Evil. On hitting the ground, this parliament would unfold and be inflated just like your rescue dinghy is supposed to do when you fall in the water. Ready to enter and take your seat, your finger still red from the indelible ink that proves you have exercised your voting duty, instant democracy would thus be delivered! The lesson of this simile is easy to draw. To imagine a parliament without its material set of complex instruments, "air-conditioning" pumps, local ecological requirements, material infrastructure, and long-held habits is as ludicrous as to try to parachute such an inflatable parliament into the middle of Iraq. By contrast, probing an object-oriented democracy is to research what are the material conditions that may render the air breathable again.

Furthermore, take the terrifying example offered by the now infamous speech former Secretary of State Colin Powell gave to the United Nations on 5 February 2003, about the unambiguous and undisputable fact of the presence of weapons of mass destructions in Iraq (Fig. 4).[10] No doubt, the first half of the representation—namely the assembly of legitimate speakers and listeners—was well taken care of. All of those sitting around the UN Security Council horseshoe table had a right to be there. But the same can't be said of the second half, namely the representation of the facts of the matter presented by the Secretary of State. Every one of the slides was a blatant lie—and the more that time has passed, the more blatant it has become. And yet their showing was prefaced by these words: "My colleagues, every statement I make today is backed up by sources, solid sources. *These are not assertions*. What we are giving you are *facts* and conclusions based on solid intelligence" [emphasis the author's own]. Never has the difference between facts and assertions been more abused than on this day.

To assemble is one thing; to represent to the eyes and ears of those assembled what is at stake is another. An object-oriented democracy should be concerned as much by the procedure to detect the relevant parties as to the methods to bring into the center of the debate the proof of what it is to be debated. This second set of procedures to bring in the object of worry has several old names: *eloquence*, or more pejorative, *rhetoric*, or, even more derogatory, *sophistry*. And yet these are just the right labels that we might need to rescue from the dustbin of history.[11] Mr. Powell tried to distinguish the rhetoric of assertions from the undisputable power of facts. He failed miserably. Having no truth, he had no eloquence either. Can we do better? Can we trace again the frail conduits through which truths and proofs are allowed to enter the sphere of politics?

Unwittingly, the secretary of state put us on a track where the abyss between assertions and facts might be a nice "rhetorical" ploy, but it has lost its relevance. It would imply, on the one hand, that there would be matters of fact which some enlightened people would have unmediated access to. On the other hand, disputable assertions would be practically worthless, useful only insofar as they could feed the subjective passions of interested crowds. On one side would be the truth and no mediation, no room for

367

Fig. 4   The United Nations Security Council meets at the UN headquarters to hear evidence of Iraq's weapons program presented by US Secretary of State Colin Powell on Wednesday, 5 February 2003. Photo: Richard Drew.

discussion; on the other side would be opinions, many obscure intermediaries, perhaps some hecklings. Through the use of this indefatigable cliché, the "pneumatic parliament" is now equipped with a huge screen on which thoroughly transparent facts are displayed. Those who remain unconvinced prove by their resistance how irrational they are; they have unfortunately fallen prey to subjective passions. And sure enough, having aligned so many "indisputable" facts behind his position, since the "dispute" was *still* going on, Powell had to close it arbitrarily by a show of unilateral force. Facts and forces, in spite of so many vibrant declarations, always walk in tandem.

The problem is that transparent, unmediated, undisputable facts have recently become rarer and rarer. To provide complete undisputable proof has become a rather messy, pesky, risky business. And to offer a *public* proof, big enough and certain enough to convince the whole world of the presence of a phenomenon or of a looming danger, seems now almost beyond reach—and always was.[12] The same American administration that was content with a few blurry slides "proving" the presence of non-existing weapons in Iraq is happy to put scare quotes around the proof of much vaster, better validated, more imminent threats, such as global climate change, diminishing oil reserves, increasing inequality. Is it not time to say: "Mr. Powell, given what you have done with facts, we would much prefer you to leave them aside and let us instead compare mere *assertions* with one another. Don't worry, even with such an inferior type of proof we might nonetheless come to a conclusion, and this one will not be arbitrarily cut short"?[13] Either we should despair of politics and abandon the hope of providing public proofs altogether, or we should abandon the worn-out cliché of incontrovertible matters of fact. Could we do better and manage to really conclude a dispute with "disputable" assertions? After all, when Aristotle—surely not a cultural relativist! —introduced the word "rhetoric" it was precisely to mean *proofs*, incomplete to be sure but proofs nonetheless.[14]

This is what we wish to attempt: Where matters of fact have failed, let's try what I have called matters of concern. What we are trying to register here in this catalog is a huge sea change in our conceptions of science, our grasps of facts, our understanding of objectivity. For too long, objects have been wrongly portrayed as matters of fact. This is unfair to them, unfair to science, unfair to objectivity, unfair to experience. They are much more interesting, variegated, uncertain, complicated, far reaching, heterogeneous, risky, historical, local, material, and networky than the pathetic version offered for too long by philosophers. Rocks are not simply there to be kicked at, desks to be thumped at. "Facts are facts are facts"? Yes, but they are also a lot of other things *in addition*.[15]

For those like Mr. Powell, who have long been accustomed to getting rid of all opposition by claiming the superior power of facts, such a sea change might be met with cries of derision: "relativism", "subjectivism", "irrationalism", "mere rhetoric", "sophistry"! They might see the new life of facts as so much subtraction. Quite right! It subtracts a lot of their power because it renders their lives more difficult. Think of that: They might have to enter into the new arenas for good and finally make their point to the bitter end. They might actually have to publicly prove their assertions *against other assertions* and come to a closure without thumping and kicking, without alternating wildly between indisputable facts and indisputable shows of terror. So let's explore realist gestures other than just thumping and kicking. Let's imagine a *new eloquence*. Is it asking too much of our public conversation? It's great to be convinced, but it would be even better to be convinced *by some evidence*.[16]

Our notions of politics have been thwarted for too long by an absurdly unrealistic epistemology. Accurate facts are hard to come by, and the harder they are, the more they entail some costly equipment, a longer set of mediations, more delicate proofs. Transparency and immediacy are bad for science as well as for politics; they would make both suffocate.[17] What we need is to be able to bring inside the assemblies *divisive* issues with their long retinue of complicated *proof-giving* equipment. No unmediated access to agreement; no unmediated access to the facts of the matter. After all, we are used to rather arcane procedures for voting and electing. Why should we suddenly imagine an eloquence so devoid of means, tools, tropes, tricks, and knacks that it would bring the facts into the arenas through some uniquely magical transparent idiom? If politics is earthly, so is science.

From Object to Things

It's to underline this shift from a cheapened notion of objectivity to costly proofs that we want to resurrect the word "Ding" and use the neologism *Dingpolitik* as a substitute for *Realpolitik*. The latter lacks realism when it talks about power relations as well as when it talks about mere facts. It does not know how to deal with "indisputability". To discover one's own real naked interest requires probably the most convoluted and farfetched inquiry there is. To be brutal is not enough to turn you into a hard-headed realist.

As every reader of Heidegger knows, or as every glance at an English dictionary under the heading "Thing" will certify, the old word "Thing" or "Ding" originally designated a certain type of archaic assembly.[18] Many parliaments in Nordic and Saxon nations still activate the old root of this etymology: Norwegian congressmen assemble in the *Storting*; Icelandic deputies called the equivalent of "thingmen" gather in the *Althing*;[19] Isle of Man seniors used to gather around the *Ting*;[20] the German landscape is dotted with *Thingstätten*, and you can see in many places the circles of stones where the Thing used to stand.[21] Thus, long before designating an object thrown out of the political sphere and standing there objectively and independently, the *Ding* or Thing has for many centuries meant the issue that brings people together *because* it divides them. The same etymology lies dormant in the Latin *res*, the Greek *aitia*, and the French or Italian *cause*. Even the Russian *soviet* still dreams of bridges and churches.[22]

Fig. 5 Althing in Thingvellir (fiingvellir), Iceland. In 930 A.D. chieftains in Iceland gathered in a natural amphitheater and formed the world's first parliament, the Althing. The meeting place was called Thingvellir ("parliament plains"), and over the next 300 years representatives journeyed here once a year to elect leaders, argue cases, and settle disputes. Photo: Sabine Himmelsbach.

Of all the eroded meanings left by the slow crawling of political geology, none is stranger to consider than the Icelandic *Althing*, since the ancient "thingmen"—what we would call "congressmen" or MPs—had the amazing idea of meeting in a desolate and sublime site that happens to sit smack in the middle of the fault line that marks the meeting place of the Atlantic and European tectonic plates (Fig. 5). Not only do Icelanders manage to remind us of the old sense of *Ding*, but they also dramatize to the utmost how much these political questions have also become questions of nature. Are not all parliaments now divided by the nature of things as well as by the din of the crowded *Ding*? Has the time not come to bring the res back to the res publica?[23] This is why we have tried to build the provisional and fragile assembly of our show on as many fault lines from as many tectonic plates as possible.

The point of reviving this old etymology is that we don't assemble because we agree, look alike, feel good, are socially compatible or wish to fuse together but because we are brought by divisive matters of concern into some neutral, isolated place in order to come to some sort of provisional makeshift (dis) agreement. If the *Ding* designates both those who assemble because they are concerned as well as what causes their concerns and divisions, it should become the center of our attention: *Back to Things!* Is this not a more engaging political slogan?

But how strange is the shape of the things we should go back to. They no longer have the clarity, transparency, obviousness of matters of fact; they are not made of clearly delineated, discrete objects that would be bathing in some translucent space like the beautiful anatomical drawings of Leonardo, or the marvelous wash drawings of Gaspard Monge, or the clear-cut "isotypes" devised by Otto Neurath.[24] Matters of fact now appear to our eyes as depending on a delicate aesthetic of painting, drawing, lighting, gazing, and convening, something that has been elaborated over four centuries and that might be changing now before our very eyes.[25] There has been an aesthetic of matters of fact, of objects, of

Gegenstände. Can we devise an aesthetic of matters-of-concern of Things? This is one of the (too many!) topics we wish to explore here.[26]

Gatherings is the translation that Heidegger used, to talk about those Things, those sites able to assemble mortals and gods, humans and nonhumans. There is more than a little irony in extending this meaning to what Heidegger and his followers loved to hate, namely science, technology, commerce, industry, and popular culture.[27] And yet this is just what we intend to do in this book: the objects of science and technology, the aisles of supermarkets, financial institutions, medical establishments, computer networks—even the catwalks of fashion shows![28]—offer paramount examples of hybrid forums and agoras, of the gatherings that have been eating away at the older realm of pure objects bathing in the clear light of the modernist gaze. Who could dream of a better example of hybrid forums than the scale models used by architects all over the world to assemble those able to build them at scale?[29] Or the thin felt pen used by draughtsmen to imagine new landscapes?[30] When we say "Public matters!" or "Back to Things!" we are not trying to go back to the old materialism of *Realpolitik*, because *matter itself* is up for grabs as well. To be materialist now implies that one enters a labyrinth more intricate than that built by Daedalus.

In the same fatal month of February 2003, another stunning example of this shift from object to things was demonstrated by the explosion of the Columbia shuttle. "Assembly drawing" is how engineers call the invention of the blueprint.[31] But the word assembly sounds odd once the shuttle has exploded and its debris has been gathered in a huge hall where inquirers from a specially designed commission are trying to discover what happened to the shuttle. They are now provided with an "exploded view" of a highly complex technical object (Figs. 6 and 7). But what has exploded is our capacity to understand what objects are when they have become *Ding*. How sad that we need catastrophes to

Fig. 6   Hangar at Kennedy Space Center in Cape Canaveral, Florida, 2003. NASA
crash investigators place debris from the Space Shuttle Columbia onto a grid
on the floor of a hangar. NASA is attempting to reassemble debris from the shuttle
to learn what caused Columbia to break up during reentry. NASA Mission Control
lost contact with the Space Shuttle Columbia during the reentry phase of mission
STS–107 on 1 February 2003 and later learned that the shuttle had broken up over
Texas. Debris from the wreckage drifted hundreds of miles from central Texas to
Louisiana. All seven astronauts onboard the shuttle died in the crash. Photo: NASA.

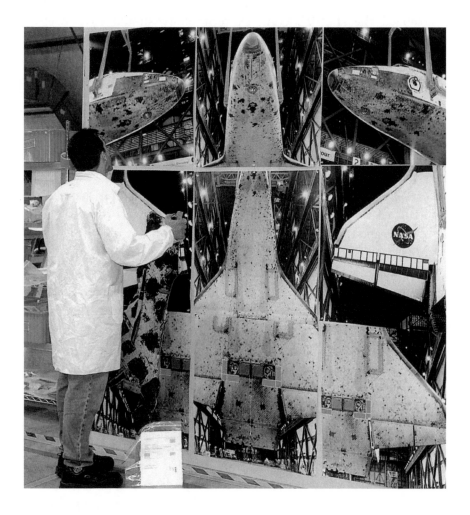

Fig. 7 NASA crash investigator, Kennedy Space Center in Cape Canaveral, Florida, 2003.
A member of the space shuttle reconstruction project team holds a piece of wreckage
and tries to locate it on pictures of the Columbia taken while the orbiter was in the vehicle
assembly building. Photo: Kim Shiflett.

remind us that when the Columbia was shown on its launching pad in its complete, autonomous, objective form that such a view was even more of a lie than Mr. Powell's presentation of the "facts" of WMD. It's only *after* the explosion that everyone realized the shuttle's complex technology should have been drawn with the NASA bureaucracy *inside* of it in which they, too, would have to fly.[32]

The object, the *Gegenstand*, may remain outside of all assemblies but not the *Ding*. Hence the question we wish to raise: What are the various shapes of the *assemblies* that can make sense of all those *assemblages*? Questions we address are to the three types of representation brought together in this show: political, scientific, and artistic.

Through some amazing quirk of etymology, it just happens that the same root has given birth to those twin brothers: the *Demon* and the *Demos*—and those two are more at war with each other than Eteocles and Polynices ever were.[33] The word "demos" that makes half of the much vaunted word "demo-cracy" is haunted by the demon, yes, the devil, because they share the same Indo-European root *da*—to divide.[34] If the demon is such a terrible threat, it's because it divides in two. If the demos is such a welcome solution, it's because it also divides in two. A paradox? No, it's because we ourselves are so divided by so many contradictory attachments that we have to assemble.

We might be familiar with Jesus's admonition against Satan's power,[35] but the same power of division is also what provides the division/divide, namely the *sharing* of the same territory. Hence the *people*, the *demos*, are made up of those who share the same space and are divided by the same contradictory worries. How could an object-oriented democracy ignore such a vertiginous uncertainty? When the knife hovers around the cake of common wealth to be divided in shares, it may divide and let loose the *demon* of civil strife, or it may cut equal shares and let the *demos* be happily apportioned. Strangely enough, we are divided and yet might have

376

Fig. 9 "Moyens expéditifs du peuple français pour démeubler un aristocrate" [The French people's quick measure of removing an aristocracy], Révolutions de France et de Brabant, engraving. While sacking a noble's house, the mob is taking a careful look at what they throw out of the windows, creating, involuntarily, a Thing around which they assemble.

Fig. 8 Saint George, San Giorgio Maggiore, Venice. Photo: Fondazione Cini.

to divide, that is to share, even more. The "demos" is haunted by the demon of division! Politics is a branch of teratology: from Leviathan to devils, from Discordia to Behemoth, and soon a whole array of ghosts and phantoms. Tricks and treats all the way down.

No Representation without Re-presentations

Michael Frayn's play *Democracy* begins with the grating noise of a worm, a little annelid that at the onset is supposed to make the whole decadent West crumble like a wooden house eaten up by termites while the sturdy and united DDR emerges from chaos.[36] The same noisy worm is heard again at the end of the play, but this time it's the whole Soviet Bloc that, unexpectedly, lies in dust while democracy—"the worst form of government, *except* for all the others", as Churchill famously said—keeps on munching and worming along.

A demon haunts politics but it might not be so much the demon of division—this is what is so devilish about it—but the demon of unity, totality, transparency, and immediacy. "Down with intermediaries! Enough spin! We are lied to! We have been betrayed." Those cries resonate everywhere, and everyone seems to sigh: "Why are we being so badly represented?" Columnists, educators, militants never tire of complaining of a "crisis of representation". They claim that the masses seem no longer to feel at ease with what its elites are telling them. Politicians, they say, have become aloof, unreal, surrealistic, virtual, and alien. An abysmal gap has opened between the "political sphere" and the "reality that people have to put up with". If this gap is yawning under our feet much like the Icelandic fault line, surely no *Dingpolitik* can ignore it.

But it might also be the case that half of such a crisis is due to what has been sold to the general public under the name of a faithful, transparent, and accurate representation.[37] We are asking from representation something it cannot possibly give, namely representation *without* any *re*-presentation, without any provisional assertions, without any imperfect proof, without any opaque layers of translations, transmissions, betrayals, without any complicated machinery of assembly, delegation, proof, argumentation, negotiation, and conclusion.

In 2002, in the course of the *Iconoclash* exhibition, we tried to explore the roots of a specific form of Western fanaticism. If only there was no image—that is, no mediation—the better our grasp of Beauty, Truth, and Piety would be. We visited the famous iconoclastic periods from the Byzantine to the Reformation, from Lenin's Red Square to Malevich's *Black Square* to less well-known struggles among iconoclasts in mathematics, physics, and the other sciences.[38] We wanted to compare with one another the various interference patterns created by all those forms of contradictory attitudes toward images. Scientists, artists, and clerks have been multiplying imageries, intermediaries, mediations, and representations while tearing them down and resurrecting them with even more forceful, beautiful, inspired, objective forms. We reckoned that it was not absurd to explore the whole Western tradition by following up such a ubiquitous double bind. Hence the neologism Icono*clash* to point at this ambivalence, this other demonic division: "Alas, we cannot do anything without image!" "Fortunately, we cannot do anything without image!" (Fig. 10).[39]

Iconoclash was not an iconoclastic show but a show *about* iconoclasm; not a critical show but a show *about* critique. The urge to debunk was no longer a *resource* to feed from, we hoped, but a *topic* to be carefully examined. Like the slave who was asked to remind emperors during their triumphs that they were mere mortals, we had asked an angel to come down and suspend in mid-air the arm that held the hammer, an angel that could mutter in the ear of the triumphant idol-breakers: "Beware! Consider what you strike at with so much glee. Look first at what you might risk destroying *instead*!" Once the destructive gesture was suspended, we discovered that no iconoclast had ever struck at the right target. Their blows always drifted sideways. For this reason, even St. George, we thought, looked more interesting without his spear.[40]

Fig. 10 *The Mercator Atlas* by Gerard Mercator, 1609, frontispiece.

Our aim was to move the collective attention, as the subtitle of the show, "*beyond* the image wars in science, religion, and art", clearly indicated. This "beyond" was drawn, very simply, by taking into consideration the other half of what they were all doing: Those we were following were never simply tearing down idols, burning fetishes, debunking ideologies, exposing scandals, breaking down old forms but *also* were putting ideas onto pedestals, invoking deities, proving facts, establishing theories, building institutions, creating new forms, and *also* destroying unexpectedly and unwittingly other things they had not known that they cherished so much. By bringing destruction, blunder, plunder, and construction together we hoped to foster a new respect for mediators.

Obviously, there is something in the way sequences of images create access to Beauty, Truth, and Piety that has been missed by idol-breakers over the ages. To summarize our attempt in one simile, I proposed to say that Moses, in addition to being tongue-twisted, might have also been a little hard of hearing and that's why he had understood "Thou shall not make unto thee any graven image" when he had been told: "Thou shall not *freeze frame*." If you stick to them, images are dangerous, blasphemous, idolatrous, but they are safe, innocent, indispensable if you learn how to jump from one image to the next. "Truth is image, but there is no image of Truth."[41] This solution might offer, we thought, a possible cure against fundamentalism, that is, the belief that without any representation you would be represented even better.

Iconoclash, however, carefully excluded politics. This was done on purpose. There is no activity where it is more difficult to pay due respect to mediators; no calling more despised than that of politicians; no sphere more inviting for irony, satire, debunking, derision than the political sphere; no idols more inviting for destruction than the Idols of the Forum; no discourse easier to deconstruct. On political rhetoric, critique has a field day. By kindergarten, toddlers have already grown cynical on all political matters. In a show that was *about* critique, adding politics would have skewed the whole project, and visitors would have left even more iconoclasts than when they had entered.

But once we have moved *beyond* the image wars, once we have regained a good grasp of the masses of intermediaries necessary to represent anything, once we have moved back to things, could we extend the same attention for mediators to the most despised activity, namely political *spin*? Is it possible now to tackle the question of political representation with care and respect? Even more extravagant: Is it possible to tackle it uncritically? Just try to imagine a show about politics that would not be about debunking, exposing, revealing, or smashing the idols down. Do you really want to take politics *positively*? Indeed.

"Disabled Persons of All Countries, Unite!"

What makes it so difficult to stare straight at the Gorgonian face of politics is that we seem to delight in adding to it some even more distorting traits. Not happy with Frankenstein, we want to hybridize it with Quasimodo. Monstrous it is, yet this is not a reason to transform it into a painting by Hieronymus Bosch. Or rather, Bosch is painting our own internal Hell, which might not bear that much of a relation with the *specific* monsters of politics.[42] What frightens us so much in collective action, the reason why we delight so much in despising it, is that we might see reflected in its distorted mirror our own grimacing faces. Are we not asking from the assembly something it cannot possibly deliver, so that talking positively of politics horrifies us because it's our limitations that we are not prepared to accept? If it's true that representations are so indispensable and yet so opaque, how well prepared are we to handle them? When hearing the call for assembling at the Thing, are we able to accept that we are radically and basically unfit to take a seat in it? Do we have the cognitive equipment required for this? Are we not, on the whole, totally *disabled*?

382

Instead of the radiant citizen standing up and speaking their mind by using solid common sense, as in Rockwell's famous painting *Freedom of Speech*, should we not look for an eloquence much more indirect, distorted, inconclusive? Let's tackle the question of politics from the point of view of our own weaknesses instead of projecting them first onto the politicians themselves! We could say that the blind lead the blind, the deaf speak eloquently to the deaf, the crippled are leading marches of dwarfs, or, rather, to avoid those biased words, let's say that we are all *politically-challenged*. How would it look if we were chanting this more radical and surely more realistic slogan: "Disabled persons of all countries, unite!"?[43] After all, was not Demosthenes, as much as Moses and many other legislators, speech-impaired?[44] Are we not all, when our time comes to speak up?

The cognitive deficiency of participants has been hidden for a long time because of the mental architecture of the dome in which the Body Politic was supposed to assemble. We were told that all of us—on entering this dome, this public sphere—had to leave aside in the cloakroom our own attachments, passions, and weaknesses. Taking our seat under the transparent crystal of the common good, through the action of some mysterious machinery, we would then be *collectively* endowed with more acute vision and higher virtue. At least that was the idea, no matter if the machinery was the social contract or some other metamorphosis: The selfish narrow-minded worm will re-emerge as a brightly colored collective butterfly.[45]

During the Enlightenment, architects took this virtual reality so literally that they actually drew and sometimes built those domes, globes, and palaces.[46] Later, during the time of revolutions, other builders gave a shape to this public sphere that was no longer limited to deputies and congressmen but included the whole people or the proletariat or the *Volk*.[47] They distributed speech differently, they imagined another way to compose the body, the procedures were modified, they arrayed much vaster masses, but it was still under a dome that they marched and chanted. From Boullée to Speer, from Pierre-Charles L'Enfant to the new Scottish Parliament, from John Soane to Norman Foster, it seemed possible for architects to provide a literal rendition of what it means to assemble in order to produce the common will (Figs. 11 and 12).[48] Individuals might be corrupted, feeble, or deficient, but above their weak heads there was a heaven, a sphere, a globe under which they all sat. Just before the French Revolution, Emmanuel-Joseph Sieyès imagined a parliament so big—and so virtual—that it extended to the whole of France, tier after tier, all the way to the farthest provinces.[49]

Unfortunately, much like the Tower of Babel, those "palaces of reason"—to use the name of many city halls in northern Italy—are no longer able to house the issues they were supposed to gather. Commentators on the "events" of May 1968 in France were amused to see that the turbulent demonstrating crowds passed by the National Assembly without even looking at it, as if its irrelevance was so great that it could not even invite abuses. How irrelevant they might seem now that the global has become the new name of the Body Politic. *Where* would you assemble the global? Certainly not under golden domes and kitsch frescoes where heroic senators and half-naked Republics are crowned by laurels descending from clouds. Why are politics always about imitation? There is Robespierre imitating Cicero, Lenin mimicking Robespierre. In the name of the common good, forests of Greek columns have been erected across the Western world—while the "mother of parliaments" in Westminster remained faithful to the dark, cramped, uncomfortable cave of stalls, spires, and gargoyles. Neo-gothic, neo-classic, neo-modern or neo-postmodern, those spaces were all "neo", that is, trying to imitate some venerated past.[50] But you might need more than imitation to build the new political assemblies. Covering the Reichstag with a transparent dome—in effect, fully opaque—as Foster did, doesn't seem nearly enough to absorb the new masses that are entering political arenas.

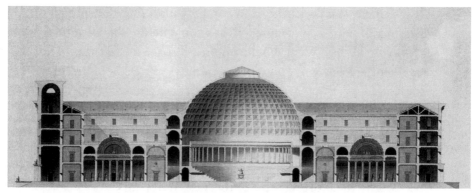

Fig. 11   Etienne-Louis Boullée, *Palais National*, plenary hall in section, 1792.

Fig. 12   Members of the International Medical Congress, London, 1881.

If it's true that a parliament is a complex machinery of speech, of hearing, of voting, of dealing, what should be the shapes adjusted to a *Dingpolitik*? What would a political space be that would not be "neo"? What would a truly contemporary style of assembly look like?

It's impossible to answer this question without gathering techniques of representation in different types of assemblies. The effect we wish to obtain is to show that parliaments are only a few of the machineries of representations among many others and not necessarily the most relevant or the best equipped.

It's likely that fundamentalists will not like the argument laid out here. They think they are safer without representation. They really believe that outside of any assembly, freed from all those cumbersome, tortuous, and opaque techniques, they will see better, farther, faster, and act more decisively. Inspired directly by the Good, often by their God, they despise the indirectness of representations. But realists might appreciate it because if we are all politically challenged, if there is no direct access to the general will, if no transparent dome gives any global visibility, if, at best, the blind lead the blind, then any small, even infinitesimal innovation in the practical ways of representing an issue will make a small—that is, huge—difference. Not for the fundamentalist but for the realists.

Ask the blind what difference it makes to have a white cane or not. Ask the deaf what difference it makes to be instrumented with a hearing aid or not. Ask the crippled what advantage they see in having a slightly better-adjusted wheelchair. If we are all handicapped, or rather politically-challenged, we need many different prostheses. Each object exhibited in the show and commented on in the catalog is such a crutch. We promise nothing more grandiose than a store of aids for the invalids who have been repatriated from the political frontlines—and haven't we all been badly mauled in recent years? Politics might be better taken as a branch of disability studies.

386

From an Assembly of Assemblies …
This article explores new possibilities with a great degree of freedom, on the ways of thought experiments, or rather *Gedankenausstellungen*. One of those attempts is to design not one assembly but rather an assembly of assemblies, so that, much like visitors of a fair, readers can *compare* the different types of representation. This is what we have attempted here.

Scientific laboratories, technical institutions, market-places, churches, and temples, financial trading rooms, internet forums, ecological disputes—without forgetting the very shape of the museum inside which we gather all those *membra disjecta*—are just some of the forums and agoras in which we speak, vote, decide, are decided upon, prove, are being convinced. Each has its own architecture, its own technology of speech, its complex set of procedures, its definition of freedom and domination, its ways of bringing together those who are concerned—and even more important, those who are not concerned—and what concerns them, its expedient way to obtain closure and come to a decision (Fig. 13). Why not render them comparable to one another?

387

Fig. 13   Arbre à palabre (Palaver Tree), Kabé, Mali, 1998.
Photo: Katherine Blouin and Vincent Demers.

After all, they have never stopped exchanging their properties: churches became temples before becoming city halls;[51] heads of state learned from artists how to create a public space through publicity;[52] it is deep inside monasteries that the complex voting procedures have been prepared and constitutions been written;[53] while laboratories are migrating to forums, the tasting of products borrows heavily from the laboratory;[54] supermarkets are taking more and more features that make them look like contested voting booths;[55] but even the most abstruse models of physics have to borrow heavily from social theories.[56] On the other hand, financial institutions seem to gather more information technologies than parliaments.[57] The quietest sites of nature have become some of the most contested and disputed battlegrounds.[58] As for the World Wide Web, it begins by being a mess and slowly imports all sorts of virtual architectures, but only very few reproduce the even more virtual space of the original parliaments;[59] artistic installations borrow more and more from scientific demonstrations;[60] technical know-how absorbs more and more elements from law.[61] There is no longer any river that flows from mountain to sea without being as equipped in speech-making instruments as humans are through opinion polls.[62] Such is the constant commerce, the ceaseless swapping, the endless crisscrossing of apparatuses, procedures, instruments, and customs that we have attempted to weave through this show and this catalog.

To collect such an assembly of assemblies, we have not tried to build around them an even bigger, a more all-encompassing dome. We have not tried to imagine that they would all be reducible to the European tradition of parliaments. On the contrary, we have offered to show how much they differ from one another by linking them through the humble and mundane back door of their representation machineries. We would like readers to move from one to the other by asking every time the three following questions: How do they manage to bring in the relevant parties? How do they manage to bring in the relevant issues? What change does it make in the way people make up their mind to be attached to things?

We hope that once this assembly of assemblies is deployed, that which passes for the political sphere—namely the parliaments and the offices of the executive branches—will appear as one type *among* many others, perhaps even a rather ill-equipped type. This approach to presenting the representation technology of parliamentary life will not seek to ridicule its antiquated ways or to criticize the European way of imagining public space. On the contrary, in the object-oriented conception, "parliament" is a technical term for "making things public" among many other forms of producing voices and connections among people. By this comparative visit, we seek to learn how parliaments—with a small "p"—could be enlarged or connected or modified or redrawn.[63] Instead of saying that "everything is political" by detecting dark forces hidden beneath all the other assemblages, we wish on the contrary to locate the tiny procedures of parliamentary assent and dissent, in order to see on what practical terms and through which *added* labor they could, one day, become pertinent. We hope readers will shop for the materials that might be needed later for them to build this new Noah's Ark: *The Parliament of Things*. Don't you hear the rain pouring relentlessly already? And Noah was a realist for sure.

... to an Assembly of Dissembling

There might just be another reason than the weak imagination of architects for not having a well-designed dome under which to assemble: Getting together might not be such a universal desire after all! No matter how wide you stretch it, the political horizon might be too small to encompass the whole Earth. Not only because parliaments are too tiny, not only because a parliament of parliaments would require the use of many different machineries now dispersed among different gatherings, but because the very idea of a political assembly might not be shareable in the end. The urge for political representation might be so much of a Western obsession that other people might *object* to being thus mobilized or called for. And this objection too has to be registered in our show.

If you read the UNESCO literature, it seems that the whole world aspires to become one under the aegis of democracy, transparent representation, and the rule of law. But what if every time this inflatable parliament was being dropped in, many other voices were raised: "No politics, please!" "No representation!" "Not with you," "No democracy, thanks," "Would you please stay as far away as possible?" "Leave us alone," "I'd rather not," "I prefer my king".[64] What if the disagreements were not the sort of issues that divide people in the normal state of things but were bearing instead on the very way to assemble at all? What if we had to imagine not an assembly of assemblies, not even an assembly of ways of assembling but an assembly of ways of *dissembling*? Would not that be a call for *disassembling* instead?

And yet this is just what happens when you begin to listen to other voices. Not because they are exotic, far-fetched, archaic, irrational, but because they too claim that making things public might be a much more protracted affair than entering into the realm of politics—even widely enlarged. Under the thin veneer of "democracy for all" will soon appear another crisis of representation, one much wider and deeper, because it will strike at the heart of what it is to represent at all.

Listen to the Japanese tradition: The very word "representation" strikes their ears as quaint and superficial.[65] Listen to the Jivaros: Their highly complex rhetoric of agonistic encounters aims at not meeting in the same assembly.[66] Listen to the Jihadists calling for the extension of the Oumma. The word "demokrata" remains an imported vocabulary that resonates more like a term of abuse than any deeply cherished value.[67] There are many other ways to assemble than under the aegis of a political intent.[68] And when highlanders of Papua New Guinea assemble to vote using a complex procedure imported by helicopter from Australian-trained scrutinizers, can we measure how much they have transformed it?[69] Even in our own lands obsessed by the transparent republic, much effort is put into doing just the opposite, that is, into making things *secret*.[70] What if one of the causes of fundamentalism were that all those other ways of gathering find themselves, in the end, badly represented? As if the usual garment of politics were too narrow for them? As if they never had room to assemble with the other things they are attached to, such as their gods, their divinities, their scruples of conscience. It's as if the whole definition of politics inherited from the conflicts between church and state had to be discussed again.[71]

To see politics as a problem of collecting, where if you don't manage it properly you disappear into chaos, seems to be the problem of only a fraction of humanity, for instance, those obsessed by the link between their cosmic and social orders.[72] And even among those, the idea of politics as speaking one's mind in the middle of an assembly seems to be a rather provincial notion. According to François Jullien, the Chinese tradition seems to ignore it entirely.[73] The Chinese, at least in their ancient learned tradition, don't want simply to add their differences to other differences. They are more than happy to take their seats in the global amphitheater of multiculturalism—similarly seated but with a tiny difference of angle to witness the same spectacle—but wish to remain *indifferent* to our own, meaning Western, ways of being all-encompassing. Differences we could absorb—we thought we could absorb under the decaying but still solid dome of the Holy Roman Empire—but *indifferences*?

To the possible dismay of political scientists, the very idea of a political assembly does not gather much interest. This is where things become really complicated and thus interesting: How to devise an assembly of *ways of dissembling* instead of sending a convocation to gather under the common dome of "One Size Politics Fits All"? Can we enlarge our definition of politics to the point where it accepts its own suspension? But who can really be *that* open-minded?[74]

And yet, do we have another course of action? It would be too easy simply to recognize the many contradictions as if we could be content with the absence or the demise of all political assemblies, as if we could abandon for good the task of composition. There must be some alternative to cheap universalism ("but surely every human is a political animal") and to cheap relativism ("let everyone gather under their own flag, and if they have no flag then let them hang themselves!").

That we have to find a way out is forced upon us by what is called "globalization": even though the Jivaros, the Chinese, the Japanese, the faithful members of the Oumma, the born-again Christians don't want to enter under the same dome, they are still, willingly or unwillingly, connected by the very expansion of those makeshift assemblies we call markets, technologies, science, ecological crises, wars, and terrorist networks. In other words, the many differing assemblages we have gathered here are *already* connecting people no matter how much they *don't* feel assembled by any common politics. The shape of the dome might be contested, because it does not allow enough room for differences and indifferences, but that there is something at work that is called "global" is not in question. It's simply that our usual definitions of politics have not caught up yet with the masses of linkages already established.

Let's probe further into this historical paradox. In earlier times, say during the Enlightenment, there existed a metaphysical globe, to use Sloterdijk's expression,[75] even though globalization was barely beginning. But now that we are indeed globalized, there is no globe anymore! To take an example, when the cartographer Mercator transformed Atlas from a distorted giant supporting the Earth on his shoulder into a quiet and seated scientist holding the planet in his *hand*, this was probably the time when globalization was at its zenith. And yet the world in 1608 was barely known, and people remained far apart. Still, every new land, every new civilization, every new difference could be located, situated, housed without much surprise in the transparent house of Nature. But now that the world is known, people are brought together by violent deeds, even if they wish to differ and not be connected. There is no global anymore to assemble them. The best proof is that there are

392

people setting up demonstrations against globalization. The global is up for grabs. Globalization is simultaneously at its maximum and the globe at its nadir. There are lots of *blogs* but no globe.

And yet, we are all in the same boat, or at least the same flotilla. To use Neurath's metaphor, the question is how to rebuild it while we are cruising on it. Or rather, how can we make it navigate when it's made of a fleet of diverging but already intertwined barges? In other words, can we overcome the multiplicity of ways of assembling and dissembling and yet raise the question of the one common world? Can we make an *assembly* out of all the various *assemblages* in which we are already enmeshed?

The Phantom Public

The cry is well known: "The Great Pan is dead!" Nature, this huge and silent parliament where all the creatures would be arrayed tier after tier from the biggest to the smallest, this magnificent amphi-theater offering to the clumsy politicians a perfect and successful original of what is rational and what is irrational, this great parliament of nature has crumbled down much as did the Tower of Babel.[76] Political philosophy has always tried to prop up its frail intuitions onto the solid and powerful pattern of some other science: It seems that everything from the metaphor of the organism to that of the brain has been tried. It has been a continuous undertaking: How to replace the dangerous trade of politics by the serious and safe knowledge of some better established science? And it has continuously failed.

A crisscrossing of metaphors from Menenius's "Fable of the Members and the Stomach"[77] to contemporary socio-biology and cybernetics[78] has tried to fasten the poor assemblies of humans to the solid reality of nature. All the organs of the body have been tried out to probe the making up of the monstrous Body Politic.[79] All the animals have been invoked in turn—ants, bees, sheep, wolves, bugs, worms, pigs, chimps, baboons—to establish a firmer ground for the whimsical assemblies of humans (Fig. 14). And yet

393

to no avail, since there are many ways to be a body, since sheep don't flock,[80] wolves are not as cruel as humans, baboons have an intense social life,[81] brains have no central direction. It seems that nature is no longer unified enough to provide a stabilizing pattern for the traumatic experience of humans living in society. No doubt, the Body Politic is a monster—so much so that it's not even a body.

But which *type* of monster is it? This is what we wish to find out. We might have transformed politics into a monstrous activity because we have tried to make it exist in a form, borrowed from nature, that it could not possibly take. "The answer was not acceptable in the nineteenth century, when men, in spite of all their iconoclasm, were still haunted by the phantom of identity," wrote Walter Lippmann in a stunning book called the *Phantom Public*.[82] In many ways our exhibition is an effort in teratology, an experiment in trying to pry apart two ghostly figures: the Leviathan and the Phantom of the Public. (Sorry, there is no way to talk about politics and to speak of beautiful shapes, elegant silhouettes, heroic statues, glorious ideals, radiant futures, transparent information—except if you want to go through, once again, the long list of grandiose ceremonies held by various totalitarianisms which, as we are all painfully aware, lead to the worst abominations. The choice is either to speak of monsters early on with care and caution, or too late and end up as a criminal. Oh Machiavelli, how right you were; let us pray that we heed your cautious lessons in realism.)

According to Lippmann and to the philosopher John Dewey in response to his book,[83] most of European political philosophy has been obsessed by the body and the state. The Europeans have tried to assemble an impossible parliament that represented really the contradictory wills of the multitude into *one* General Will. But this enterprise suffered from a cruel lack of realism. Representation, conceived in that total, complete and transparent fashion, cannot possibly be faithful. By asking from politics something it could not deliver, Europeans kept generating aborted monsters and

394

Fig. 14 The rats council, fables from La Fontaine, illustrations by Gustave Doré, 1868.

ended up discouraging people from thinking politically. For politics to be able to absorb more diversity ("the Great Society" in Dewey's time and what we now call "Globalization"), it has to devise a very specific and new type of representation. Lippmann calls it a Phantom because it's disappointing for those who dream of unity and totality. Yet strangely enough, it is a *good* ghost, the only spirit that could protect us against the dangers of fundamentalism. Long before the United States degenerated into its present conservative revolution, it had a much more sturdy and contemporary tradition. Those American philosophers call their tradition *pragmatism*, meaning by this word not the cheap realism often associated with being "pragmatic" but the costly realism requested by making politics turn toward *pragmata*—the Greek name for Things. Now that's realism!

We aim at *giving flesh* to the Phantom of the Public. Readers should feel the difference there is between expecting from the Body Politic something it cannot give—and that surely creates a monster—and being moved by the Phantom Public. The idea is to take the word Phantom and to grant this fragile and provisional concept more reality—at least more realism—than the phantasmagorical spheres, globes, common good and general will that the Leviathan was supposed to incarnate, tackling the problem of composing one body from a multitude of bodies.

Why do we attach so much importance to the difference between Body Politic and Phantom? It is due to the fact that for the new eloquence to become a habit of thought, we must be able to distinguish two ways of speaking. To raise a political question often means to reveal a state of affairs whose presence was hitherto hidden. But then you risk falling into the same trap of providing social explanations and do exactly the opposite of what is meant here by political flow. You use the same old repertoire of already-gathered social ties to "explain" the new associations. Although you seem to speak *about* politics you don't speak *politically*. What you are doing is simply the extension one step further of the same small repertoire of already standardized forces. You might feel the pleasure of providing a "powerful explanation," but that's just the problem: You yourself partake in the *expansion* of power not the re-composition of its content. Even though it resembles political talk, it has not even begun to address the political endeavor since it has not tried to assemble the candidates into a new assembly adjusted to their specific requirements. "Drunk with power" is an expression not only fit for generals, presidents, CEOs, mad scientists, and bosses—it can also be used for those commentators who are confusing the expansion of powerful explanations with the composition of the collective. This is why we might need still another slogan: "Be sober with power." In other words, abstain as much as possible from using the notion of power in case it backfires and hits your explanations instead of the target you are aiming to destroy. No powerful explanations without checks and balances.

Politics of Time, Politics of Space

Going back to things and speaking positively of the "phantom of the public", is this not, in the end, terribly reactionary? It depends on what we mean by progressive. Imagine that you have the responsibility of assembling together a set of disorderly voices, contradictory interests, and virulent claims. Then imagine you are miraculously offered a chance, just at the time when you despair of accommodating so many dissenting parties, to get rid of most of them. Would you not embrace such a solution as a gift from heaven?

This is exactly what happened when the contradictory interests of people could be differentiated by using the following shibboleths: "Are they progressive or reactionary? Enlightened or archaic? In the vanguard or in the rear guard?" Dissenting voices were still there, but most of them represented backward, obscurantist, or regressive trends. The cleansing march of progress was going to render them passé. You could safely forget two-thirds of them, and so your task of assembling them was simplified by the same amount.

397

In the remaining third, not everything had to be taken into account either, since most of the positions were soon made obsolete by the passage of time. Among the contemporary parties to the dispute, progressive minds had to take into consideration only those few seen as the harbingers of the future. So, through the magical ordering power of progress, politics was a cinch, since 90 percent of the contradictory passions had been spirited away, left to linger in the limbo of irrationality. By ignoring most of the dissenters, you could reach a solution that would satisfy everyone, namely those who made up the liberal or revolutionary avantgarde. In this way, the arrow of time could safely thrust forward.

Philosophers define time as a "series of successions" and space as a "series of simultaneities". Undoubtedly, while we filed away everything under the power of progress, we lived in the time of succession. Chronos would eat away all that was archaic and irrational in his own progeny, sparing only those predestined for a radiant future. But through a twist of history that neither reformists nor revolutionaries ever anticipated, Chronos has suddenly lost his voracious appetite.[84] Strangely enough, we have changed time so completely that we have shifted from the time of Time to the *time of Simultaneity*. Nothing, it seems, accepts to simply reside in the past, and no one feels intimidated any more by the adjectives "irrational", "backward", or "archaic". Time, the bygone time of cataclysmic substitution, has suddenly become something that neither the Left nor the Right seems to have been fully prepared to encounter: a monstrous time, the time of cohabitation. *Everything has become contemporary.*

The questions are no longer: "Are you going to disappear soon?" "Are you the telltale sign of something new coming to replace everything else?" "Is this the seventh seal of the Book of Apocalypse that you are now breaking?" An entirely new set of questions has now emerged: "Can we cohabitate with you?" "Is there a way for all of us to survive together while none of our contradictory claims, interests, and passions can be eliminated?"

398

Revolutionary time, the great Simplificator, has been replaced by cohabitation time, the great Complicator. In other words, space has replaced time as the main ordering principle.

It's fair to say that the reflexes of politicians, the passions of militants, the customs of citizens, their ways to be indignant, the rhetoric of their claims, the ecology of their interests are not the same in the time of Time and in the time of Space. No one seems prepared to ask: What should now be simultaneously present?

How different, for instance, to deal with religion if you wait for its slow disappearance into the faraway land of fairies, or if it explodes before your very eyes as what makes people live and die now—now and also tomorrow. What a difference it makes if nature, instead of being a huge reservoir of forces and a bottomless repository of waste, turns suddenly into something that interrupts any progression: something to which you cannot appeal and can't get rid of. "*Comment s'en débarrasser?*" Ionesco asked during the "Glorious '30s".[85] It has now become the worry, the *Sorge*, the *souci* of almost everyone in all languages. We can get rid of nothing and no one. Ecology has probably ruined forever the time of Succession and has ushered us into the time of Space. Yes, everything is contemporary. Progress and succession, revolution and substitution, neither are part of our operating system any longer.

And yet where is the alternative OS? Who is busy writing its lines of code? We sort of knew how to order things in time, but we have no idea of the space in which to collect ourselves.[86] We have yet to channel new political passions into new habits of thought, new rhetoric, new ways of being interested, indignant, mobilized, and pacified. Whenever we are faced with an issue, the old habits still linger and the voice of progress still shouts: "Don't worry, all of that will soon disappear; they're too archaic and irrational." And the new voice can only whisper: "You have to cohabit even with those monsters, because don't indulge yourself in the naive belief that they will soon fade away; space is the series of simultaneities, all of that has to be taken into account *at once*."

This does not mean that there is no progress in the end, or that no arrow of time can be thrust forward. It means that we slowly proceed from a very simple-minded form of cohabitation—such as the evolutionary or revolutionary ones—to a much fuller one, where more and more elements are taken into account. There is progress, but it goes from a mere juxtaposition to an intertwined form of cohabitation: How many contemporary elements can you build side by side, generating the series of simultaneities? Communism might have been wrong not in the quest for the community but in the hasty way it imagined what is the Common World to be shared.

What is Dingpolitik?
Back to things. *Demon* and *demos*, as I said earlier, have the same etymology. If you follow the first division, you multiply the occasions to differ and to dissemble; if you follow the second division, you multiply the occasions to agree, to compose, to assemble, to share. The difference between the two is as thin as a knife. In both cases the *Ding* will disband—and so will this exhibit. If the "demon of politics" has taken you over, a certain pattern will emerge: too much unity, too much disunity. But if you manage to feel the passage of the Phantom Public through your actions, another pattern will emerge: fewer claims to unity, less belief in disunity. The quest for composition has begun again just as in the times of Father Nicéron. This is at least the effect we wish to produce on visitors and readers.

So what is *Dingpolitik* in the end? It is the degree of realism that is injected when:

a. Politics is no longer limited to humans and incorporates the many issues to which they are attached;
b. Objects become things, that is, when matters of fact give way to their complicated entanglements and become matters of concern;

400

c. Assembling is no longer done under the already existing globe or dome of some earlier tradition of building virtual parliaments;

d. The inherent limits imposed by speech impairment, cognitive weaknesses, and all sorts of handicaps are no longer denied but prostheses are accepted instead;

e. It's no longer limited to properly speaking parliaments but extended to the many other assemblages in search of a rightful assembly;

f. The assembling is done under the provisional and fragile Phantom Public, which no longer claims to be equivalent to a Body, a Leviathan, or a State;

g. And, finally, *Dingpolitik* may become possible when politics is freed from its obsession with the time of Succession.

If fundamentalism is the conviction that mediations may be bypassed without cost, then it's the ultimate "ding-less" mode of doing politics. In the end, one question especially interests us: Can fundamentalism be undone? When will the horsemen of the apocalypse stop meddling in politics?

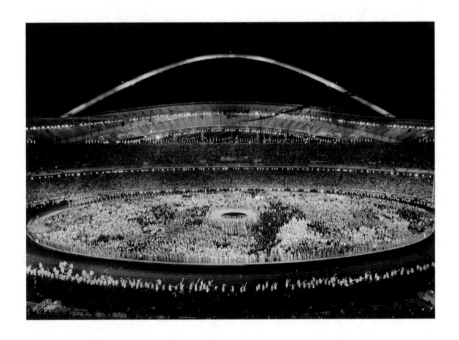

Fig. 15   Athens, Greece, opening ceremony of the 2004 Olympic Games.
Athletes from countries all over the world assemble inside the stadium during the
opening ceremony of the 2004 Olympic Games in Athens, Friday, 13 August 2004.
Photo: David J. Phillip.

1. The term "fluid" was introduced in Annemarie Mol and John Law, "Regions, Networks and Fluids: Anaemia and Social Topology" (1994). See also Zygmunt Bauman, *Liquid Modernity* (2000). The word "fluid" allows analysts to insist on the circulation and on the nature of what is being transported better than if they used the word "network".

2. This is why the notion of affordance, introduced in James G. Gibson, *The Ecological Approach to Visual Perception* (1986), has been found so useful. The multiplicity of modes of action when dealing with technology—hard and soft— is marvelously followed by Lucy Suchman, *Plans and Situated Actions* (1987), Charles Goodwin and Marjorie H. Goodwin, "Formulating Planes: Seeing as a Situated Activity" (1996), and Bernard Conein, Nicolas Dodier, and Laurent Thevenot, *Les objets dans l'action. De la maison au laboratoire* (1993).

3. There is a bit of anthropocentric bias in using the expression *non*-humans. I have explained in detail elsewhere how *human/non-human* should be substituted for the insurmountable dichotomy between subject and object (see Bruno Latour, *Politics of Nature* (1999)). No extra meaning should be looked for in this notion: it does not specify any ontological domain, but simply replaces another conceptual difference. For a complete panorama of human/non-human relations, see Philippe Descola, *La nature des cultures* (2005).

4. Horst Bredekamp, *Thomas Hobbes Visuelle Strategien. Der Leviathan: Urbild des modernen Staates. Werkillustrationen und Portraits* (Berlin: Akademie Verlag, 1999); Simon Schaffer, Bruno Latour et. al., *Making Things Public*, chapter 3; about Nicéron's machine: Jean-François Nicéron, *La perspective curieuse à Paris chez Pierre Billaine Chez Jean Du Puis rue Saint Jacques à la Couronne d'Or avec l'Optique et la Catoptrique du RP Mersenne du mesme ordre Oeuvre très utile aux Peintres, Architectes, Sculpteurs, Graveures et à tous autres qui se meslent du Dessein* (1663).

5. Dario Gamboni, in Latour et.al., *Making Things Public*, chapter 3.

6. Steven Shapin and Simon Schaffer, *Leviathan and the Air-Pump. Hobbes, Boyle and the Experimental Life*, (Princeton: Princeton University Press, 1985).

7. Quentin Skinner, *Ambrogio Lorenzetti: The Artist as Political Philosopher*, (Cambridge: Cambridge University Press, 1986); Anne-Marie Brenot, *Sienne au XIV siècle dans les fresques de Lorenzetti: la Cité parfaite* (Paris: L'Harmattan, 1999); Giovanni Pavanello, *Il Buono et il Cattivo Governo. Rappresentazioni nelle Arti dal Medioevo al Novecento*, exhibition catalogue (Venice: Fondazione Cini, Marsilio, 2004), and his paper in Latour et.al., *Making Things Public*, chapter 2.

8. Peter Sloterdijk, *Sphären III – Schäume. Plurale Sphärologie* (Frankfurt: Suhrkamp, 2004).

9. Peter Sloterdijk, in Latour et.al., *Making Things Public*, chapter 15.

10. Full text is available at: http://www.state.gov/secretary/rm/2003/17300.htm

11. Barbara Cassin, *L'effet sophistique* (Paris: Gallimard, 1995), and her contribution to Latour et.al., *Making Things Public*, chapter 14.

12. Simon Schaffer, in Latour et.al., *Making Things Public*, chapter 5.

13. See the complex set of assertions offered by Hans Blix, *Disarming Iraq* (New York: Pantheon Books, 2004).

14. "Enthymem" is the name given to this type of incomplete proof: Aristotle, *Treatise on Rhetorics* (New York: Prometheus Books, 1995).

15. Hans-Jörg Rheinberger, *Toward a History of Epistemic Thing. Synthesizing Proteins in the Test Tube* (Stanford, CA: Stanford University Press, 1997; Hans-Jörg Rheinberger and Henning Schmidgen, in Latour et.al., *Making Things Public*, chapter 5.

16. It's a striking feature of the 2004 American election to have witnessed the drift of the meaning of the word "convinced" from an objective to a subjective status. One now designates by it the inner wholesomeness of an interior soul and no longer the effect on one's mind of some indirect and risky evidence: the "convinced" Bush won over the "flip-flopper" to-be-convinced Kerry.

17. Hanna Rose Shell about Marey's instrumentarium, Latour et.al., *Making Things Public*, chapter 5; Peter Galison about the Wall of Science, in Latour et.al., *Making Things Public*, chapter 5.

18. See the Oxford Dictionary: "ORIGIN: Old English, of Germanic origin: related to German *Ding*. Early senses included 'meeting' and 'matter', 'concern' as well as 'inanimate objects'." Martin Heidegger, *What is a Thing?*, trans. W. B. Barton, Jr. and Vera Deutsch (Chicago: Regnery, 1968); Graham Harman, in Latour et.al., *Making Things Public*, chapter 4.

19. Gísli Pálsson, in Latour et.al., *Making Things Public*, chapter 4.

20. Elizabeth Edwards and Peter James on Benjamin Stone's photographs, ibid., chapter 2.

21. Barbara Dölemeyer, ibid., chapter 4.

22. Oleg Kharkhordin, ibid., chapter 4.

23. "When [the res] appears in this function, it is not as a seat where the unilateral mastery of a subject is exercised [...] If the res is an object, it has this function above all in a debate or an argument, a common object that opposes and unites two protagonists within a single relation." And, further on: "Its objectivity is ensured by the common agreement whose place of origin is controversy and judicial debate." Yan Thomas, "Res, chose et patrimoine (note sur le rapport sujet-objet en droit romain)", in *Archives de philosophie du droit*, 25 (1980) 413–426.

24. Frank Hartmann, in Latour et.al., *Making Things Public*, chapter 12.

25. Lorraine Daston and Peter Galison, "The Image of Objectivity", in *Representation*, 40 (1992) 81–128; Lorraine Daston, in Latour et.al., *Making Things Public*, chapter 12; Jessica Riskin, ibid., chapter 12.

26. Peter Weibel, ibid., conclusion.

27. Richard Rorty, ibid., chapter 4; Graham Harman, ibid., chapter 4.

28. Pauline Terreehorst and Gerard deVries, ibid., chapter 11.

29. Albena Yaneva, ibid., chapter 9.

30. Emilie Gomart, ibid., chapter 12.

31. Wolfang Lefèvre, *Picturing Machines 1400–1700* (Cambridge, MA: The MIT Press, 2004).

32. Wiebe E. Bijker, in Latour et.al., *Making Things Public*, chapter 9.

33. Marcel Detienne (ed.), *Qui veut prendre la parole?* (Paril: Le Seuil, 2003).

34. Pierre Lévêque, "Repartition et démocratie à propos de la racine da-", in: *Esprit*, 12 (1993) 34–39.

35. "Every kingdom divided against itself is laid waste, and no city or house divided against itself will stand; and if Satan casts out Satan, he is divided against himself; how then will his kingdom stand?" (Matthew 12: 25–26).

36. Michael Frayn, *Democracy* (London: Methuen Drama, 2003).

37. Noortje Marres, in Latour et.al., *Making Things Public*, chapter 3.

38. Bruno Latour and Peter Weibel (eds.), *Iconoclash. Beyond the Image Wars in Science, Religion, and Art* (Cambridge, MA: The MIT Press, 2002).

39. This illustration has been kindly provided by Erica Naginski, "The Object of Contempt", in: Yale French Studies, No. 101, *Fragments of Revolution* (2001) 32–53.

40. Jerry Brotton, "Saints Alive. The Iconography of Saint George", in Latour, Weibel (eds.), op. cit., 155.

41. Marie José Mondzain, "The Holy Shroud. How Invisible Hands Weave the Undecidable", ibid., 324–335.

42. Joseph Leo Koerner, "Impossible Objects: Bosch Realism", in: *Res*, 46 (2004) 73–98.

43. Michel Callon, in Latour et.al., *Making Things Public*, chapter 5.

44. "How then should Pharaoh heed me, a man of impeded speech." (Exodus 6: 12) According to Marc Shell (personal communication), all great statesmen had some speech defect.

45. Chantal Mouffe, in Latour et.al., *Making Things Public*, chapter 13.

46. Jean-Philippe Heurtin, *L'espace public parlementaire. Essais sur les raisons du législateur* (Paris: PUF, 1999); and in Latour et.al., *Making Things Public*, chapter 13; Ludger Schwarte, ibid., chapter 13.

47. Ana Miljacki, in Latour et. al., *Making Things Public*, chapter 3.

48. Deyan Sudjic, *Architecture and Democracy* (Glasgow: Lawrence King Publishing, 2001).

49. See excerpt, Latour et. al., *Making Things Public*, chapter 13.

50. Christine Riding and Jacqueline Riding, *The Houses of Parliament. History, Art, Architecture* (London: Merrell, 2000); James A. Leith, *Space and Revolution: Projects for Monuments, Squares, and Public Buildings in France, 1789–1799* (Montreal: McGill-Queens University Press, 1991).

51. Joseph Leo Koerner, in Latour et.al., *Making Things Public*, chapter 7.

52. Lisa Pon, ibid., chapter 12.

53. Christophe Boureux, ibid., chapter 7.

54. A. Hennion, G. Teil, F. Vergnaud, ibid., chapter 11.

55. Franck Cochoy and Catherine Grandclément Chaffy, ibid., chapter 11.

56. Pablo Jensen, ibid., chapter 5.

57. Daniel Beunza and Fabian Muniesa, ibid., chapter 11; Alex Preda, ibid., chapter 11.

58. Vinciane Despret, ibid., chapter 6; Isabelle Mauz and Julien Gravelle, ibid., chapter 6.

59. Richard Rogers and Noortje Marres, ibid., chapter 14.

60. XPERIMENT!, ibid., chapter 14.

61. Susan S. Silbey and Ayn Cavicchi, ibid., chapter 10.

62. Christelle Gramaglia, ibid., chapter 8; Cordula Kropp, ibid., chapter 8; Jean-Pierre Le Bourhis, ibid., chapter 8; Matthias Gommel, ibid., chapter 8.

63. Delphine Gardey, ibid., chapter 13; Michael Lynch, Stephen Hilgartner, Carin Berkowitz, ibid., chapter 13.
64. Isabelle Stengers, ibid., chapter 15.
65. Masato Fukushima, ibid., chapter 1.
66. Philippe Descola, ibid., chapter 1.
67. Gilles Kepel, Fitna. *Guerre au coeur de l'Islam* (Paris: Gallimard, 2004).
68. Anita Herle, in Latour et.al., *Making Things Public*, chapter 2; Amiria Henare, ibid., chapter 1.
69. Pierre Lemonnier and Pascale Bonnemère, ibid., chapter 1.
70. Peter Galison, ibid., chapter 10.
71. Olivier Christin, ibid., chapter 7.
72. Philippe Descola, *Par delà la nature et la culture* (Paris: Gallimard, 2005).
73. François Jullien, *The Propensity of Things. Toward a History of Efficacy in China* (Cambridge, MA: Zone Books, 1995).
74. Compare Isabelle Stengers' definition of politics (Latour et.al., *Making Things Public*, chapter 15) with Ulrich Beck, *Der kosmopolitische Blick* (Frankfurt: Suhrkamp, 2004).
75. Peter Sloterdijk, *Sphären II – Globen* (Frankfurt: Suhrkamp, 1999).
76. John Tresch, in Latour et.al., *Making Things Public*, chapter 6.
77. William Shakespeare, excerpt in Latour et.al., *Making Things Public*, chapter 3.
78. Eden Medina, ibid., chapter 12.
79. Francisco Varela et al., "The Brainweb: Phase Synchronisation and Large-Scale Integration", in: *Nature Reviews Neuroscience*, 2 (2001) 229–239; Michael Hagner, in Latour et.al., *Making Things Public*, chapter 2.
80. Vinciane Despret, in Latour et.al., *Making Things Public*, chapter 6.
81. Shirley Strum, *Almost Human. A Journey into the World of Baboons* (New York: Random House, 1987).
82. Noortje Marres, in Latour et.al., *Making Things Public*, chapter 3.
83. John Dewey, *The Public and Its Problems* (Athens, OH: Swallow Press, Ohio University Press, 1991 [1927]).
84. Francis Fukuyama (*The End of History and the Last Man* (New York: Free Press, 1992)) was right in diagnosing the end of history but wrong to believe it would simplify the political tasks ahead: Exactly the opposite happened. Simultaneity is much harder to crack than succession because you can't get rid of any contradictions.
85. Eugène Ionesco, *Amédée ou Comment s'en débarrasser* (Paris: Gallimard, 1954).
86. Witness how clumsy is the effort of Samuel Huntington (*The Clash of Civilization and the Remaking of World Order* (New York: Simon & Schuster, 1998)) to project into geography the history that Fukuyama had declared moot.

Manuel de Solà-Morales
Urbanity of Things

1. Manuel de Solà-Morales, *A Matter of Things* (Rotterdam: Nai Publishers, 2008), 18–29, 72–79, 108–111, 142–143, 146–149, 152–153.

The City, a Matter of Things

I. 26 The contemporary city is not becoming more ugly every day: it grows ever richer. The impossibility of imaging it that is so regretted need not be an objective limitation, but it may simply be the consequence of a considerable lack of information. If, in order to interpret the form of the contemporary city, we try to reinvent a new catalogue of spaces, the prototypes that we thought we had discovered have disappeared by the next day. The formal cohesion proper to the good old conventional spaces or the reciprocal relation between form and matter are less common today. Thus, many commentators repeat the tired old mantra that the city is in retreat, indeed that historically it is already worn out. And sometimes they even go so far as to say that it has become a virtual territory, a dynamic cyberspace without a place.

On the contrary, there are more places every day. Extension and occupation are increasing exponentially.

There are also more contacts every day. And more activities, uses, constructions, movements, areas, urban images. The number of urban objects is multiplying. We need new perspectives in order to get used to this multiplicity.

If Calder (Fig. 1) with his mobiles could be a metaphor for space as a system of interdependencies in movement (the city as system), and Braque (Fig. 2) with his collages anticipated the figures of the city created by superimposing and juxtaposing fragments (mosaics), Malevich (Fig. 3) and above all Miró (Fig. 4) recognized space as a constellation of objects, as a field of free forms, as a table full of things.

The list of urban things that could be enumerated may well be at least as diverse as that set out by Borges. But if we concentrate with attention—or even with devotion—scenes of the contemporary city lacking visual coherence or apparent meaning become in fact fortuitous ensembles that take on

Fig. 1 Alexander Calder, *A Universe*, 1934.

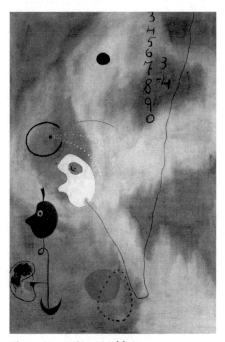

Fig. 4 Joan Miró, *L'Addition*, 1925.

Fig. 3   Kasimir Malevich, *Suprematist Composition*, 1915–1916.

Fig. 2   Georges Braque, *Le Petit Provençal*, 1913.

interdependence by virtue of their material reality. As in painted still lifes of a tabletop with an arrangement of disparate objects (an apple, a pitcher, a magazine, fabric), urban things establish direct, immediate relations with one another. The city is the table that supports them and that presents them to us in their pure materiality, as realities identifiable in their differences, their relative position, and their mutual reflections—reflections that refer to an external, immense, and polysemic field.

A pavement, a glass façade, a wall, a ramp, or a distant perspective interrupted by obstacles, a silhouette against the sky and a closed patio, bare, unfinished roads half-occupied by provisional pieces of furniture, a whole range of banal situations, of insignificant postcards, a series of "peripheral" or "unconnected" or "informal" spaces are urban still lifes if we look at them through the eyes of a painter or naturalist lost in thought. They are syntagmata of the language of urban spaces. Respect for urban things brings with it the appreciation of corners and vacant spaces, of environments, scaffolding, railings, garages, basements and platforms, gateways and warehouses, ramps and railings, corridors and gardens and fences, not as anecdotes of a landscape, but as urban forms that today's architecture frenetically produces even though lacking a name so far. And perhaps it is this taxonomic weakness that prevents us from recognizing them in their materiality, in their disturbing presence.

The crossroads and corners as places of reference and of exchange; the ramps and gaps which conjoin different levels, the intermittent appearance of tunnels, bridges, and railway lines, rigid components of the fluidity, the intervals of pavements and boulevards as a primary support, the rows of trees or parked cars, all suggest a logic of the physical city that operates through differentiated elements. Without failing to include the regular directions or the continuous façades and

414

the major traffic axes, it is the truncated episodes, the dislocated elements, the ambiguous spaces, and the heaps of objects, as well as their transience in space and time, which are the formal characteristics that make our cities territories of things, fields of elements.

Paying attention to urban things is what enables us to make the urban "quantity" translated into variety the main characteristic of the metropolitan territory. Masses of houses and buildings, office districts, endless zones of single-family homes, open extensions without planning, the hubbub of maritime littorals, industrial estates, commercial centers, holiday resorts, big car parks, and stations are sums of things—urban things in which we can recognize the energy of urbanity today.

That the city is composed of things seems less useful in the face of the evidence for the growing interdependence of activities and landscapes. None of that is denied; on the contrary. But my work usually teaches me that it is precisely the things in the city that determine the relations, and that a vision of the city as composed of elements is today particularly useful for integrating the urban complexity to be superimposed on the post-structuralist schematic logic of flows and systems.

Neue Sachlichkeit [New Objectivity] wanted to make immediate objects objective presences in themselves. A piece of fruit, a pitcher, or a portrait become absolute realities. Any still life of elements forms both a space and a matter (Fig. 5). It is the Husserlian *zu den Sachen selbst*: go to the things themselves!

That is why the contemporary urban project has to fight for far greater recognition, to make sure that those urban things become the material of its own work and the content of its proposals. Here lies the possibility of difference, even within the uniformity imposed by the functional and economic systems of modern cities. And difference is quality. Perhaps.

Fig. 5   George Brecht, *Valoche*, 1975.

I work on the skin of cities. Their epidermis is what I study and enjoy and what enables me to discern their deepest structures. The architecture of surface textures is the raw material of my urban projects.

The skin of cities is composed of constructions, textures, and contrasts, of streets and empty spaces, of gardens and walls, of contours and voids. "Bricks and mortar" is how the perspicacious geographer Maximilien Sorre defined the city. Plus movements and crossroads, vehicles and façades, basements and subterranean ducts. Shops, offices, empty building sites, apartments, museums, theaters and all kinds of empty buildings. Curbs and pavements, warehouses and storage depots, factories and markets, monuments and ruins, stations, stadiums, studies. [...] It is precisely the contact between our bodies and these forms of physical matter that constitutes the urban experience. *"Flesh and Stone* is the title of one of Richard Sennett's most beautiful writings on the city. This is why the ramps and staircases, the gateways and corners are so important, because in them we feel with our weight the shape and size of the city.

I am interested in material urbanity, urbanity made of touch and vision, of sensations and suggestions. It is different from the idea of "urban structure" on which so much planning has been based, or the notion of "urban system" which is applicable above all to the interdependence of activities and positions, or from the "functional areas" used for the classification and allocation of spaces. These are all approaches which have monopolized a large part of urban studies in the last half century. In trying to make out supposedly more important internal structures beneath the appearances, they have proposed hierarchies of concepts to interpret the urban from a structuralist and/or formalist and/or economist position.

It now appears that today, with a change of terms, when what used to be called communication, channel, or mesh is now called flux, connection, or network, what is presented as new often turns out to be the same old semantic reduction that the systemic structuralism of the 1960s imposed on the physical city.

So the surface of the city, the urban skin, is considered "superficial", that is, light, inconsistent, insignificant, incapable of having a content worthy of serious study. Reduced to the status of a bearer of only "superstructural", "aesthetic", or "environmental" values, the skin of the city is for today's neo-structuralists a consequence rather than a subject, a phenomenon rather than anything material.

And yet, in the urban matter, in the surface of the city experienced in its tangible materiality, in its physical sensations and in all it suggests, lie the origin and form of any kind of urbanity. It is the urban matter that transmits to us, at its most sensitive points and in its most neutral zones, the qualitative energy that accumulates collective character on certain spaces, charging them with complex significance and cultural references and making them semantic material, social constructions of inter-subjective memory.

It is the composition of the urban skins that indicates to us their characteristics and their differences, their weight, form, texture, format, their morphology and their tectonics. But we have to look at them insistently and with sufficient attention for them to reveal to us, as Jacques Derrida has already explained, their hidden replies, their caverns.

Urban Acupuncture?

The skin of the city is not a flat envelope. It is in itself, and as a skin, a qualitative network, a membrane of differences that are subject to interventions and strategies, whether they be rough or smooth.

The ancient oriental practice of acupuncture regards the skin of the human body as the principal energy transport system, with 361 sensitive points scattered over the surface of the body transmitting their sensory impressions to the rest of the organism, exterior and interior, by means of twelve meridians or pathways.

The urban skin ("the epidermis of the earth" that Jean Tricart studied) also channels qualitative energy. And if acupuncture speaks of "cold" and "hot" energy, the qualities of the urban epidermis are also blunt or sharp, mental or sensorial.

As in therapeutic acupuncture, the location of the sensitive point is the first step in the strategic treatment of the urban skin. It is dexterity in the identification of the spot and the channels of influence in the fabric that enable us to add new qualities, adequate energy, whether cold or hot, and to empower urbanity in its various modes.

Project acupuncture is less concerned with the small, the minute, or the delicate than with the strategic, the systemic, and the interdependent. Actions performed on the ear, the Chinese experts say, will have beneficial effects on the lung or the knee. Acupuncture is above all about a much higher appreciation of the epidermis as a rich, complex, and enormously influential membrane. In the skin of the city, our architectural instruments, our experience as city dwellers and our bodily sensations are the real working material, useful and substantial in themselves, even for cause-and-effect relations of the most abstract kind. So there is a certain analogy between intervening in the skin of the city and the techniques of acupuncture—not because it involves using needles or making small incisions, but because the epidermis is understood to form a system.

For acupuncturists, the skin is not the covering of the interior but the principal structure of the organism, the clearest expression of its nature. To act with punctures, pressures, injections is to distribute energy through the skin. It is the epidermis of the urban fabrics that enables us to transform internal metabolisms of its organism which others express in abstract socio-economic, symbolic-cultural, infrastructural, or historic-political terms.

The analogy with acupuncture—needles and points—can become trivial if it is reduced to small-scale local sewing interventions in the urban fabrics or low-cost reforms. Conversely, it is sometimes extrapolated to the scale of the political and the social when the same term—urban acupuncture—is used to refer to political tactics that, although isolated, transform the general functioning of the city: transport, housing, refuse. I think this is a much more generic analogy. Some of my works entail urban acupuncture as a specific project proposal and as a methodological attitude of a physical, if not physiocratic urbanism.

The skin of cities has to be observed with the attention of a detective who scrutinizes the tiniest clues in its wrinkles and in their apparent lack of connection. The masters of the whodunit can teach us the art of revealing description, always intriguing even though unconnected to anything else. It is precisely from the apparently incidental nature of their data that they extract the threads of narrative interest. By the power of enumeration with which novelist Henning Mankell's Inspector Wallander, for example, makes us see objects and situations, mixing the surprise of the murder with his pile of washing for the laundry, the broken ignition of his car, or his frequent bar snacks. We should concentrate on some fragment of a city or of a project, without knowing whether that topographical incident or that sequence of walls will be decisive in the resolution of our puzzles for the simple reason that surprise and intuition are as important in the urban project as coherence and getting to the bottom of things. It is not only the ensemble of relations that links the complexity of the steps, but paying simultaneous attention to things themselves, appreciating each of them one by one, because they are already in essence beautiful constituents of reality, making us feel that "l'amore delle cose" in the city which Felice Casorati and the painters of the *Neue Sachlichkeit* movement wanted to express.

Michel Foucault the philosopher or Victor Erice the film director tell us that paying attention to things, respecting the material culture is a way to rescue the purely physical along with our view of matter, our preoccupation and our understanding, our love of things. Doing projects in the city is for me a part of this act of paying attention. To operate on the skin of the city is to be constantly attending to the way things are, and to questions about which things need adding, removing, or modifying, or how better to rearrange them. There is no way of finding out other than to plunge into the strategy of things, of urban things.

I. 152Hence, today's urban project can lie more in the strategic and the material, with the intention of acting like acupuncture on the skin to affect the underlying organ. It is an urban project that in order to be effective is concentrated and specific, limited in the time and space of its intervention, but open and extensive in its influence beyond itself, with the technical, budgetary, infrastructural, and architectural facets of the constructional project, with the functional layering and collective condition of use, with the expiry of an executive program. This idea of a project as being like acupuncture involves leaving behind the schematism of functionalist structural planning and the reductionism of contextualism to entrust the capacity to construct a contemporary urbanity to the richness of the urban material.

For a "Material" Urbanity

I. 146There is an urbanity that applies to people. There is also an urbanity that applies to places, the one that sociologists and geographers talk about. And there is an urbanity in the forms of life, taste, and fashions that different social groups choose, with tastes that vary with the times, and that they find more attractive as places and forms rather than as their shared practices. There are those who hate urbanity too. For the sociologists, from Georg Simmel to Francois Ascher, the urban character would be more or less that of a constructed and accessible public place, adapted and suited to the social practices of the majority.

But that is not what we are talking about here. Those are tangential urbanities. We want to speak about the urban qualities of things, of the urbanity of urban things, about why and how the urban is urban. We accept the challenge of the sociologists when they sometimes play down the values of space to give primacy to behavior, forgetting that behavior is derived from models that, in their "urbanity", are spatial, dimensional, and physical.

Simultaneity, temporality, and plurality are the attributes of the city. We have to think in these terms when it comes to making a city. And "making a city" is the object of the urban project, at whatever scale, in whatever country, with whatever program, even though only rarely attained. There is a lot of confusion and hot air concerning what constitutes the urban. A lot of architects talk about "urban architecture" as they clumsily project buildings full of confusion. Bewilderment and complication are confused with supposed urban complexity. Nouvel's gherkin on a corner of the extension of Barcelona is an elementary, autistic, and self-referential building. Norman Foster's almost identical gherkin in London establishes such a richness in its complex relation with the context that one can readily call it urban architecture of the first order. The tertiary growth in the Pudong of Shanghai that has come under so much criticism organizes the use of the free spaces in relation to a metropolitan project which confers on it a modern and very civic condition of new urbanity in the face of the strange society that is emerging in social-capitalist China: the opposite of the laconic Canary Wharf, a pure department store of postmodern buildings and jobs without the slightest urban temporality or simultaneity. The absence of subjectivism in the Tate Modern is urban: the anecdotal recent projects in Barcelona by Toyo Ito or David Chipperfield, far from it. Los Angeles is urban, Berlin 2000, what a pity! Etc., etc.

Urbanity is articulation, complexity and difference. Articulation of floors, pavements, roadways, itineraries, supports, empty spaces. Buildings and activities are like qualifications, but in the end they are complementary to the urban base. The materials

422

and the relations between the materials are what counts: distances, rhythms, continuities, sequences, conflicts. Space that is socially shared, yes, but not only that. Intensity of use, and of participation in the detail, the variety of the parts—almost the opposite of monumentality, except, perhaps, when it becomes conventional, repetitive, innocuous.

Temporality is in the walls and the levels. In the city, the walls talk to the levels. Their textures and differences break the uniformity of the spaces and create intersection and conflict. It is in the relation between floor and level, it might be argued, that exhibition and emphasis are created. To pay attention to the walls as contours of urban space is to recognize the unquestionable role of the ground floors, the location of the dissolution of the boundary between public and private, of the diversity and spatial control of traffic, the ways in which interior and exterior are enmeshed.

Articulation of articles which do not lie in functions or activity, but in the material of walls and corners, in differences of level and façades, in roadsides and traffic islands, windows, doorways, and displays, in ramps and traffic lights, in alignments and recesses, in moldings and cantilevers, in silhouettes and billboards, in platforms and empty spaces, gaps and wastelands.

The urbanity of the material lies today, above all, in the extensive, empty and discontinuous periphery as much as in the dense and compact city, both in the commercial centers or housing blocks and in the margins of solitary infrastructures or of intensive hubs.

But, beware: urbanity is a concept that is often misinterpreted. It is sometimes used as a synonym of correction, conventionalism, traditional urbanism. It is associated with the compact, dense, centralized European city. Not at all. We are interested in a new concept of urbanity, precisely as something that contemporary (global, territorial, hybrid, and scattered) urbanization regards as its major resource. It is the new urbanity of the distances and silences of the incipient peripheries, the internal brilliance in intersections, in wastelands, of the mute presence of industrial-ized construction and of banal architecture.

An urbanity that is not made up of conviviality, of com-mercial axes and historic centers of laid-out parks, lively bars, and prestigious public buildings, but of the new material com-plexity of the inhabited areas (complexity of structures, uses, empty spaces, levels, dimensions, references). Creating projects for this "material urbanity" presupposes, provisionally, turning confusion into clarity and opaqueness into language. Proceeding in the opposite direction would mean falling back on complica-tion, that short-sighted refuge of so many urban projects, and, consequently, clarifying and expressing the conceptual layered characteristic of the contemporary city in real material diagrams of that complexity.

Qualitative density is of more importance than quantita-tive density to intense urbanity; a qualitative density that refers to the variety and number of superimposed references in a place, building or zone. Not just any densification guarantees a better intensity; indeed, at times, it simply becomes congestion or confusion. It is in the coexistence of differences that qualitative urban energy emerges. It is "mixity" rather than "density" that can characterize contemporary urbanity, and it is particularly absent in the speculative peripheries or tourist areas thematized ad nauseam by promoters and architects.

In reasserting "material" urbanity, I am thus distancing myself from a conventional and bland idea of urbanity as an ethereal quality, almost as idealized and attractive as tourist advertising, in which shopping, fashion, and animation are taken to be the current version of the discrete charm of the bourgeoisie that characterized many of the prosperous urban centers of the nineteenth and twentieth centuries in Europe and the United States. That ideological fantasy has very little that is material in its origin, and involves too much sociological wishful thinking and an assault on the true expression of modern urbanity.

Fig. 6   Palermo, 1987. Photo: Roberto Collova.

Fig. 7   La Coruña, 2003. Photo: Miguel Moran.

Fig. 8   Passeio Atlantico, Porto, 2002.
Photo: Rosa Feliu.

Fig. 9   Via Brasso, Milan, 2000.
Photo: Cino Zucchi.

The urban project does not reside in the formal unity of the whole, nor in pure congestion, nor in a respect for the context in itself, but in the specific elements and episodes that relate people to things. And for this project or its handling we have to practice paying attention to things in the most down-to-earth sense of the term. Like in the critical realism of Raymond Carver's stories, or in the filmed backgrounds in some passages by Jim Jarmusch or Michael Winterbottom. For this purpose, we draw the urban projects in detail; the scrupulous realism is not ingenuousness but blind rage, a condemnation of vagueness and a clear presentation of the material to enable it to communicate its force. It is respect for the material that underlies a certain new critical realism. New objectivity?

Material urbanity is also a function of the use value, an old Marxist concept employed here in a more direct sense. It is the use of places that gives them collective meaning, so not only their location but also their real utilization by their users (frequency, diversity, itinerary, contribution, cost, publicity) forms an important part of the character, references, meaning and semantic charge that, as I have already indicated, are aspects of material urbanity.

The value of the intensity of urban use is always connected with the constant interdependence that the city establishes and reestablishes between the public and the private domains. A lot has been said on this subject. Traditionally, the city has been a means of bringing them together, to the advantage of one or the other at different times and in different places. But if the public spaces are the social image of the city, and the private plots are the privilege of the individual citizen, where contemporary urbanity may perhaps appear at its highest level in what we define as "collective spaces", hybrid spaces that are simultaneously public and private, where the force of urbanity as a spatial mechanism to mediate social differences becomes tangible, material, and sometimes conflict-ridden (Figs. 6, 7, 8, and 9).

426

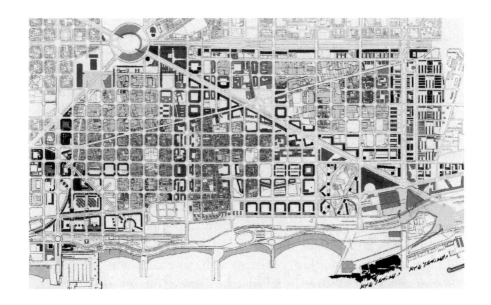

The Gaze Upon the City

I. 18 I want to reflect, above all, on the effort made to understand and to serve the interests of cities by an insistent and eager gaze, and of the difficulty of carrying this out. Underlying all my work is an attentive and cautious approach to the richness of urban sites—both their existing richness and, above all, potential richness (Fig. 10). This assiduous gaze becomes the starting point for resolutions, which though distinct in every case are always bound up with the city that lies beyond. Deep down then, there is a breath of optimism, a naive confidence in the richness of urban facts (urban in the generic sense, of course, without preferred models); a confidence surely born of the very same eager gaze that the sage astronomers fixed on the heavens.

427

Fig. 10   Plan of Barcelona, 2000.

Operating on the city does not mean solving problems; it means I. 72 increasing clarity while creating ambiguity at the same time in order to bring the great wealth of significance contained in places to the forefront, creating places where before there were none; introducing unsuspected scales of reference, taking advantage of anything that strikes the senses in order to augment the mental significance of the site.

The way of life in Saint-Nazaire is indifferent. In Porto people live strictly and ceremoniously. In Trieste, conventionally but nervously. In Groningen, people dress elegantly and with sophistication. And just as in the way someone dresses, so the form of a city creates the character of its places. I find that maintaining an intention consistent with this character is difficult, sometimes too subtle to be relied upon, but essential even so to the task of developing projects in cities.

The lack of proportion between the gigantic submarine base and the townhouses in Saint-Nazaire demanded a strategy of connection and transition. The north–south orientation of the huge concrete bunker breaks the harbor apart, leaving it tangential to the city. To reverse this orientation, it was necessary to challenge the hierarchy of spaces, to turn around Lemaresquier's planning. Reaching the pen's roof would introduce it into the sequence of large public spaces; yet, above all, its great mass would be made accessible, as would be the transparent interior (Fig. 11).

In tracing out a wide and powerful shape for the new Largo Cavour between the station and the Riva, a replica of the façade of the Borgo Teresiano, the hinge between the city and the Porto Vecchio becomes an evident emblematic main urban space, generally stimulating the residents' economic, sociological, and functional use of the whole section behind it. For the rest, it will find its way. As far as the project is concerned, what matters here is marking the intersection, the starting point, the reference point from which the

Fig. 11　The condition of "historical periphery" or better said "periphery
of history", showing the non-central, non-empty, non-closed, and non-precise
character of the area. A history of human and urban facts brought together
has made this area inert and fit for burning. That is the historical city of a minor
city but made of huge urban facts. Transformation of the Submarine Base,
Saint-Nazaire, 1996–2002. Photo: Rosa Feliu.

Fig. 12 The Largo Cavour building creates continuity between the harbor façades and allows the entrance of the maritime front along the urban façade. Porto Vecchio, Trieste, 1999–2001.

new relationships between the station and its square, the Borgo and its façades, and the Riva and its traffic become clear and effective.

The proposal is to build a mass that meshes. The volume and quantity of a built frontage are the elements that guarantee the later transformation of the warehouses and streets beyond for diverse uses. It constitutes a façade to the city, to the Borgo Teresiano, rather than to the sea.

The strategy in Trieste is about replacing the former material to "urbanize" it more. It has a good character that can now be put to an urban use. Most important is to break through the visual obstruction, the wall of buildings and the closed physical and administrative boundaries and to entertain only those activities which extend the mixed and collective everyday urban use of derelict industrial structures once meant for shipping and long lying empty (Fig. 12).

The Saint-Nazaire and Trieste projects both proclaim urban relations as their main subject, and the transformation of this urban relation is what defines the characteristic strategies of the proposal. How is it possible to relate a small residential town with a huge military bunker, deserted and inert, or to integrate the large spread of the eighteenth-century harbor warehouses with the urban panel of the city center (Figs. 13 and 14)?

There is a strategic gesture behind the demolition of the highway along the breakwater road in the case of Porto's Atlantic Marginal; we are losing a wall that shields an introverted terrain from the waves and gaining instead a low arc of a beach that comes together topographically with the green park of the interior beneath an autonomous and transparent viaduct (Fig. 15).

There is plenty of topographical conviction in this project to challenge the engineering urge to gather stone defense work in front of the sea and, in the other direction, to propose the extraction of tons of soil to bring the natural profiles of the valley forward into the sea, in the vertical, and of the beach towards the inside in the horizontal.

The relationship between community park and shore, which had been one of mutual ignorance has been reversed, recreated. The same goes for the renewed contact between Porto and Matosinhos, as well as for the awareness of the urban coast, now a setting for cultural experiences, a setting that is intellectually prepared and artificially naturalized (Fig. 16). This strategy deals with the perception and imagination of space, seeking out a contemporary significance for a space initially having no meaning other than the apparent amassing of practical defects.

There is, however, a far more specific relation between public ways (avenue, road, street) and location, which I have always studied with interest: the visual perception of the changing totality of a place as experienced while driving on the road. When driving down a stretch of an avenue or a dual highway, we not only see its length and the geometry of its layout, we perceive the measure of its corresponding surrounding space. And this vision comes to be one of the most significant for understanding the city (or the territory). What deserves to be called a panoramic view is something that only the road alignment, by opening a wide space, can offer as a view ahead of us. "The view from the street" was a behaviorist analysis of the changing vision and the explaining capacity of kinetic perception. But I'm talking about a different thing here: the capacity for understanding the urban space by the transversal relationship the road establishes between its edges, especially if they are not façades. From Porto's Marginal, we understand the coast, its irregularity and constancy, the sea in its movements, its colors and waves, its far away character and its proximity to the people who approach its shore and in the slow rhythm of their walk. All this taken together provides us with the scale of the space, its physical relationships, and the complexity of its events.

And taken in reverse, from the walk, from its own walking and resting platforms, it is perceived as the place where traffic crosses. The static or slow condition of the crossed spaces shares

432

in this vision of movement and of the impressions of connection and interdependence suggested by its presence. That is why it is so very important to reaffirm this mutual vision between roads and walkways by its doubling at varying levels so that one becomes the "stage" for the other; from the walking spaces you can see the cars and when driving you will notice the walkways, different but complementary, different materials, distinctly urbanistic (Figs. 17 and 18).

The aim is to reinvent these walkways in a contemporary way, taking advantage of the cities' everyday technological and cultural revolution. In my original project, for the Moll de la Fusta in the Port of Barcelona, I had already applied this doubling of traffic and walks (in a literal way there) and, where the transversal section between Ciutat Vella's façades and the port dock articulate a vertical relationship that hides the parking space and some of the traffic lanes, created the idea of an urban balcony above the sea as a strategy of double tension between spaces and levels of mutual integration. The observation upwards and downwards creates a place and a scale where there was only a road surface before and where the city–sea transversal quality was ignored and/or denied (Figs. 19 and 20).

The act of establishing four lanes of slow urban traffic, two central lanes reserved for public transport, and a further four lanes of fast traffic, semi-concealed in the 180-meter-wide strip, though not buried, where vehicles remain integral to the place and contribute to the creation of it, constitutes a typological invention of urban elements (walkways, sidewalks, platforms, docks, terraces, small buildings, bridges, skylights, viewpoints, etc.) which are linked by superposition, contact, or rhythm. The merging of disparate types of roads and spaces makes the site new.

In Genoa too, the proposal of a "sottocorso", a new intermediate carriageway between the level of the harbor and its workshops (the *cantieri navali*) and the dual highway (*sopraelevata*), besides offering a solution to the problem of functional

433

Fig. 13   General plan of the intervention and new spatial configuration, Porto Vecchio, Trieste, 1999–2001.

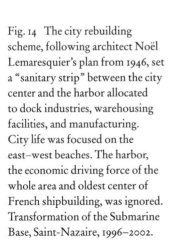

Fig. 14   The city rebuilding scheme, following architect Noël Lemaresquier's plan from 1946, set a "sanitary strip" between the city center and the harbor allocated to dock industries, warehousing facilities, and manufacturing. City life was focused on the east–west beaches. The harbor, the economic driving force of the whole area and oldest center of French shipbuilding, was ignored. Transformation of the Submarine Base, Saint-Nazaire, 1996–2002.

Fig. 15 The viaduct, a two-winged white concrete slab on a single asymmetrical pillar, offers a very thin profile of only 90 centimeters for all of its almost 150 meters of length, allowing a clear view of the sea and the sky. Passeio Atlantico, Porto, 1999–2002. Photo: Rosa Feliu.

Fig. 16 The greatest interest, and difficulty, in the Porto project is to articulate the natural form of the park's interior with the marine front. The proposal lays out a transition from the greenery, the rocks, and the sand through the topographical neck that forms the banks of the valley and which is reinforced by the viaduct's horizontal orientation. Passeio Atlantico, Porto, 1999–2002.

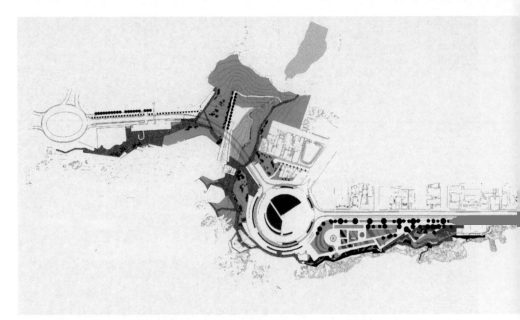

Fig. 17 Masterplan of the coastline, Passeio Atlantico, Porto, 1999–2002. The aim is a double walking experience along the coast, with transforming gardens at the higher level, along Avenida Montevideu, and a light pedestrian walkway on the lower level, right next to the beaches.

Fig. 18 Example of a garden and the pedestrian promenade along Avenida Montevideu. Photo: Rosa Feliu.

Fig. 19   Relationship between the new public facilities and infrastructure, Moll de la Fusta, Barcelona 1987.

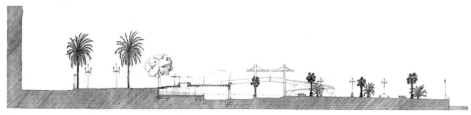

Fig. 20   Urban and constructive section showing the relationship between different levels at the Moll de la Fusta , Barcelona, 1987.

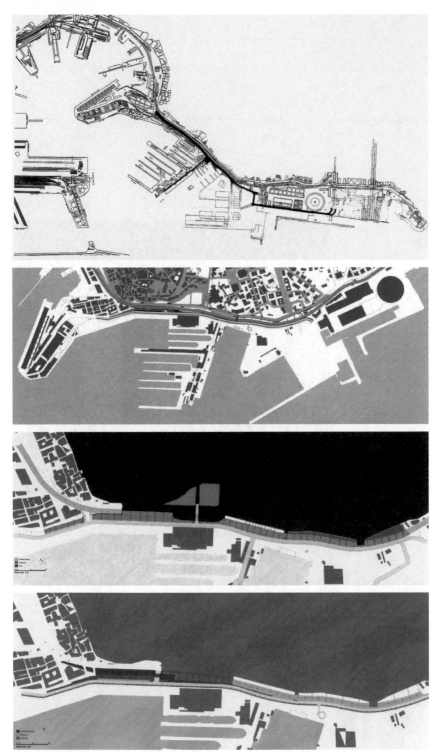

Fig. 21 General plans of the different levels of the intervention, Cantieri Navali, Genoa, 1998–1999.

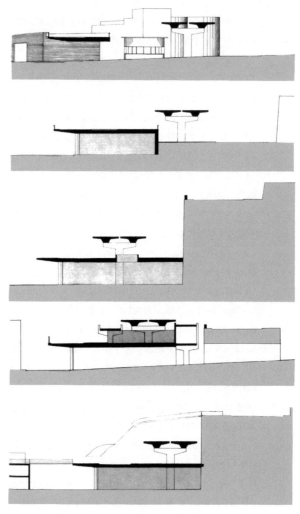

Fig. 22 Proposed new profiles and relationships with the old docks, Cantieri Navali, Genoa, 1998–1999.

Fig. 23 Section with the proposed new use, joining the new Sotto-Corso with the existing Sopraelevata. Cantieri Navali, Genova, 1998–1999.

independence and of the modernization of each one of its levels, creates a panoramic balcony where traffic and parking provide visual cognizance of the place (Figs. 21, 22, and 23). This simultaneous awareness of the harbor in both of its two environments— the new and the old—and of the urban topography, affords an understanding that has only become possible due to the scale provided by the new traffic way. Because simultaneity is not a concept found in the vocabularies of the civil and architectural syntactic works, we should instead turn to the intellectual, the emotional, or even the poetic references to the urban condition (size, complexity, diversity, and conflict) they transmit, and of which they are a result.

The millimetric adjustment between the levels of the dock, the *sopraelevata*, and the corso suggests a similar strategy of urban intervention. Indeed, it is by assimilating the conflict and confusion of its structures, pillars, ramps, warehouses, properties, domains, movements, barriers, gradients, and, above all, its images and visual references that we can come right to the point of the urban substance, to the very roots of any idea. Only by appreciating the significant value of each one of these urban objects as components of a mental cataclysm, is it possible to approach urbanistic creativity.

Doubling spaces, adding things instead of eliminating them, (in Genoa, all mayors begin their terms by promising to demolish the *sopraelevata*; but here it is the opposite: double it) enriching places, while specializing them, creating urbanity in the things themselves, in their own material.

The strategic project is derived from an attempt to step beyond designed objects. The scale of a project is not a result of the dimensions of the work but rather of the relationships it is capable of bringing into play. Scale, let us repeat it again, is relative, the respective proportions of the transformations that we are proposing and their incidence in the general urban structure, in the mental comprehension of the overall built space.

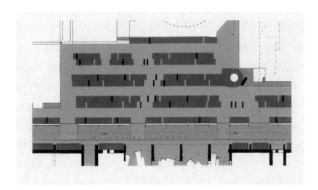

In these projects I found that four preliminary self-reinforcing conditions had to be met: the required distances between structural elements to provide interior transparency, the abundant penetration of daylight, clarity in the circulation of vehicles and pedestrians, and a clear relationship with the surface from both the visual and the functional viewpoint.

The new nexus between urban use and the awareness of territory, landscape, and periphery which is formed through and on top of Saint-Nazaire's U-boat pen (Fig. 24) is far more meticulous, even though the material size of its elements would seem to imply the contrary. Bringing the loneliness of the industrial harbor together with the homogeneity of the residential city called for a strategy of the half, of the scarcely just begun, and then only indirectly appropriated. The tense dialogue between heavy construction bulk and a parking void was silenced by the total absence of any conventional urban elements. A strategy was required that employed the calm of raw cement and its everlasting character as mass.

This way of thinking could be called inductive structuralism, a comprehension of the systemic condition of urban facts and, at the same time, an operational intent focused on neuralgic points. Acupuncture maybe, though not in its misleading interpretation as the practice of multiplying and sewing small elements; rather in

441

Fig. 24 The piano-shaped parking lots confer centrality, considering access and parking facilities as a spatial relationship typical of peripheral centrality. Transformation of the Submarine Base, Saint-Nazaire, 1996–2002.

its true clinical sense of acting on one point in order to cure many others precisely by virtue of having affected the nervous system and the metabolism in their entirety (Figs. 25 and 26).

Looking for a structural strategy does not of course deny a project's further intentions. The formal search for place, the attention to precursors as narrative possibilities is an underlying constant. Because of its strategic character, a project will always leave open certain unaddressed questions, loose ends and unmarked traps, such that time and use will override the hand of the project author.

442

Fig. 25 Overall view of the Almere waterfront proposal, 1998.
Fig. 26 The logic of the acupuncture: diversity of uses shaped by the sequence of public spaces in the Almere project.

I. 108   The city is a heavy magma that flows or seeps like a sea or sand bank, rising and falling according to the energy of its own interior mass. Its sensitivity to the gravity of urban forms finds meaning and beauty in the density of events, buildings, open spaces, and volumes in the urban landscape.

The desire to accumulate the whole functional and expressive load of a strong mixed program into a façade of 340 meters is, as in the Illa Diagonal or the Maquinista projects, an attempt to give form to this oscillating magma. These projects read their surroundings as anonymous and compact, and they consider that a reliance on the customary Barcelona skyline of six-to-seven-story buildings allows for little comprehension of its extensive mass. And they believe that, whenever possible, the exhibition of a continuous front of such considerable dimensions will establish a scale rarely seen in the common fabric and is therefore capable of evoking references to the total city in the imagination.

The manipulation of qualitative density—that is, the mingling of the conflict between, and the concentration of diverse quantitative densities of construction, of activity, of population, of movement—is, I think, an interesting path for the urban project to take. For the structural form of the Barcelona metropolis, the large scale of elements, such as the Diagonal and the Pare de la Sagrera, play an important role in establishing the main relationships between the city's old town, the Eixample, as well as the incorporated nuclei and neighborhoods, and I'm interested in forcing a muscular distillation of urban form upon them.

In Badalona, or in Alcoi, the creation of a neighborhood from scratch along the outlines of the former fabric condenses a variety of forms of buildings and of roadways of small, medium, and large dimensions into a limited space. The task of the project is to achieve density of form and its insertion into the general

443

morphological system. The effect is the condensation of many urban referents (congestion, style, publicity, permanence, service) into the same place.

The specificity of Alcoi is related to the tiny fabric of its old town. Everything there seems to have been built using a meter rule only 80 centimeters long. The streets, the open spaces, the housing, and the commercial spaces are all miniscule. The slopes, on the other hand, are exaggerated. This minuteness will be important as input and in pursuit of the condensed form. In Badalona, a reading of the city picks up, above all, its grid morphology, its delta-like flatness and, as a result, its propensity towards regular form organized according to regular shapes and sizes, to syntactical continuities. The proposed Cyber District on the footprint of the domestic airport in Herrera, Santo Domingo is another bet playing with the same cards.

In l'Illa Diagonal in Barcelona, the project proposes an occupation of the site that does not imply its splitting into parts but instead a reinforcement of its singularity as a center of the city's interest.

The project, shared with Rafael Moneo, concentrates on the weight of the building and its uses, providing la Diagonal with the largest possible façade in length, height. and depth, and the maximum of activities. Perforating this front, and acquiring presence in it, an inner park announces the location of the residential hotel of low height, with dining rooms on the ground floor, at park level, rather than the usual vertical business hotel (Figs. 27 and 28).

Cultural, service, and educational uses add to the depth of the park and the hotel. All these are aggregated in the prioritized orientation that acquires architectonic expression in the double game of the big façade and its penetrations into the park.

The exceptional characteristics of the site, a block of land about 420 meters long, and its proximity to the new Gran Parque Lineal de la Sagrera necessitate a large architectional project

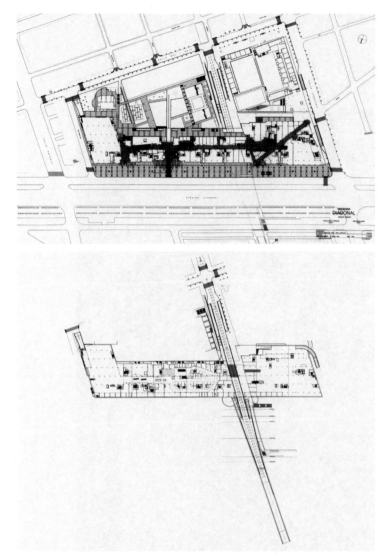

Fig. 27   Plans of the ground and underground levels, illustrating the interdependence between public space, infrastructure, and building interiors. Illa Diagonal, Barcelona, 1992.

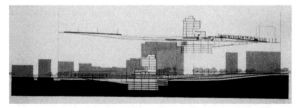

Fig. 28   Section across Carabela de la Niña street showing the profile of Illa Diagonal, Barcelona, 1992.

Fig. 29   Implementation in the urban context of Sagrera's new urban park, Barcelona, 2003.

which simultaneously takes into account the tertiary, commercial and residential premises alongside the hotel facilities (Fig. 29).

The proposed planning joins built volumes into a single linear building of broken aspect, looming over the park as a very large façade on an urban scale. The importance of this public space as an access to the central city and to Sagrera's TGV station, and as an imposing landmark within the built fabric of the district, requires both suitable planning in accordance with the mobile perceptions of pedestrians and an overall conception of landscape that allows us simultaneously to perceive its sheer size and variety.

The cantilevers of vertical blocks appearing over the horizontal bar and the sequence of passages below them in the interior of the project confer on every visitor a variety of effects and contrasts: light and shadow, a sense of space and confinement, near and distant effects, all of which display the advantages of having chosen an open and continuous building system.

In the Sant Andreu district of Barcelona, the project of state-subsidized housing is a city project. Residences and parking lots are a public service, but they also have to raise capital.

The modernization of the old industrial and proletarian area on the eleven-hectare site of the ancient Sant Andreu's Barracks in Barcelona proposes an intensive program of public facilities and 2,000 state-subsidized apartments. The combination of such a variety of needs has demanded radical options in the aggregation of residences and shops along a central axis that links with the main avenue of the borough, and which, according to the unities of arbitrary verticality, is able to accommodate the great height. At either end some low-rise public-use buildings—schools, hospital centers, library, swimming pool, sports center, and a hostel—will be added, organized in a lineal boulevard in an innovative urban typology (Figs. 30 and 31).

The modal interchange point of trains, buses, cars, taxis, cyclists, and pedestrians in Leuven, translated into an urban complex of stations, tunnels, garages, ramps, platforms, and

447

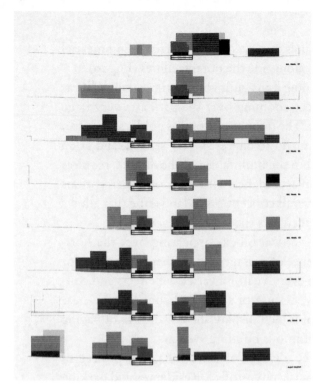

Fig. 31 Transversal design profiles of the Sant Andreu project, Barcelona, 2005.

Fig. 30 The project's guidelines for the urban layout along a central axis. Sant Andreu, Barcelona, 2005.

squares is intended to condense the accumulation of flows at the intersection of the two façades, in combination with the empty interior space formed by the stations, into a reference point for the city. The memorable and undoubtedly canonical presence of the old station's volume on the pedestrian square, in conjunction with the system of accesses and waiting rooms in the underground areas, proposes a sequential reading of multiple paths that results in an explicit and stable urban form.

The fact that in these projects the design mechanism and the attention to façades and intersections are central techniques underlines their consciously conventional processes. Perhaps it is precisely this methodological neutrality that enables these projects to maximize innovative efficacy and singularity as urban products.

The Anxious Gaze

I. 142

I have found myself in situations in which projects, from the outset and instinctively, have emerged as a reaction, as a counter-attack, as a confrontation with some given situation; circumstances which though presented as problematic, nevertheless present no greater problem than their own faulty conceptualization.

Against urbanistic frigidity: promiscuity. Against sclerotic functional schematics: heterogeneous accumulation.

Like the deserted space at Alexanderplatz seen against Berlin's encyclopedic splendor, the qualitative low density of Rotterdam's Alexanderpolder is a prototypical example of disappointed intelligence (Figs. 32 and 33). For the strict branch of the CIAM, for Bakema, it served as the model for the perfect residential city—in the crossroads of Europe joining Paris, London, and Moscow. The Y-shaped block and the associated open spaces were urbanistic utopianism with a basis in social engagement.

449

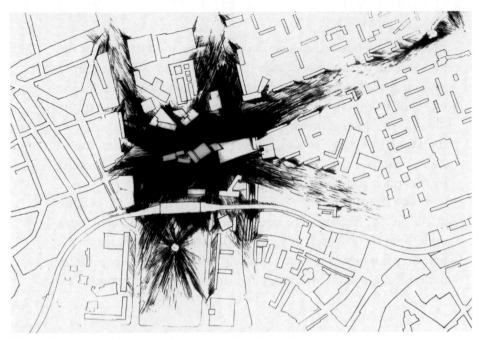

Fig. 32 The Alexanderplatz as congestive place of buildings, in tension across
the Stalin Allee and Karl-Marx Platz. It has been suggested that the void
be transformed into a conflict of public activities and housing, Berlin, 1990.

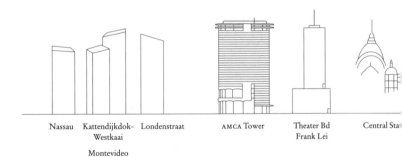

Nassau   Kattendijkdok- Londenstraat   AMCA Tower   Theater Bd   Central Sta
         Westkaai   Frank Lei

         Montevideo

Fig. 33   Axonometric projection of two density
proposals, taking the conflict between
the road system and the buildings to the limit.
Alexanderpolder, Rotterdam, 1990.

Fig. 34   Layout plan of the Falcon–Nassau axis,
Antwerp, 1993.

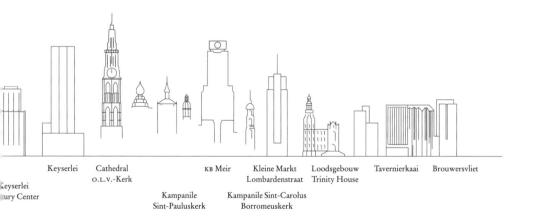

| Keyserlei | Cathedral | | KB Meir | Kleine Markt | Loodsgebouw | Tavernierkaai | Brouwersvliet |
| | O.L.V.-Kerk | | | Lombardenstraat | Trinity House | | |

Keyserlei
tury Center

Kampanile
Sint-Pauluskerk

Kampanile Sint-Carolus
Borromeuskerk

Fig. 35   Comparison with other urban profiles, Het Eijlande, Antwerp, 1990–1993.

Then came the rules, the distances, the repetitions. Parallel bands of defensive spaces barring all contact. Please! Let's provoke promiscuity. It's not impossible! But not as rule; as an opportunity.

What a great opportunity for Genoa, too, to be able to add a *sopraelevata*, a corso, and the ramps from the old town in the hills down to its base, crammed full of port warehouses, customs houses, silos, fish markets, captains' headquarters, and sheds. All of it descending almost vertically towards the port. Increasing the contradiction by accumulating more form, with the necessary strategic precision, allows for a reinterpretation of the problem, a pinning down of the conflict, at the same time opening up new possibilities of use. Less times less is more.

A certain heterogeneous accumulation is also sought in the transformation of larger areas, as in the projects for Antwerp or Arnhem. This is a quite different thought from the "collage" and the "patchwork". Far from it. Here, by contrast, there are articulation and difference, sequential contrasts and mutual references. Here there must be no arbitrary self-satisfaction towards rupture, or comfortable pleasure in the fragment (Figs. 34, 35, and 36). For examples of those, twenty years of postmodern architecture offer us today a panorama of interventions that are as strident in their origins as they are disgraceful or irrelevant in their results.

In order to operate in the contemporary city, we need to think about adding, complicating, insisting. Accumulating strata. Superimposing languages and references. Multiplying traces even though they may seem incompatible, provoking unprecedented juxtapositions. It is not enough to mix uses and functions; sometimes it will be necessary to create conflict and congestion among material contacts, mental references, the many orders of urbanity, with so many different identities.

Fig. 36   Night view, Het Eijlande, Antwerp, 1990–1993.

Copyright Information and Credits

Christopher Alexander
A Pattern Language

Oswald Mathias Ungers
A Thematic Repertoire

List of Images

Fig. 1. Christopher Alexander, Sara Ishikawa, and Murray Silverstein, *A Pattern Language: Towns, Buildings, Construction* (New York: Oxford University Press, 1977), 163.

Fig. 2. Ibid., 165.

Fig. 3. Ibid., 166.

Fig. 4. Ibid., 167.

Fig. 5. Ibid., 270.

Fig. 6. Ibid., 271.

Fig. 7. Ibid., 272.

Fig. 8. Ibid., 272.

Fig. 9. Ibid., 273.

Fig. 10. Ibid., 273.

Fig. 11. Ibid., 274.

Fig. 12. Ibid., 310.

Fig. 13. Ibid., 312.

Fig. 14. Ibid., 313.

Fig. 15. Ibid., 451.
 Photo by Eugene Atget.

Fig. 16. Ibid., 453.

Fig. 17. Ibid., 453.

List of Images

Fig. 1: Oswald Mathias Ungers, *Morphologie: City Metaphors* (Cologne: Verlag der Buchhandlung Walther König, 1982), 60–61. Left image: Plan of the city of St. Gallen, Merian, 1809.

Fig. 2: Ibid., 124–125. Left image: Tenecmitlen.

Fig. 3: Ibid., 76–77. Left image: General plan of Riverside, 1890.

Fig. 4: Ibid., 92–93. Left image: Toulouse le Miraille, Candilis, Josic, Woods, 1958

Fig. 5. Oswald Mathias Ungers, *Architettura come tema/Architecture as theme* (Milan: Electa, 1982), 8. Copperplate engraving by Gabriel Krammer, 1600.

Fig. 6. Oswald Mathias Ungers, Stefan Vieths, *Die dialektische Stadt* (Braunschweig/Wiesbaden: Vieweg, 1999), 9.

Fig. 7. Ibid., 11. Plans by Walter Gropius, 1929; Le Corbusier, 1922; Ivan Leonidov, 1930.

Fig. 8. Ibid., 12. Painting by Giovani Paolo Pannini, 1756.

Fig. 9. Ibid., 14. Plans by Cancellotti, Montuori, Piccinato, and Scalpelli, 1933–1934 and Hans Bernhard Reichow, 1948.

Fig. 10. Ibid., 15.

Fig 11. Ibid., 17.

Fig. 12. Ibid., 19.

Fig. 13. Ungers, *Architecture as theme*, 30.

Fig. 14. Ibid.

Fig. 15. Ibid.

Fig. 16. Ibid.

Fig. 17. Ibid., 32.

Fig. 18. Ibid.

Fig. 19. Ibid.

Fig. 20. Ibid., 34

Fig. 21. Ibid.

Fig. 22. Ibid., 36.

Fig. 23. Ibid.

Fig. 24. Ibid., 38.

Fig. 25. Ibid., 39.

Fig. 26. Ibid., 36.

Fig. 27. Ibid.

Fig. 28. Ibid.

Fig. 29. Ibid., 50.

Fig. 30. Ibid., 52.

Fig. 31. Ibid., 53.

Fig. 32. Ibid., 50.

Fig. 33. Ungers et al., *Die dialektische Stadt*, 81.

Fig. 34. Ibid., 82.

Fig. 35. Ibid., 85.

Fig. 36. Ibid., 86.

Fig. 37. Ibid., 87.

Fig. 38. Ibid., 88–89.

Fig. 39. Ibid.

Fig. 40. Ibid., 90.

Fig. 41. Ibid.

List of Images

Fig. 1. Fumihiko Maki, *Investigations in Collective Form*, Special Publication of the School of Architecture (St. Louis: Washington University, 1964), 6.

Fig. 2. Ibid., 7.

Fig. 3. Ibid.

Fig. 4. Ibid., 10. Model by Kenzo Tange et al., 1960.

Fig. 5. Ibid., 12.

Fig. 6. Ibid., 14. Model by Noriaki Kurokawa, 1960.

Fig. 7. Ibid., 17. Photo by Susumu Higachi.

Fig. 8. Fumihiko Maki and Mark Mulligan (eds.), *Nurturing Dreams. Collected Essays on Architecture and the City* (Cambridge: MIT Press, 2008), 69. Photo by ASPI.

Fig. 9. Ibid. Photo by Maki & Associates.

Fig. 10. Ibid., 71. Photo by Shinkenchiku-sha.

Fig. 11. Ibid., 73. Photo by Maki & Associates.

Fig. 12. Ibid., 75. Photo by Maki & Associates.

Fig. 13. Ibid., 79. Photo by Maki & Associates.

All materials © Alison Smithson
and Peter Smithson, 1993 and 1997,
reproduced with kind permission
of the Smithson Family Collection.

List of Images

Fig. 1. Alison Smithson and Peter
Smithson, *Italienische Gedanken,
weitergedacht* (Basel: Birkhäuser
Verlag, 2001), 27. Drawing by Charles
Waldstein, 1902.

Fig. 2. Alison Smithson and Peter
Smithson, *Italian Thoughts* (London:
Alison and Peter Smithson
Architects, 1993), 58. Drawing by
S. Smithson, 1983.

Fig. 3. Ibid. Photo by Peter Smithson, 1983.

Fig. 4. Ibid., 59. Drawings by G.
Coscarella and F. C. Franchi, 1981.

Fig. 5. Ibid., 60.
Photo by Peter Smithson, 1954.

Fig. 6. Ibid., 61. Sketch by
Peter Smithson, August 1983.

Fig. 7. Original map from a tourist shop
in Siena, 1983. Digital scan received
from the Smithson Family Collection,
10 February 2020.

Fig. 8. ILA&DU document, 1980s. Digital
scan received from the Smithson
Family Collection, 10 February 2020.

Fig. 9. Smithson and Smithson,
*Italienische Gedanken, weiterge-
dacht,* 32. Drawings by G. Coscarella
and F. C. Franchi, 1981.

Fig. 10. Photo by Peter Smithson, 1983.
Digital scan received from the
Smithson Family Collection,
10 February 2020.

Fig. 11. Photographer unknown. Digital
scan received from the Smithson
Family Collection, 10 February 2020.

Fig. 12. Photo by Alison and Peter
Smithson, 1960s. Digital scan received
from the Smithson Family Collection,
10 February 2020.

Fig. 13. Smithson and Smithson,
*Italienische Gedanken, weiterge-
dacht,* 45. Painting by unidentified
Dutch painter, ca. 1480–1485.

Fig. 14. Photo by Peter Smithson, 1995.
Digital scan received from
the Smithson Family Collection,
10 February 2020.

Fig. 15. Image from an unidentified
American magazine, 1950s. Digital
scan received from the Smithson
Family Collection, 10 February 2020.

Fig. 16. Smithson and Smithson,
*Italienische Gedanken, weiterge-
dacht,* 75. Photo from a postcard.

Fig. 17. Photo by Peter Smithson, 1992.
Digital scan received from the
Smithson Family Collection,
10 February 2020.

Fig. 18. Photo by Peter Smithson, 1985.
Digital scan received from
the Smithson Family Collection,
10 February 2020.

Fig. 19. Smithson and Smithson,
*Italienische Gedanken, weiterge-
dacht,* 72. Photo by Peter Smithson,
1972.

Fig. 20. Photo by Peter Smithson, 1978.
Digital scan received from
the Smithson Family Collection,
10 February 2020.

Fig. 21. Smithson and Smithson, *Italienische Gedanken, weitergedacht*, 82. Drawing by D. G. Cavallero, 1985.

Fig. 22. Photo by Peter Smithson, 1968. Digital scan received from the Smithson Family Collection, 10 February 2020.

Fig. 23. Collage by Peter Smithson, 1972. Digital scan received from the Smithson Family Collection, 10 February 2020.

Fig. 24. Collage by Peter Smithson, 1972. Digital scan received from the Smithson Family Collection, 10 February 2020.

Fig. 25. Collage by Peter Smithson, 1972. Digital scan received from the Smithson Family Collection, 10 February 2020.

Fig. 26. Smithson and Smithson, *Italienische Gedanken, weitergedacht*, 98. Diagram by Peter Smithson, 2000.

Fig. 27. Photo by Peter Smithson, 1990. Digital scan received from the Smithson Family Collection, 10 February 2020.

Fig. 28. Photo from a postcard. Digital scan received from the Smithson Family Collection, 10 February 2020.

Fig. 29. Smithson and Smithson, *Italienische Gedanken, weitergedacht*, 46. Drawing from a postcard.

Fig. 30. Photo by Peter Smithson, 1994. Digital scan received from the Smithson Family Collection, 10 February 2020.

All materials reproduced from *The Concise Townscape*, first paperback edition by Gordon Cullen, published by Routledge. © The Architectural Press, 1961, 1971; Reproduced by arrangement with Taylor & Francis Books UK.

List of Images

Fig. 1. Gordon Cullen, *The Concise Townscape*, first paperback edition with new material (London: The Architectural Press, 1971), 17. Photo by Gordon Cullen.

Fig. 2. Ibid., 18. Photo by Gordon Cullen.

Fig. 3. Ibid. Photo by Gordon Cullen.

Fig. 4. Ibid., 19. Photo by Gordon Cullen.

Fig. 5. Ibid., 20. Photo by Gordon Cullen.

Fig. 6. Ibid., 21. Photo by Eric de Mare.

Fig. 7. Ibid., 22. Photo by I. de Wolfe.

Fig. 8. Ibid. Photo by H. Dennis Jones.

Fig. 9. Ibid., 23. Photo by Cas Oorthuys.

Fig. 10. Ibid. Photo by Eric de Mare.

Fig. 11. Ibid. Photo by H. I. de Wolfe.

Fig. 12. Ibid., 29. Photo by Gordon Cullen.

Fig. 13. Ibid. Photo by Gordon Cullen.

Fig. 14. Ibid. Photo by Gordon Cullen.

Fig. 15. Ibid., 32. Photo by H. de Burgh Galwey.

Fig. 16. Ibid. Photo by Gordon Cullen.

Fig. 17. Ibid., 33. Photo by G. E. Kidder Smith.

Fig. 18. Ibid. Photo by Gordon Cullen.

459

Fig. 19. Ibid., 34.
   Photo by Gordon Cullen.
Fig. 20. Ibid. Photo by Ian Nairn.
Fig. 21. Ibid., 35. Photo by Ian Nairn.
Fig. 22. Ibid. © Cambridge
   University Press.
Fig. 23. Ibid., 44. © The Architectural
   Review.
Fig. 24. Ibid. © The Architectural
   Review.
Fig. 25. Ibid., 45. Photo by Gordon
   Cullen.
Fig. 26. Ibid. Photo by Gordon Cullen.
Fig. 27. Ibid., 49.
   Photo by Gordon Cullen.
Fig. 28. Ibid., 50.
   Photo by Gordon Cullen.
Fig. 29. Ibid. Photo by Gordon Cullen.
Fig. 30. Ibid. Photo by Gordon Cullen.
Fig. 31. Ibid., 51.
   Photo by Gordon Cullen.
Fig. 32. Ibid. Photo by Gordon Cullen.
Fig. 33. Ibid., 183.
   Photo by Gordon Cullen.
Fig. 34. Ibid., 184.
   Photo by Gordon Cullen.
Fig. 35. Ibid. Photo by Gordon Cullen.
Fig. 36. Ibid. Photo by Gordon Cullen.
Fig. 37. Ibid., 185.
   Photo by Gordon Cullen.
Fig. 38. Ibid. Photo by Gordon Cullen.
Fig. 39. Ibid., 186.
   Photo by Gordon Cullen.
Fig. 40. Ibid. Photo by Gordon Cullen.
Fig. 41. Ibid., 187.
   Photo by Gordon Cullen.
Fig. 42. Ibid. Photo by Gordon Cullen.
Fig. 43. Ibid. Photo by Gordon Cullen.

All materials © Lucius Burckhardt,
1975, 1979, 1981, 1995, 1996, and 1998,
reproduced by arrangement with
Martin Schmitz Verlag, Berlin.

List of Images
Fig. 1. Lucius Burckhardt,
   "Strollological Observations on
   Perception of the Environment and
   the Tasks Facing Our Generation",
   in Jesko Fezer and Martin Schmitz
   (eds.), *Lucius Burckhardt Writings.*
   Rethinking Man-made
   Environments. Politics, Landscape
   & Design (Vienna/New York:
   Springer, 2012), 241. Drawing
   by Lucius Burckhardt.
Fig. 2. Ibid., 240. Drawing by
   Lucius Burckhardt.

List of Images

Fig. 1. Bruno Latour, "From Realpolitik
to Dingpolitik or How to Make
Things Public", in: *Bruno Latour
and Peter Weibel, Making Things
Public—Atmospheres of Democracy*,
exhibition catalogue (Cambridge,
MA: MIT Press, 2005), 15. © AP Photo,
Greg Gibson.

Fig. 2. Ibid. © AFP/E-Lance Media.
Photo by Luke Frazza.

Fig. 3. Ibid., 17. © Comune di Siena.
Photo by Foto Lensini Siena.

Fig. 4. Ibid., 18. © AP Photo/
Richard Drew.

Fig. 5. Ibid., 19. Photo by
Sabine Himmelsbach.

Fig. 6. Ibid., 20. © NASA/Getty Images.

Fig. 7. Ibid., 22. © AP Photo/NASA,
Kim Shiflett.

Fig. 8. Ibid., 24. © Fondazione Cini.

Fig. 9. Ibid., 25. © Bibliothèque Nationale
de France.

Fig. 10. Ibid., 27. Photo by Bruno Latour.

Fig. 11. Ibid., 28. © Bibliothèque
Nationale de France.

Fig. 12. Ibid. © Wellcome Library,
London.

Fig. 13. Ibid., 32–33. © Katherine Blouin
and Vincent Demers.

Fig. 14. Ibid., 36. © Bibliothèque
Nationale de France, Département
des estampes et photo.

Fig. 15. Ibid., 42–43. © AP Photo,
David J. Phillip.

461

List of Images
Fig. 1. Manuel de Solà-Morales,
   A Matter of Things (Rotterdam:
   Nai Publishers, 2008), 27.
   Original artwork by
   Alexander Calder, 1934.
Fig. 2. Ibid., 26. Original artwork
   by Georges Braque, 1913.
Fig. 3. Ibid., 27. Original artwork
   by Kasimir Malevich, 1915–1916.
Fig. 4. Ibid. Original artwork
   by Joan Miró, 1925.
Fig. 5. Ibid., 29. Original artwork
   by George Brecht, 1975.
Fig. 6. Ibid., 149.
   Photo by Roberto Collova.
Fig. 7. Ibid. Photo by Miguel Moran.
Fig. 8. Ibid. Photo by Rosa Feliu.
Fig. 9. Ibid. Photo by Cino Zucchi.
Fig. 10. Ibid., 21.
Fig. 11. Ibid., 39. Photo by Rosa Feliu.
Fig. 12. Ibid., 44.
Fig. 13. Ibid.
Fig. 14. Ibid., 34.
Fig. 15. Ibid., 49. Photo by Rosa Feliu.
Fig. 16. Ibid., 48.
Fig. 17. Ibid., 56.
Fig. 18. Ibid., 57. Photo by Rosa Feliu.
Fig. 19. Ibid., 74.
Fig. 20. Ibid., 75.
Fig. 21. Ibid., 60.
Fig. 22. Ibid., 61.
Fig. 23. Ibid., 59.

Fig. 24. Ibid., 40.
   Photo by Rosa Feliu.
Fig. 25. Ibid., 76.
Fig. 26. Ibid.
Fig. 27. Ibid., 112–113.
Fig. 28. Ibid., 113.
Fig. 29. Ibid., 110.
Fig. 30. Ibid., 99.
Fig. 31. Ibid.
Fig. 32. Ibid., 118.
Fig. 33. Ibid., 122.
Fig. 34. Ibid., 126.
Fig. 35. Ibid., 127.
Fig. 36. Ibid.

Library of Congress Control Number 2019955725

Bibliographic information published by the German National Library

The German National Library lists this publication in the Deutsche Nationalbibliografie; detailed bibliographic data are available on the Internet at http://dnb.dnb.de.

ISBN 978-3-0356-2076-4

© 2021 Daniel Kiss, Simon Kretz, and Birkhäuser Verlag GmbH, Basel P.O. Box 44, 4009 Basel, Switzerland Part of Walter de Gruyter GmbH, Berlin/Boston

9 8 7 6 5 4 3 2 1 www.birkhauser.com

Editors
Daniel Kiss (D. Sc. ETH Zurich, M.Arch. Harvard University)
Simon Kretz (D. Sc. ETH Zurich, dipl. Arch. ETH Zurich)

The editors of this anthology are architects, urban designers,
researchers, and educators who have been collaborating
for over a decade to teach design and theory and conduct joint
scientific inquiries into theories of urban form and methods
of its design.

With contributions by
Christopher Alexander, Lucius Burckhardt, Gordon Cullen,
Daniel Kiss, Simon Kretz, Bruno Latour, Fumihiko Maki,
Alison Smithson, Peter Smithson, Manuel de Solà-Morales,
Oswald Mathias Ungers

Acquisitions Editor
David Marold, Birkhäuser Verlag, A–Vienna

Content and Production Editor
Angelika Gaal, Birkhäuser Verlag, A–Vienna

Translation from German into English
Ada St. Laurent, A–Vienna

Copy editing
Ada St. Laurent, A–Vienna

Graphic concept and design
Jauneau Vallance, F–Paris

Lithography
Christophe Girard, F–Villeneuve-lès-Avignon

Printing
Holzhausen, die Buchmarke der Gerin Druck GmbH,
A–Wolkersdorf

Printed with the financial support of ETH Zurich,
Department of Architecture